Bloom's Modern Critical Interpretations

Bloom's Modern Critical Interpretations

William Shakespeare's
Julius Caesar
New Edition

Edited and with an introduction by
Harold Bloom
Sterling Professor of the Humanities
Yale University

BLOOM'S
LITERARY CRITICISM
An imprint of Infobase Publishing

Bloom's Modern Critical Interpretations: Julius Caesar—New Edition
Copyright © 2010 by Infobase Publishing
Introduction © 2010 by Harold Bloom

Bloom's Literary Criticism
An imprint of Infobase Publishing
132 West 31st Street
New York NY 10001

Library of Congress Cataloging-in-Publication Data

William Shakespeare's Julius Caesar / edited and with an introduction by Harold Bloom.
— New ed.
    p. cm. — (Bloom's modern critical interpretations)
  Includes bibliographical references and index.
  ISBN 978-1-60413-639-5
  1. Shakespeare, William, 1564–1616. Julius Caesar. 2. Caesar, Julius—In literature. 3.
Assassination in literature. 4. Rome—In literature. I. Bloom, Harold. II. Title: Julius
Caesar. III. Title. IV. Series.
  PR2808.W54 2010
  822.3'3—dc22   2009022143

Contributing editor: Pamela Loos
Cover designed by Takeshi Takahashi

Printed in the United States of America
IBT IBT 10 9 8 7 6 5 4 3 2 1

This book is printed on acid-free paper.

Contents

Editor's Note

My introduction follows Dr. Samuel Johnson, in admiring *Julius Caesar* while wondering at its Stoic restraint.

Terrence N. Tice centers on Calpurnia's dream, which he reads as an index to Caesar's and the play's "largely hidden conflicts."

The Forum scene is judged by Robert F. Willson Jr. as a theatrical vision of destructive passion, while Jan H. Blits explores the limits of masculine friendship in the play.

Mob politics in *Julius Caesar* is raised to an integral dignity by Nicholas Visser, after which R.F. Fleissner broods on the questions that endlessly intrigue me: Was not Brutus the natural son of Caesar and Hamlet the illegitimate son of Claudius?

John Roe contrasts Machiavelli, who desired a republic, with Shakespeare, who hoped to free conscience, while Lloyd Davis sees *Julius Caesar* as a complex testing ground for masculine selfhood.

Barbara J. Baines intricately studies the ways language is misconstrued by the characters of *Julius Caesar*, after which Daniel Juan Gil contrasts the play's political orders and disorders.

HAROLD BLOOM

Introduction

James Joyce, asked the question of which writer's works he would take with him to a desert island, replied that he would like to select Dante but would have to take Shakespeare, because he is *richer*. That extraordinary wealth of the creation of personalities by Shakespeare can blind the reader-playgoer to the most fascinating (for me) quality of Shakespearean art: the elliptical or leaving-out element. Why do we not see Antony and Cleopatra alone onstage together? How is it that Lear and Edmund never address a word to each other? Is the marriage of Othello and Desdemona consummated? What happens to Lear's Fool? Why does Shakespeare have Macbeth slain offstage? What do we make of an undergraduate Hamlet in act 1 and a thirty-year-old in act 5, a few weeks later? There are many other leavings-out, but these will suffice.

Shakespeare's source for *Julius Caesar* was North's translation of Plutarch's *Lives*. Plutarch tells us that Marcus Brutus was Caesar's illegitimate son, as was recognized by all in Rome, Brutus and Caesar included. Many in the audience had read Plutarch or learned this fascinating gossip from one another. Shakespeare seems to ignore this in the play. Why? It certainly makes a difference. Hamlet does not know when the sexual relationship of Gertrude and Claudius began, nor do we. The Prince rarely says what he means or means what he says, but is that another cause for his delay in revenge? Contra Freud, there is no Oedipal aspect to this drama unless Hamlet fears that Claudius indeed may be his phallic father. There certainly is an Oedipal struggle in *Julius Caesar*, even though Shakespeare allows it to be implicit.

Angus Fletcher, a great literary critic of my generation, remarks that what matters most in *Hamlet* is what doesn't happen. I would expand that observation to all of Shakespeare, even to *King Lear*. In *Julius Caesar* what does not happen is any confrontation between Brutus and his likely father. Only once do they share the stage alone together, in an amazingly banal exchange, which is subtly deliberate. Caesar asks Brutus the time of day, Brutus obliges and is gravely thanked for his courtesy.

Surveying the criticism of the play, from Ben Jonson through Dr. Samuel Johnson and on to Goethe, Hazlitt, Coleridge, Nietzsche, Wilson Knight, Kenneth Burke, Frank Kermode, and other distinguished hands, I find no realization among them of this ellipsis. And yet there are hints scattered throughout *Julius Caesar*, as I note in my book *Shakespeare: The Invention of the Human*. So sly was William Shakespeare that he allows his best auditors and readers the labor of assimilating the irony of what may constitute the deepest ambivalences and ambiguities in Brutus's motivations.

Admirable as everyone in the play finds Brutus to be (including Brutus) he is at least as flawed as great Caesar himself, who now is in decline. But Caesar's attitude toward danger is another extraordinary ellipsis in the play. Why are there no guards to protect Caesar? He is vainglorious yet still a great realist, and he knows Cassius and some of the others are his enemies. I wonder if Shakespeare, endlessly subtle in his ironies, does not give us a Julius Caesar who courts assassination as a step toward becoming a god?

Dr. Johnson found this to be a *cold* play, missing the passions. Even the Grand Cham's misses are any other critic's palpable hits. Something is repressed throughout *Julius Caesar*, and it could be one of several evasions. Brutus's desperate pride in his antityrannical family heritage is overstressed by him because he cannot be certain as to whose family he belongs. Cassius, who keeps yielding to Brutus's wrong-headed tactics, loses because his own political and military skill is countermanded by Brutus's blunders. Brutus has inherited Caesar's pride but not the would-be monarch's brilliance at seeing that politics and war are the same enterprise. There are intimations that Cassius, allied to Brutus through Portia, is helpless to govern Brutus because of a homoerotic attachment to him, never expressed as such.

By tradition, this epitome of the "well-made" play is the tragedy of Brutus and not of Caesar. As always, Shakespeare writes no genre, and therefore Johnson was not wholly off the track; this is too cold to be tragedy. Like *Coriolanus* and *Antony and Cleopatra*, this is no tragedy but a history play, like the tetralogy *Richard II, Henry IV, Parts I* and *II,* and *Henry V,* which scholars call the Henriad. I myself prefer to title *Henry IV*'s two parts as the Falstaffiad, since I join William Hazlitt and A.C. Bradley in judging Prince Hal/Henry V to be a Machiavelli and a dark one at that. A.D. Nuttall whitewashes Hal/King Henry, but he remains what Hazlitt charmingly called "an amiable monster."

Nuttall is refreshingly free of the New Historicist delusion that Michel Foucault was more intelligent than William Shakespeare. There is no Falstaff to heat up *Julius Caesar*, but Brutus seems to me closer to Henry V than he is to Hamlet. Shakespeare hardly wrote a major tragedy in Brutus's blunders, and yet I doubt if "tragedy" was Shakespeare's true mode, though here again I part from most Shakespearean scholarship. We never will catch up with Shakespeare, and that is his glory, or part of it.

TERRENCE N. TICE

Calphurnia's Dream and Communication with the Audience in Shakespeare's Julius Caesar[1]

Shakespeare's 1599 play *The Tragedy of Julius Caesar*, though a mere year away from *Hamlet*, is only a bridge to the more deeply existential later plays; and, as such, it has won less thoroughgoing attention among recent critical scholars. Yet, as Harold Bloom has recently stated, it is "a very satisfying play, as a play, and is universally regarded as a work of considerable aesthetic dignity."[2] Moreover, this drama bearing the name of the historical figure most often mentioned by Shakespeare, and about whose life circumstances the playwright showed sustained interest, continues to move audiences profoundly. Certainly it evokes strong feelings of recognition and concern during any time marked by high anxiety about the public's future, by revelations of self-justifying evil connivance among powerful men in whom the public has placed its trust, and by ambitious, prideful, incautious decisions on the part of leaders. These conditions would appear to be even more pronounced and worrisome for present-day audiences than for Shakespeare's own. Thus the play bears a special capacity to connect with contemporary moods encompassing failure, loss, hurt, or impending disaster.

I wish to use some remarks on the dream of Caesar's wife, Calphurnia, a dream portending his murder, in order ultimately to suggest an underlying depressive theme in the work and, along the way, to indicate where both merits and limits in psychoanalytic contributions to interpreting literature may

From *Shakespeare Yearbook* 1 (Spring 1990): 37–49. © 1990 by the Edwin Mellen Press.

be found. The focus is placed on communication of affect-laden awarenesses to the audience—first by the writer, then by subsequent directors and actors. Sometimes, I believe, this occurs by extraordinarily subtle means, even in a reputedly "simple" drama like *Julius Caesar*, often the awareness is absorbed unconsciously by the audience, and occasionally it appears to be purveyed unconsciously by the author or later surrogates.

Analysis of Dream Material in Shakespeare

Calphurnia's dream itself has attracted very little notice in the literature. The chief reasons are probably that its function as a portent has been thought to be self-evident—sufficient in itself—and that psychoanalytic interpretations of Shakespeare have tended to focus on Shakespeare and his characters rather than on other material that is to me more fully and legitimately analyzable: notably, relations between events in the plays and expectable audience responses. The latter I take to be an important, more nearly supportable function of such interpretation, which has often tended, without real warrant, to import schema normally suitable only for an extended analysis of a living person.[3] I have selected Calphurnia's dream precisely because extremely little is told of her, so that the interpreter must look almost exclusively at its actual manifest content and at plausible associations within the play as a whole.

Over the past three decades and more, three books have purported to emphasize dreams and visionary content in Shakespeare, and a search for articles has yielded only bits and pieces (e.g., Camden and Rubenstein). Only one, by Marjorie Garber, has dealt with dream in *Julius Caesar*, of necessity referring to Calphurnia's dream, though John Arthos also alludes to the dream and many others mention it in passing. Arthos winsomely interprets a poem and four plays, including *Julius Caesar*, as conveying "metaphysical matters"—"the sense of realms of being across the threshold of the waking sight" (13, 9). Kay Stockholder cleverly offers a psychoanalytically informed interpretation of the plays, but not specifically treating *Julius Caesar*, as "dream works." In doing this she attempts to show "ways in which the most private passions depicted in Shakespeare's figures are shaped by and expressed in the most public conventions and ideological conflicts" (x).

Garber's 1974 chapter "Dream and Interpretation: *Julius Caesar*" aptly expounds the following thesis: "The play is full of omens and portents, augury and dream, and almost without exception these omens are misinterpreted. Calpurnia's [*sic*] dream, the dream of Cinna the poet, the advice of the augurers, all suggest one course of action and produce its opposite" (see, perhaps most conveniently, in Bloom 43).[4] Her statement is not quite accurate, in that such material, as she herself indicates, is used accurately to foretell disaster and its aftermath and in that the material itself does not "produce" the oppos-ing actions, but *reactions to the material*, both deliberate (Decius Brutus) and unconsidered (Caesar), do.

The theme of misinterpretation is important nonetheless, though to my mind the varied, numerous interactions between interpretation and event are what loom large throughout; the chief transactions of play and audience fol-low. As Garber herself contends: "More and more it becomes evident [in the play] that signs and dreams are morally neutral elements, incapable of effect without interpretation. By structuring his play around them, Shakespeare invites us to scrutinize the men who read the signs—to witness the tragedy of misconstruction" (Bloom 47). As she points out, this is "the last of his plays to use dreams and omens primarily as devices of plot" (Bloom 52), whereas in the later plays the movement is to dream as a universalizing, transcendent state of mind, which ultimately serves powerfully in metamorphosis of the self through imaginative effort. Thus it is of value to see exactly how Shake-speare carries out this earlier use.

Calphurnia's Dream

By the second scene of Act Two, plans, omens, and portents of Caesar's impending death have already built up to a high pitch, but so far his house-hold has not been touched by them. As the scene opens Caesar reports:

> Nor heaven nor earth have been at peace to-night:
> Thrice hath Calphurnia in her sleep cried out,
> "Help, ho! They murther Caesar!"
>   (2.2.1–3)

Calphurnia enters, and in pleading for him to stay home speaks of signs that should deter him; he at first resists, then relents. She says to him:

> Caesar, I never stood on ceremonies,
> Yet now they fright me. There is one within,
> Besides the things that we have heard and seen,
> Recounts most horrid sights seen by the watch.
> A lioness hath whelped in the streets,
> And graves have yawn'd and yielded up their dead;
> Fierce fiery warriors fight upon the clouds
> In ranks and squadrons and right form of war,
> Which drizzled blood upon the Capitol;
> The noise of battle hurtled in the air,
> Horses did neigh, and dying men did groan,

And ghosts did shriek and squeal about the streets.[5]
O Caesar, these things are beyond all use,
And I do fear them.

. . . .

When beggars die, there are no comets seen;
The heavens themselves blaze forth the death of princes.
     (2.2.13–26, 30–1)

Then comes a discussion with Decius Brutus, wherein Caesar lays out the dream Calphurnia has related to him, but Decius offers a flattering counter-interpretation and Caesar decides to go forth to the Capitol after all. This is the dream itself, as Caesar gives it:

She dreamt to-night she saw my statue,
Which like a fountain with an hundred spouts
Did run pure blood; and many lusty Romans
Came smiling, and did bathe their hands in it.
And these does she apply for warnings and portents
And evils imminent; and on her knee
Hath begg'd that I will stay at home to-day.
     (2.2.76–82)

Such is the dream and its setting in the play, which embellishes greatly on the report by Plutarch though following his outline of events: the sleep-talk-ing and a dream, both portending Caesar's death, Caesar's fear and indeci-sion, his consulting augurers, and Decius' fateful influence. In Plutarch she was simply reported to have "dreamed Caesar was slain and that she had him in her arms" and, regarding a pinnacle that the Senate had placed on the top of Caesar's house, that "she saw it broken down." Decius there advises Caesar to make only a brief appearance to salute the Senate "and return again when Calpurnia should have better dreams." The rest, includ-ing the recital of signs, is all masterfully Shakespeare's.

Interpretation of Calphurnia and her Dream
Calphurnia, Cato's daughter, was Caesar's fourth wife, probably younger than Caesar, who was then fifty-six. She had borne no child, and Caesar's only legitimate child, Julia, whom he had given to the great Pompey in mar-riage, had died. All that we learn of her earlier in the play, however, is that Caesar has humiliated her by asking Antonius to "touch" her in the Luper-calian race (to strike her with white leather thongs carried by the naked runners, explains Plutarch), in order to rid her of her "sterile curse," as was

the custom (1.2). This is the same occasion wherein Caesar thrice refuses the laurel crown that the runner Antonius would place on his head, to indicate his kingly status. Brutus reports that Caesar is angry and "Calphurnia's cheek is pale" (1.2.183).

Apart from Zelda Teplitz's unpublished paper presented at the 1972 annual meeting of the American Psychoanalytic Association, Garber's 1974 chapter employs Calphurnia's dream more fully than any study I have encountered (see in Bloom 48–51). This is what she does. She regards the dream as a crux of the play; it is a portent, among others, of unnatural events, "an apocalypse of sorts, the last judgment of Rome." Calphurnia has been established as an accurate and lyrical prophetess. As is the case in other Shakespearean dreams, hers makes the dead man into a statue, and she views the spouting of blood as death. The ambiguity in her dream enables the irony that Decius' interpretation, "that from you great Rome shall suck / Reviving blood," is "as true in its way as Calpurnia's." Its significance lies not only in its functional role of furthering the action but also in that it "symbolically foreshadows events to come, supporting the theme of 'all amiss interpreted' which is central to the play's meaning." However, Garber finds the later scene of Cinna the poet, who also has a portentous dream, "the most symbolically instructive of the whole play," for he has the premonition but chooses to disregard it, and when he goes out he meets a bad end simply through a playing with his name (like Caesar, the private and public name). Thereby "the whole myth of the play is concisely expressed."

In contrast, I do not believe that this highly complex play can be reduced to a single myth, though Garber's reading of the scenes involving Calphurnia and Cinna seems entirely accurate and helpful short of that claim. Although a great many associations to Calphurnia's dream and to the other signs she indicates can be made throughout the play, alongside those by Casca, Cinna, and others, I shall restrict myself to a few additional features of special importance.

First, partly through her earlier, 1958 work on sleep-talking, Teplitz was able to discern what hidden hostility the barren Calphurnia might have felt toward Caesar, who sports aspirations to supremely royal status, wishes for a blood heir, and has humiliated her publicly. That is, her active sleep-talking would replace more passive fears regarding hostile, murderous impulses toward her husband. In possible support, one might add that Plutarch, though he does not mention Calphurnia among the noble women to be touched, tells of Calphurnia's dreaming that she held the slain Caesar "in her arms" (perhaps at once wife, mother, and fantasied murderer?). This detail Shakespeare omits, but it could well have influenced him. The possible feature is plausible, given the action of the play, but it is only weakly supportable.

Second, it would also be relevant to expand on the following: on the association Shakespeare (but not Plutarch) has her give of a lioness reported to have "whelped in the streets," one of the "horrid sights seen by the watch"; on the lion Casca describes as glaring at him on the Capitol, where Caesar would be murdered, but passing by without harming him (in Shakespeare's day lions were a tourist attraction at the Tower of London, an edifice it was said Julius Caesar had bestowed); and on Caesar's symbolic description of himself as a twin lion "littered in one day" with danger yet danger's master. These and the numerous other interlocking images of augury and fury to be found in the play intensify the sense of frightening danger that often accompanies murderous or ambitious feelings. So do the conflicts that Caesar experiences over his decision to go to the Capitol. Decius the flatterer—similar to those who served the childless, aging Queen Elizabeth, who was in 1599 over sixty-five years old—tries to smooth it all over with a "vision fair and fortunate" of the living king from whom Rome shall draw revitalizing substance. Caesar had been sufficiently affected by his wife's dream and the servant's report from the augurers to think that he would play it safe and stay home. Were it not for his regard for Decius, he could scarcely have admitted this to him as the occasion for his decision. However, Caesar claims to make the decision, either way, as an expression of his own sovereign will. Thus he blunders into disaster just as those closest to him (Decius, Brutus, perhaps Calphurnia as well) secretly or openly desire him to. Of such human frailties—his and theirs—is tragedy made.

Third, strictly speaking, Decius' interpretation of the dream denies and obscures the bloody criminal result of Caesar's decision, both for him and for his assassins. Decius largely fails to perceive the revengeful quality of Caesar's ensuing immortality. Robed in flattery, Decius' interpretation accentuates the problems that Caesar's immense ambition, popularity, and pretentiousness are seen to create for virtually everyone in the dream: Caesar's conspiring rivals, his wife, his alarmed friends, and later on even Cinna the poet, the innocent bystander. Were the play's structure not so wonderfully complicated—every image and relationship that emerges creating ripple effects throughout the remaining scenes—it might even be appropriate to suggest that Decius' interpretation bespeaks the earlier conspiracy scenes and that Calphurnia's interpretation foreshadows the scenes that follow. However, it does not appear that Shakespeare really prepares us for the literally mortifying ironic immortality of Caesar's spirit by either interpretation: for the agonizing outburst of short-lived triumph and sudden revenge, or for the ghostly, inexorable presence of Caesar even beyond the play's end. Calphurnia's dream and her attendant anxieties have such a powerful effect precisely because they reveal the terribly confused, uncertain consequences of letting Caesar have his way—consequences nonetheless so intractable that even his wished-for death cannot halt their influence.

Fourth, unquestionably Shakespeare used Calphurnia's dream and its interpretations to deepen the integration of the play. The second scene of Act Two is especially well placed for that effect. However, he used other structural devices as well: (1) an unparalleled close description of vitality (the exciting, never gruesome or disgusting talk of blood; fire; eating, drinking, waking from sleep, the brother of death; spirit effort; even the details of peoples' clothing and faces)—of vitality versus disorder, sickness, and infirmity;[6] (2) cold-blooded resolve versus sympathizing tears; (3) the favorite Elizabethan conflict of immortal spirituality, nobility, and reason with unruly passion and the attendant consequences of self-deception and misjudgment; (4) a continuous mixture of mythic savagery and ceremony, of emplacement and displacement; (5) the long shadow of Pompey, himself never present but constantly alluded to; (6) men's proud, twisted construing of events versus the surprising, promiscuous determination of destiny by the events themselves; (7) a series of exciting, explosive encounters; (8) the cumulative contrasts between public and private life, between stoic invulnerability and the outbreak of emotion, between willful detachment and forced involvement, as well as the monstrous exploitation of friendship for imagined honor or glory; (9) the redistribution of the dominating personalities and their conflicts from act to act; (10) the orations of Brutus and Antony; and (11) the continuing dread disturbances of the night. All but a couple of these devices are spread throughout the play, eliciting a direct emotive response from the audience. It is striking to notice how raw and elemental, how full of what Freud called *primary process* most of this material is, as is true in the dream. In this sense, there is a distinct dream quality about most of the play, so that Calphurnia's actual dream fits right in place.

Fifth, I have already referred to the theme of blood, which also serves as a powerful connection between Calphurnia's discourse and the rest of the play—not least to the self-bloodletting of Portia, the wife of that other powerful man, Brutus, whose presence dominates much of the play. In his 1951 study *The Imperial Theme* G. Wilson Knight makes much of the blood imagery and of this general connection (45–51). As he points out, the loss of Caesar's blood is a costly business, the loss of a noble, vital, spiritual force. In the end, however, Caesar bleeds to death, but his spirit lives on to haunt and inspire. More is to be said about this blood. For one thing, David Shelley Berkeley has surveyed the characteristics and means of diminishing high, noble, superior blood in Shakespeare's work and in other related English literature. "Shakespeare's plays suggest with few exceptions," he summarizes, "that the poet especially desiderated the potentialities inherent in the bright red, hot, thin, fast-flowing, sweet-tasting blood of divinely sanctioned kings, and rated every departure from this blood, by the extent of its divergence, as a diminution in human quality" (14). Likewise, in his plays no gentle person is ever said to smell (52). Berkeley comments further:

> Julius Caesar in Shakespeare's play, although not a king because of Rome's republican traditions, is physiologically fit to occupy this exalted place because, although old enough to be Brutus' father and therefore supposedly possessed of little blood, he bleeds so much at his stabbing that the conspirators bathe their hands in his blood ... "up to the elbows." Moreover, Calpurnia's dream of Caesar's statue, "Which like a fountain with a hundred spouts / Did run pure blood, and many lusty Romans / Came smiling and did bathe their hands in it" ..., implies by its strong emphasis on abundant, flowing blood, rendered even more prominent by Decius' interpretation, that Caesar is physiologically legitimate (and therefore naturally legitimate) to be king or ruler of Rome. The conspirators are ill advised to tamper with the primate of nature. (87)

Another sign of high blood, Berkeley notes, is the ability to experience heartbreak, like Lear:

> In *Julius Caesar*, Antony tells the mob that Caesar, who had lost much blood from his several wounds in the Forum, yet possessed enough blood to "burst his mighty heart" (3.2.186) if grief at the sight of Brutus among his murderers had not overcome him. The implications is that Caesar's age is no bar or hindrance to his being worthy of being ruler of Rome, crown or no crown, because he has the cachet of being able to experience heartbreak in the autumn of his life. (88–9)

This information from Berkeley's study is the kind that enables accurate reconstruction and an understanding of what an original audience was likely to have in mind. Less successful in this respect, though highly suggestive nonetheless, is Gail Kern Paster's attempt to equate the then-supposed demeaning, grotesque, unstoppable menstrual flow and lactation with Caesar's blood and thus his planned feminization and diminution as a person. These characteristics of the blood could possibly be listed among the many determinants of meaning by play's end. They by no means comprise all, or, by all evidence, even set the main point. The blood in this play is variously feminine and masculine, ordinary and regal; above all, it is exciting, vital, plenteous in its outflow toward death and life, and even ritually redeeming.

All these latter qualities, save the very last, Shakespeare has the anxious Calphurnia announce.

Finally, we must ask why Calphurnia, a woman, should serve these functions? Juliet Dusinberre emphasizes that despite Shakespeare's inherited skepticism about women in view of his society's notion of women as a separate, inferior species, he took the best of the Calvinistic Puritanism of his time and tended to see them as equal with men. Thus, for him both men and women express "an infinite variety of union between opposing influences" (308). In this perspective, she reports, he was at one with the general trend in drama within the 1590–1625 period, "feminist in sympathy" and treating women as individuals (5). Juliet Cook, in seeming agreement, emphasizes the striking "independence" of Shakespeare's women and (for his time) the unmatched variety of roles he gave them. In the historical plays they have "very subordinate roles," however; and in the Roman plays, drawing from Plutarch, Shakespeare makes all of them relatively insignificant and powerless compared to the men—in short, they are typical Roman wives (all but Volumnia). Calphurnia and Portia are "classic vignettes of the Roman wife," though in Calphurnia Shakespeare emphasizes women's "intuition and even foreknowledge of events" (64–5). In a study of gender in Shakespeare's writings, Linda Bamber adds still another feature: "In the comedies Shakespeare seems if not a feminist then at least a man who takes the woman's part. Often the women in the comedies are more brilliant than the men, more aware of themselves and their world, saner, livelier, more gay. In the tragedies, however, Shakespeare creates such nightmare female figures as Goneril, Regan, Lady Macbeth, and Volumnia" (2). R. S. White points to other female characters as "innocent victims." Understandably missing from each contrasting treatment of female figures is the middling but focal figure of Calphurnia.

Perhaps the most secure answer to our question—why Calphurnia, a woman, serves these functions—is threefold. (1) Plutarch has her there. (2) Shakespeare had been developing an interest, as Caesar is made to do, though less trustingly, in the intuitive aspect of things, represented in his mind especially by women. (3) The audience was sufficiently varied and open to sympathetic portrayals of women's contributions for him to make at least this slight venture. All these statements are, in any case, quite true. In *Julius Caesar*, moreover, neither Calphurnia nor Portia is a nightmarish figure, but as wives of powerful men they are indeed set in the midst of nightmarish events.

* * *

The major thrust of this play, dealing as it does with the conflicting mortality/immortality of Caesar, is patently a deliberate design of its author, enriched not by one but by many unconscious meanings. These often ambiguous meanings the action of the play partly nudges into consciousness. These meanings, along with what remains unconscious but is nonetheless communicated, become the audience's possession however they may have arisen for Shakespeare, however Shakespeare may have imagined them to arise for his characters, or however they may have emerged for the historical figures themselves.

As a philosopher greatly interested in the arts and in educative impacts of aesthetic means, I feel that the major contribution that psychoanalytically oriented criticism can make to the interpretation of art is to focus not so much on the artist or on the artist's characters as on the ground for vital communication between artist and audience.[7] As with an actual psychoanalysis, one wants to keep as close to the current derivatives of the more deeply lodged material of experience as possible. One must hover over the material listening for unconscious themes, not jumping too quickly to an ad hoc interpretation of symbols and actions. One must expect the material to be multiply determined, thus subject to several layers or facets of interpretation. Thus, interpretation can arise variously and afresh with each new generation because the grounds of communication, continuously opened up though also limited by the actual material of the art work, are ever shifting with changes in experience.

In closing, I should like to point out something else that, to my knowledge, no interpreter has yet indicated in psychoanalytic terms. I refer to the overwhelming depressive, sometimes alternatively manic mood that pervades most of this play—precisely in all the details that Edith Jacobson brilliantly outlines in her 1971 papers on moods and depression. According to Jacobson, a depressive mood necessarily involves aggressive conflict. This becomes amalgamated with an experience of loss or failure or the like and may persist through various narcissistic identifications. Moods tend to flood ego functioning. They are a "barometer of the ego state," displaying detachment from specific object cathexes and effecting blanket appraisals of self and object representations (notably alternating dependence on an idealized love-object and pseudo-independence of superego functioning). They may express themselves in words and actions as well as in affects. Now in a more general sense, as Charles Brenner has more recently indicated, the more depressive and the more anxious side of our affects are temporally two sides of the same coin, the one tending to point back and the other to point forward; furthermore, the two qualities of affect as they emerge within a mind in conflict may be closely associated and are probably never wholly isolated from each other.

It is this general feature of the affective quality in *our* experience that enables us as audience to apprehend representations of depression and anxiety in art, not only their occasional existence as moods. In *Julius Caesar* we see the characters under a cloud of depression interspersed with elation. As the pivotal second scene of Act Two opens, Shakespeare has Caesar himself depict the all-encompassing mood by crying: "Nor heaven nor earth have been at peace to-night." Caesar himself does not seem to experience much of a sense of failure or loss or hurt or disaster, though the aggressive, strutting, expansive qualities of his conflicts are obvious enough, but we the audience are made to feel this both through the other characters and through the very setting of Shakespeare's play. What is communicated above all, as has been only partly indicated in the themes outlined in this essay, is a set of moods and their underlying, largely hidden conflicts.

Notes

1. The occasion for an early version of this essay was a paper on Calphurnia's dream by Zelda Teplitz, a psychoanalyst and devoted Shakespeare scholar, at the American Psychoanalytic Association annual meeting in New York, December 1, 1972. I was then a candidate at the Michigan Psychoanalytic Institute and offered some extended comments. To my knowledge, her paper remains unpublished. I am grateful for the stimulus of her work, though I must take responsibility for my own, rather different, ideas. As a philosopher-historian who works especially with educators and planners, my critical interest in the possibilities and limits of psychoanalytic interpretation has continued to grow in the intervening years. This essay is intended to serve as a brief indicator of what I have learned. In immediately practical terms, I hope that the findings presented here may be of particular help to secondary school teachers, since *Julius Caesar* is in the curriculum of almost every high school in America, as frequently elsewhere, and does contain elements of special appeal to adolescents.

2. Harold Bloom, *William Shakespeare's Julius Caesar*, 1. Bloom here collects nine of the best among studies on the play from 1969 to 1985. In 1951 Harold C. Goddard had already depicted the play as Shakespeare's "bridge" to the later tragedies, explaining this in these terms: "From *Julius Caesar* on, his greater characters and greater plays are touched with the dream-light and dream-darkness of something that as certainly transcends the merely human as do the prophets and sibyls of Michelangelo" (308). Of unusual breadth among earlier psychoanalytic essays treating of the play is a 1966 study by Andrew Wilkinson in which he pays comparatively greater notice to Calphurnia than usual but not so much in psychoanalytic terms.

3. In his 1966 *Psychoanalysis and Shakespeare* and later works, Norman N. Holland has taken a position close to mine, except that he prefers to use psychoanalysis on our own reactions as readers or audience. I believe that it can also serve purposes of historical reconstruction and in detail, subject both to rigorous canons of evidence and to provisos, recently emphasized by Marjorie Garber, having to do with the "uncanny," multi-determined, in-varying-degrees-lost origins of authorship. Also compare Holland's *The Shakespearean Imagination*, wherein Chapter 8 is on *Julius Caesar*.

4. For convenience, page references are to Garber's chapter included in Bloom, as probably the more accessible source. Her entire work, however, is of one piece and is an outstanding account of the changing nature and function of dreams in Shakespeare's writings.

5. Compare these lines from *Hamlet*, a year later: "In the most high and palmy state of Rome, / A little ere the mightiest Julius fell, / The graves stood tenantless, and the sheeted dead / Did squeak and gibber in the Roman streets" (1.1.113–6).

6. G. Wilson Knight, who had a great eye for metaphoric detail, notes that "nearly everyone in the play is ill" (40).

7. For example, though not resorting to psychoanalytic tools, Phyllis Rackin offers a substantial analysis of "The Role of the Audience in Shakespeare's *Richard II*," *Shakespeare Quarterly* 36 (1985): 262–81.

Works Cited

Arthos, John. *Shakespeare's Use of Dream and Vision*. Totowa, N.J.: Rowman and Littlefield, 1977.

Bamber, Linda. *Comic Women, Tragic Men: A Study of Gender and Genre in Shakespeare*. Stanford: Stanford UP, 1982.

Berkeley, David Shelley. *Blood Will Tell in Shakespeare's Plays*. Graduate Studies, No. 28. Lubbock: Texas Tech University, 1984.

Bloom, Harold, ed. *William Shakespeare's Julius Caesar*. New York: Chelsea House, 1988.

Brenner, Charles. *The Mind in Conflict*. New York: International Universities P, 1982.

Camden, Carroll, Jr. "Shakespeare on Sleep and Dreams." *Rice Institute Pamphlet* 23 (1936): 106–33.

Cook, Judith. *Women in Shakespeare*. London: Harrap, 1980.

Dusinberre, Juliet. *Shakespeare and the Nature of Women*. London: Macmillan, 1975.

Garber, Marjorie B. *Dream in Shakespeare: From Metaphor to Metamorphosis*. New Haven: Yale UP, 1974.

———. *Shakespeare's Ghost Writers: Literature as Uncanny Causality*. London: Methuen, 1987.

Goddard, Harold C. *The Meaning of Shakespeare*. Chicago: U of Chicago P, 1951.

Green, David C. *Julius Caesar and Its Source*. Salzburg: Institut für Anglistik und Amerikanistik, Universität Salzburg, 1979.

Holland, Norman N. *Psychoanalysis and Shakespeare*. New York: McGraw-Hill, 1966.

———. *The Shakespearean Imagination*. New York: Macmillan, 1964.

Jacobson, Edith. *Depression: Comparative Studies of Normal, Neurotic, and Psychotic Conditions*. New York: International Universities P, 1971.

Knight, G. Wilson. *The Imperial Theme: Further Interpretations of Shakespeare's Tragedies Including the Roman Plays*. London: Methuen, 1951.

Paster, Gail Kern. "'In the spirit of men there is no blood': Blood as Trope of Gender in *Julius Caesar*." *Shakespeare Quarterly* 40 (1989): 284–98.

Rubinstein, Frankie. "Shakespeare's Dream-Stuff: A Forerunner of Freud's 'Dream Material'." *American Imago: A Psychoanalytic Journal for Culture, Science, and the Arts* 43 (1986): 335–55. [The subject matter is similar to that in the author's book, *A Dictionary of Shakespeare's Sexual Puns and Their Significance* (London: Macmillan, 1984), not on dreams in the plays.]

Shakespeare, William. *Julius Caesar*, The Arden Edition, 6th edn., ed. T. S. Dorsch. London: Methuen, 1955. [Compare this volume in *The Oxford Shakespeare:* Julius Caesar, ed. Arthur Humphreys (Oxford: Oxford UP, 1984).]

Stockholder, Kay. *Dream Works: Lovers and Families in Shakespeare's Plays*. Toronto: U of Toronto P, 1987.

Teplitz, Zelda. "The Ego and Motility in Sleepwalking." *Journal of the American Psychoanalytic Association* 6 (1958): 95–110.

White, R. S. *Innocent Victims: Poetic Injustice in Shakespearean Tragedy.* Rev. edn. London: Athlone P, 1983.

Wilkinson, Andrew M. "A Psychological Approach to Julius Caesar." *Review of English Literature* 7 (1966): 66–78. [Rpt. in Melvin D. Faber, *The Design Within: Psychoanalytic Approaches to Shakespeare* (New York: Science House, 1970), 63–78.]

ROBERT F. WILLSON JR.

Julius Caesar: *The Forum Scene as Historic Play-within*

That Brutus, Cassius, and the other conspirators see themselves as actors in a precedent-setting, historical drama is revealed in Cassius' exclamation following the assassination:

> How many ages hence
> Shall this our lofty scene be acted over
> In states unborn and accents yet unknown. (3.1.111–3)[1]

To amplify Cassius' prophetic claim, Brutus echoes the sentiment in a characteristically philosophical observation:

> How many times shall Caesar bleed in sport,
> That now on Pompey's basis lies along
> No worthier than the dust! (114–6)[2]

Such theatrical metaphors are of course common to Shakespearean tragic poetry. Hamlet affirms his "motive and . . . cue for passion" by adapting a play to sting his uncle's conscience. Lear speaks of "this great stage of fools" onto which crying infants are ushered at their birth. Macbeth compares his Herod's role to that of a "poor player" uttering an hour's worth of bombast,

From *Shakespeare Yearbook* 1 (Spring 1990): 14–27. © 1990 by the Edwin Mellen Press.

then disappearing forever. And Cleopatra, like Cassius glimpsing the future, shrinks from the vision of "Some squeaking Cleopatra who will boy my greatness / I' th' posture of a whore."

These reflexive references to the world as stage are so numerous in the canon that they are generally regarded as commonplaces.[3] Yet such allusions often serve as essential guides to reading the significance of pivotal scenes in major plays. We quickly grasp the clue that Hamlet's mousetrap, for instance, reveals as much about the hero's inability to distinguish between reality and illusion as it does about Claudius' guilt.

Obsessed with the moral impact of Gonzago on Claudius (and, lest we forget, on Gertrude), Hamlet dispels the theatrical vision by directing Lucianus to speak his lines and stop making "damnable faces" (3.2.253). This overmanaging of the actors by Hamlet exposes his uncontrollable impulse to force his uncle's confession—and Gertrude's conversion. (The God-playing syndrome is further revealed in his prayer-scene decision not to send Claudius' apparently repentant soul to hell.) During the play-within, moreover, the prompting of Lucianus, nephew to the king, signifies Hamlet's desire to "prompt" action by a created image of himself. His threats are Lucianus', yet they are empty without attendant action. Hamlet's inability to distinguish between the actor's art and real-world performance becomes the quicksand of inaction into which he sinks ever deeper. This reading of the play-within's function suggests that Shakespeare may have had in mind more than just a convenient poetic lexicon when he employed theatrical allusion.[4] We comprehend Hamlet's state of mind through terminology that places him in a staged or performed "life."

Shakespeare also employs the theatrical metaphor as a means of representing Macbeth's ambitious career. By killing Duncan and seizing the crown, the thane succeeds in usurping a king's role. But what Shakespeare clarifies through subsequent events (i.e., the murder of Banquo; of Lady Macduff and her children) is that this performer has degenerated into a "poor player," a common Elizabethan label for inept actor. His ineptitude—a term that carries both professional and moral significance—is dramatized in the banquet scene (3.4), where Macbeth's fear-inspired ranting parallels histrionic excess. (As Emrys Jones sees it, Banquo's appearance has caused Macbeth to behave like an actor unable to recall his lines.[5]) The hurried departure of the Scottish lords can be likened to the embarrassed escape of an audience no longer willing to tolerate this bombastic amateur. When Macbeth later characterizes himself as just such a failure, he stresses the briefness of his "stage" career, his departure for oblivion. Without an heir to succeed him, Macbeth cannot even console himself with the thought of lineal immortality. This cutting-off can likewise be appreciated with reference to playhouse practice: As an unsuccessful player, he cannot expect to have even an apprentice take his place.

The preeminence of the world-as-stage metaphor in creating a context for interpreting prominent sequences in Shakespeare's tragedies gives readers a useful decoding language. We can reasonably assume, for instance, that Shakespeare, like many of his contemporaries, recognized how successful politicians fashioned public roles which enhanced their ability to lead. This is not to say that he readily applauded histrionic talent without the stuff of character necessary to its legitimate use—in monarchs or actors, one might say. Richard Gloucester's pious impersonation (3.7), so energetically stage-managed by Buckingham, demonstrates that acting has its despotic, demonic side as well. It is the Thespian *and* Satanic art. Richard's appearance, "aloft, between two bishops," serves only as a disguise, not as a true representation of the Christian prince. We witness the apparently monkish Richard refusing to assume the yoke of worldly power, characterizing himself as unfit for the part:

> Yet so much is my poverty of spirit,
> So mighty and so many my defects,
> That I would rather hide me from my greatness— (159–61)

This poor player speaks truer than he knows, as Shakespeare ironically exposes the pretender's nature in the language of rehearsal. When the citizens-as-audience threaten to undertake violent steps to keep the "illegitimate" princes from the throne, Richard relents and agrees to

> ... buckle Fortune on my back,
> To bear her burthen, whe'er I will or no,
> I must have patience to endure the load; (228–30)

The allusion to Hercules underscores Richard's claim that the world is about to be dropped on his shoulders. However, the vision of a hunchback so burdened undercuts Richard's assumed heroic identity, transforming the god-like image into a seriocomic one. Buckingham and Richard's power play becomes an afterpiece, a parody of the coronation ritual.[6]

By contrast Prince Hal proves highly skilled as an actor, one seasoned in the art of fitting the role to the occasion. In *1 Henry IV*, the impromptu tavern-house play-within starring Falstaff and Hal (2.4.376ff.) demonstrates the hero's knack for both assuming his father's identity (thus foreshadowing his ready assumption of the crown) and using the interlude as a means of moral instruction. On the other hand, Falstaff shows himself woefully unable to jettison his monstrous ego in taking on either the princely or kingly part.

What starts as a playful, time-wasting game for fat Jack grows into a serious morality play in which his fate is sealed. Abruptly ending the scene in his guise as player-king, Hal, in answer to his "son's" plea not to banish him, declares "I do, I will." This chilling period closes the performance and allows us to see that Hal clearly perceives the distinction between counterfeiting and true action.

Later, in *Henry V*, Hal's public and private performances—the tennis ball episode, the outwitting and arrest of Cambridge, Grey, and Scroop—reveal his awareness of the value of decorous acting in the consolidating and exercising of power. The political and personal identities (see the doctrine of the king's two bodies) meet as one in him, a ruler without rival on the imperial stage. If Richard is all show, obliterating the monarch's spiritual body, Hal epitomizes the happy union of show and substance, of the illusionary and real. In Hamlet's words, he suits "the action to the word, the word to the action" and does not "o'erstep . . . the modesty of nature." Richard ends ranting in "King Cambyses' vein."

1

With these theatrical or stage-as-world guides in mind, we turn to the assassination and Forum scenes in *Julius Caesar* equipped to understand the characters and events in terms that are central to Shakespeare's political theme. That is, the "lofty scene" described by Cassius changed the course of history and thereby influenced the lives of Shakespeare and his contemporaries. We need only remember the Elizabethans' ancestral identification with Rome through the legend of Britain's founding by Brutus, great-grandson of Aeneas. On the world stage, moreover, the assassination of Julius Caesar deserved the title of tragedy—and so the playwright dubbed it through association with the murder of Jesus Christ. That such blows against God should be acted over in succeeding ages demonstrates how imperfectly their lessons (about social and political disruption) have been learned. Thus to return to the event is to take up old material, "a moldy tale," and once again rehearse its meaning, grapple with its complexities. Whether Shakespeare's additional motive was to warn his contemporaries about the danger of popular rebellion or to present the case for republicanism can never be finally known.[7] But by evaluating the assassination and Forum scenes from the perspective of theatrical metaphor, we may better appreciate the playwright's habit of interpreting events and characters by employing familiar analogues from his and the audience's playhouse experience.

What strikes one immediately in assessing the dynamics of the conspiracy is the parallel between this group of plotters and a company of actors—

even "sharers," if one adopts the language of the profession. If indeed these men are actors of a "lofty scene," it is probable that Shakespeare invites us to compare them to a cry of players.[8] The term "sharers" takes on even greater weight if we think of its professional connotation: All the "actors" are presumed to be "full adventurers" in the enterprise of assassination.[9] And while the conspirators appear to number no more than seven or eight, they could be said to approximate the size of a company of fellows.[10] These men appeal to Brutus (at Cassius' urging) to lead them in their scheme to rid Rome of its despot, regarding him as chief actor and manager of the enterprise. Given this analogue, we in the audience might well be inclined to judge Brutus' skill at both playing and managing in the company's behalf.

In this connection, we are given some early clues that Brutus is wanting. He must be persuaded by Cassius and the others that he is capable of performing the lead part. When the conspirators meet for rehearsal, moreover, Brutus refuses to allow the swearing of an oath, by which the company would have become incorporated:

> No, not an oath! If not the face of men,
> The sufferance of our souls, the time's abuse—
> If these be motives weak, break off betimes,
> So let high-sighted tyranny rage on,
> Till each man drop by lottery. (2.1.114–9)

Such bold defiance of convention sounds noble, but it fails to recognize the vital importance of—and the word is critical here—incorporating the plotters. Without such a bond, each man would then be free to choose his own course following the performance of their historic interlude. Just as the players must swear an oath to undertake the business of the company, so must the conspirator-actors agree to share equally the profit and expense of their deed.[11] By failing to secure such an oath, as well as refusing to kill Antony with Caesar, Brutus shows himself ill-equipped to lead the company. Even though he later invites the assassins to bathe their hands in Caesar's blood (3.1.105–10), Brutus fails to comprehend that this outward badge of unity means nothing without the bond of an oath. Indeed, so attired the actors do appear as the bloody butchers of "a savage spectacle" to the waiting audience of citizens.

Though he aspires to act out his philosophical beliefs, then, Brutus emerges from the assassination scene a poor player. To further reinforce this impression, Shakespeare has him agree to allow Antony to deliver the eulogy over fallen Caesar. He assents despite the wise prompting of Cassius:

[*Aside to Brutus*]
  You know not what you do. Do not consent
  That Antony speak in his funeral.
  Know you how much the people may be mov'd
  By that which he will utter. (3.1.232–5)

Brutus here is the actor who must be reminded of his proper role by a stage manager aware of the whole plot and the rhetorical power of another actor.

So Antony, at least in Cassius' eyes, qualifies as an interloper, an outsider who because of his recognized loyalty to Caesar threatens the unity of the group. But Shakespeare may have intended a more particularized identity for Antony, one related to the acting troupe analogue. He could be regarded as the hired man brought in by Brutus for a special production.[12] This analogue helps us to fully comprehend the significance of the coup Antony effects. Not a member of the company of sharers, he is engaged to perform a minor role; in the Forum scene, however, Antony usurps the central role—which Brutus intended to play—in the historical drama. Cassius senses the danger, but Brutus assures him that the citizens will believe him when he declares that Antony speaks only by their permission: "It shall advantage more than do us wrong." A key to successful performing (as the playwright knew) is gauging the reaction of one's audience, something Brutus lacks the insight to do.

Had Antony been invited to join the conspiracy in its early stages, his state of mind and behavior might have been different (though Shakespeare affords no evidence that he possessed the motive or intellectual capacity to bring about the fall of the tyrant). Had he been murdered with Caesar, the plotters could then have used the occasion of their deaths to characterize Antony and Caesar as equally ambitious. But by giving him a role in the upcoming ceremonial interlude, Brutus has made possible the transformation of the scene from solemn funeral to outraged revolt, of the kind we witness in *2 Henry VI*. The actor who leads this rebellion proves to be one who, in Hamlet's words, "out-herods Herod":

  Blood and destruction shall be so in use,
  And dreadful objects so familiar,
  That mothers shall but smile when they behold
  Their infants quartered with the hands of war. (265–8)

This ranting vow is delivered over the body of dead Caesar; on the Forum stage, Antony seeks to "Suit the action to the word, the word to the action."

With Antony's assurance to Caesar's spirit that he will prove an apt instrument of revenge (see Hamlet's promise to his father's spirit), our attention is directed to the public play about to be performed and away from the murder itself. Indeed, Shakespeare depicts the assassination as something of a backstage event. True, we have witnessed the butchery, experienced the horror of the bloody spectacle. Yet the characters of Brutus and Cassius have preoccupied us from the beginning. In reality, Caesar dead emerges as a more significant force than Caesar alive.[13] So the assassination per se might be described as a kind of rehearsal, the true tragedy—Rome's dislocation?—waiting to be played out before the populace.[14] Act Three, scene two, depicts events that determine the course of the rebellion, the fate of those republican ideals Brutus holds so dear. Given Antony's "private" eulogy in 3.1, especially his "Woe to the hand that shed this costly blood!," we are led to expect not a funeral rite but a revenge tragedy.

2

When that play begins, Brutus seems to arrest the plebeians' full attention. Yet he commences the ceremony by dividing the company, sending Cassius with a group of citizens to whom he will explain the meaning of their act. That this too is an unwise decision is later confirmed when Brutus chooses to leave the stage while Antony speaks. For the moment, however, he appears to be in control. Spoken in prose, Brutus' explanation affirms his noble motive, his love of Rome and freedom. The best skills of an academic rhetorician are here exhibited: parallelism ("As Caesar lov'd me, I weep for him; as he was fortunate, I rejoice at it"); antithesis ("Not that I lov'd Caesar less, but that I lov'd Rome more"); repetition ("Believe me for mine honor, and have respect to mine honor, that you may believe"); and the inevitable rhetorical question ("Who is here so base that he would be a bondman?"). There is even an artful pause while Brutus waits for those who are offended to accuse him: "None, Brutus, none." With this reply the self-confident speaker concludes that all is settled and that the murder has been duly justified.

But what we recognize and the plebeians seem to sense is that Brutus' speech, especially its artful structure and reasoned tone, suits better the ears of Senators than those of rude mechanicals. Rendered in dispassionate prose, the justification exposes the speaker's blindness to the reality of human emotion. He does not touch their hearts but is satisfied instead that he has lectured to them on the consequences of ambition. Thus Brutus demonstrates beyond doubt that his proper forum is the hall, not the public stage. Antony entering with Caesar's gashed body in his arms need not speak a word to begin eroding the foundation of Brutus' argument.

Yet when Brutus leaves the Forum, he is acclaimed the new Caesar, an irony that the naive conspirator appears not to discern. While he has acted to save the people from bondage, they respond by urging the kingly part on him. How ignorant he is of the motives of those he seeks to serve! And his departure from the stage at this critical point highlights yet another irony, this one recalling the theatrical analogue. Brutus believes he has spoken the crucial lines of the scene, leaving Antony to perform the simple elegaic rite of burying Caesar. We realize instead that Brutus has delivered only the prologue or chorus and is unaware that he merely prepares the way for the main action and actor, who is now free to speak his vengeful mind without prompting. The change of role from Caesar's successor to prologue-speaker underscores how ill-suited Brutus is to perform the public show necessary to the consolidation of power.

On the other hand, Antony exhibits a gift for playing that stirs his hearers to sudden, violent action. He uses the same rhetorical tools as Brutus, but he makes heavier use of repetition and personal reminiscence (see especially "You all did see that on Lupercal . . . ," 95–7) than did his rival. He repeats two words—"honorable" and "ambitious"—so adeptly that he soon has his audience wondering whether Caesar or Brutus was truly ambitious. More calculatingly, Antony employs a pun to register a shocking picture of the horrible deed in his audience's mind: "O judgment! thou [art] fled to brutish beasts." Now the conspirators are no longer honorable men but destructive animals, a transformation achieved solely by Antony's trenchant poetic art. Like Brutus, Antony also pauses, but not to hear an answer to his rhetorical question. *His* pause is dramatic, an opportunity to choke back tears while his words sink in (105–7). During this pause one of the hearers (*2 Pleb.*) delivers possibly the baldest understatement in the canon: "If thou consider rightly the matter, Caesar has had great wrong."

Thus aroused, the audience stands ready to change its mind about Caesar and the assassination. Antony need only produce the will, an ideal actor/politician's prop, to win the plebeians utterly to his side. But before he will consent to read it (here he reminds us of Richard Gloucester or Iago in his gesture of calculated restraint), Antony descends from the pulpit with the body in his arms. This masterstroke takes our breath away, but it also breaks the imaginary plane between stage and audience. Antony joins the mechanicals as if he were one of them and not a player in the historical drama. More important, as the plebeians make a ring around him and the body, Antony succeeds in creating another stage, with victim and revenger at its center. Now he retells the tragedy of the assassination, pointing to the wounds and identifying the conspirators who made them. Brutus' "most unkindest cut" recalls the "brutish beasts" pun of his earlier remarks and reinforces the moral that in striking down Caesar, Brutus has murdered his own father. Beside pointing to the unnaturalness of such a deed, Antony reminds his auditors that Caesar's fall was theirs: "Then I, and you, and all of us fell down, / Whilst bloody treason flourished over us" (191–2). How vividly this statement echoes Brutus' earlier claim that he was forced to act for fear of tyranny pressing down the citizenry! Shakespeare's irony here intimates that both men embrace their own selfish or sophistic motives for acting, ignoring all the while the good of Rome.

But Antony's inspired touch of scene-painting—traitors covered with innocent blood—confirms his ingenuity as an actor and poet. He has won the audience to his cause in a *coup de théâtre* that blatantly violates the end of playing. Witnesses of a tragedy should leave the playhouse purged of their emotions; instead these hearers are roused to destructive fury by Antony's words. By further associating Caesar's fate with Pompey's—"Even at the base of Pompey's statue / (Which all the while ran blood) great Caesar fell"—Antony seems to justify the citizens' lust for revenge, chronicling the act of treachery as if it were part of a Fall of Princes interlude. The mantle and wounds are assigned choric identities, moreover; they are voices crying against the inhumanity and unnaturalness of the sacrifice. Antony remembers that Caesar first wore the mantle on the day he overcame the Nervii, a tribe renowned for *its* pagan fierceness. The implied comparison between the barbarous Nervii and the assassins is obvious. But Antony's anecdote also underscores his resourcefulness: How did he manage to dredge up such an apparently trivial detail? Had he in fact been waiting for just such a moment to spring this memory on unsuspecting ears? Similarly, his opportunism prompts him to catalogue the wounds made by each conspirator, even though he was not a witness to the killing. How can he or we be sure of these attributions? The question goes unasked and unanswered, of course, because the citizens have been trapped in the web of deep-seated emotion aroused by the speaker. Each rent in the robe qualifies as a piece of evidence of the conspirators' cruelty.

At just the right moment, Antony pulls off the mangled robe (196) to reveal the "marred" body of Caesar himself. While Brutus had represented this event as a funeral, the somber interring of their dead leader's bones, Antony seizes the occasion (as Richard did the funeral of Henry VI) to transform the ceremony into a trial. The body, uncovered and gory, issues as the main piece of evidence in that trial of "honorable" men. (Surely Shakespeare wants *his* audience to associate Caesar's murder with the sacrifice of Christ, whose savaged body revealed the extent of barbarous destructiveness.[15]) When the First Plebeian exclaims "O piteous spectacle!" we recognize that Antony has succeeded brilliantly in creating his play-within-the-play by concurrently exceeding the bounds of art. Shakespeare's playhouse audience's attitude toward him should be shifting—away from admiration toward suspicion—with the increasing hyperbole of his words and actions. Not Caesar's but his own cause motivates him now.

This suspicion of Antony's motives is further confirmed with his disclaimer of oratorical or histrionic powers of speech (210–30). He only speaks "right on," assuring all that he lacks the persuasive skills of Brutus. By now this claim is as hollow and ironic as his affirmation that all the conspirators are "honorable men." (We likewise suspect none of the ingenuousness that attends remarks about his "rude speech" by Othello.) In place of his ill-trained speech, Caesar's wounds have mouths to rouse Romans to mutiny. This corporeal allusion refocuses the citizens' eyes on the body; their immediate reaction is to seek out Brutus' house and burn it down. The wheel has turned suddenly and decisively, and Antony assumes the central role once reserved for Brutus. It is now "most noble Antony!" whom the plebeians urge one another to heed.

As the crowning achievement of his performance, Antony once again reminds the citizens of Caesar's will. This prop, like Caesar's muffled body, arrests the hearers' attention, even though it too seems suspiciously like a sham. Such a document is cited by Plutarch, but Shakespeare introduces it at a time convenient to Antony's political purposes. By possessing it, he substantiates his claim of being Caesar's successor, the executor of his will. Knowing as well that nothing can stop the mob from trampling Caesar's "private arbors, and newplanted orchards," Antony simply lends legal status to civil disobedience. Caesar's will has become the will of the people, a dangerous principle for the state to condone. But Antony too now holds the script of events in his hands, symbolizing his possession of rule. The actor and avenging prince have merged in one identity, a reality confirmed by Antony's *ubi sunt*–like question: "When comes such another?" As the auditors spill out from the Forum stage into the Roman streets, Ambition and Revenge assume the mantle of leadership.

3

To underscore the representation of the Forum scene as play-within on the theme of destructive passion, Shakespeare creates an afterpiece or *coda* depicting the murder of Cinna the poet. The aroused mob ignores this victim's disclaimer that he is not a conspirator, electing instead to tear apart their prey for his bad verses. The scene's didactic purpose seems to be to illustrate the consequences of disorder, the threat to innocent citizens caught in the tide of fury. But the murder of a poet also symbolizes Antony's willful distortion of the end of art. Murdering poets, as Orpheus was dismembered by the Bacchic women, signals the destruction of those charged with chronicling, not making, history. Coming as it does after the Forum interlude, the episode reveals just how completely Antony's actions have perverted the stage/state function. Not only is the play broken, but so is the playwright. The motif is comparable to the beating-of-messengers device in *Antony and Cleopatra*, where such behavior reveals the same blindness.

What began as stately ritual—a noble funeral—in *Julius Caesar* has degenerated into rule by a headless mob killing innocents along with combatants. Antony has shown just how potentially threatening events in the public playhouse can be to the public safety, a point which seems to suit well the moral goal of *Julius Caesar*. By shaping the scene to his own purposes—which prove both vengeful and ambitious—Antony has ravaged the very setting in which historical tragedy carries meaning and purpose. Likewise, the poet/playwright's artistic voice has been stilled by men whose emotions have not been purged but roused to perform yet more horrible deeds.[16] Both Brutus and Antony have in the end failed as actors, one for his inability to understand his audience, the other for manipulating its psyche only too well. In judging both leaders and actors, Shakespeare seems to say, we must look to that Aristotelian balance or "mean" so vital to the proper ruler. (Antony will soon confront such a mediated personality in the figure of Octavius, true inheritor of Julius Caesar's spirit.) Failing such a leader, the state suffers the consequences; Rome falls as the central victim of the tragedy. That men are prone to ignore this dramatic and historical truth is then aptly confirmed by Cassius' memorable comment:

> How many ages hence
> Shall this our lofty scene be acted over
> In states unborn and accents yet unknown.

NOTES

1. All quotations are from G. Blakemore Evans, ed., *The Riverside Shakespeare* (Boston, Mass.: Houghton Mifflin, 1974).

2. That theatrical reenactment of the murder was a commonplace Shakespeare and his audience readily recognized is hinted at in Polonius' self-satisfied pronouncement: "I did enact Julius Caesar: I was kill'd i' the Capitol; Brutus killed me" (*Ham.* 3.2.108). E. K. Chambers cites the performance of "a storie of Pompey" at Court on Twelfth Night of 1581 (*The Elizabethan Stage* 4:158). This play may have depicted Caesar as Pompey's nemesis. Henslowe identifies a play called "seser and pompie" on November 8, 1594, as well as "the 2 pte of sesore" on 18 June 1595 (see *Henslowe's Diary*, ed. W. W. Greg, 1:20). These plays do not survive, however.

3. James L. Calderwood has written extensively on the subject of metadrama. See his *Metadrama in Shakespeare's Henriad* (Berkeley: U of California P, 1979) and *To Be and Not To Be: Negation and Metadrama in* Hamlet (New York: Columbia UP,

1983). See as well Wendy Coppedge Sanford, *Theater as Metaphor in* Hamlet (Cambridge: Harvard UP, 1967).

4. Maynard Mack speaks directly to the linguistic and dramatic implications of the word "acting" in his "The World of *Hamlet*," *Yale Review* 41 (1952): 502–23.

5. *Scenic Form in Shakespeare* (Oxford: Oxford UP, 1971), 226. I have suggested that *Macbeth*'s banquet scene fits the play-within formula as well, Macbeth failing to maintain his mask of kingship and the order of the state. See my *"Macbeth*: The Banquet Scene as Frustrated Play Within," *Shakespeare Jahrbuch* (Weimar) 114 (1978): 107–14. S. Viswanathan explores the related idea of clothing imagery and its relationship to the theatrical metaphor in "Macbeth in the Tiring House: The Clothes and Actor Motifs in the Play," *Anglia* 100 (1982): 18–35.

6. The concept of the citizens as reluctant audience is established earlier in this scene when Buckingham informs Richard of his failed attempt to coax from them a proclamation of kingship. In answer to Buckingham's "God save Richard, England's royal king!" they "spake not a word" (See *R3* 3.7.5–41.) J. L. Styan argues convincingly that this scene, along with others in which Richard assumes roles, "tests . . . the theatre's power of elasticity: how far can an audience be persuaded by mere convention to lend itself to villainy?" See *Drama, Stage and Audience* (Cambridge: Cambridge UP, 1975), 176–7.

7. One is inclined to believe that Shakespeare's consistent belief is that rebellion invites chaos, which can only result in blind destruction of existing order. Stephen Greenblatt's list of instances of self-fashioning includes a description of the "alien" (#4) which seems to apply to Shakespearean rioters. See *Renaissance Self-Fashioning: From More to Shakespeare* (Chicago: U of Chicago P, 1980), 9.

8. G. E. Bentley, *The Profession of Player in Shakespeare's Time, 1590–1642* (Princeton: Princeton UP, 1984), 25.

9. The term "adventurer" had a commercial connotation as early as the 1480s, when Henry VII established the Society of Merchant Adventurers. See *OED*.

10. Ten sharers signed the debt contract of the Lord Admiral's men in 1598. See Bentley, 27.

11. Bentley, 26.

12. Though hired men performed a variety of services useful to the company—players, musicians, book holders or prompters, gatherers—those who acted were given unassigned roles in most productions. See Bentley, 68–112.

13. Nicholas Brooke observes that "Caesar's arrogance and weakness are part of an insistent naturalism set against another order governed by storm and blood" (*Shakespeare's Early Tragedies* [London: Methuen, 1968], 145).

14. The assassination was referred to in the 1587 edition of the *Mirror for Magistrates*, a collection of tragedies dramatized in the manner of Lydgate's rendering of Boccaccio's *Falls of Princes*.

15. See T. S. Dorsch, ed. *The Arden Julius Caesar* (London: Methuen, 1961), xxxviii–xxxix.

16. That Shakespeare had a clear sense of the purging purpose of tragedy is exhibited in Hamlet's speech to the players, 3.2.1–45. Antony's performance might be called "overdone" (26), leading the "judicious" to "grieve" (27).

JAN H. BLITS

Manliness and Friendship
in Julius Caesar

The city of Rome had besides its proper name another secret one, known only to a few. It is believed by some to have been "Valentia," the Latin translation of "Roma" ["strength" in Greek]; others think it was "Amor" ("Roma" read backwards).
      —G. W. F. Hegel, *The Philosophy of History*, Part III, Section 1

Shakespeare's *Julius Caesar* examines the lives and souls of the sort of men who made republican Rome the foremost model of political greatness and glory. The men we see in the play have the strongest desire for worldly glory and, regarding honor as the highest good, relentlessly strive to win it. They look up to the things that make men strong and, having tremendous pride and trust in their own "strength of spirit" (I.iii.95),[1] jealously contend with one another for outstanding distinctions. Their hearts are, as Cassius says, "hearts of controversy" (I.ii.108). Loving victory, dominance, and honor, they characteristically equate manliness and human excellence. Cassius sums up their view of their humanity when, bemoaning Rome's acquiescence to Caesar, he says,

> But, woe the while! our fathers' minds are dead,
> And we are govern'd with our mothers' spirits;
> Our yoke and sufferance show us womanish.
>   (I.iii.82–84)

From *The End of the Ancient Republic: Shakespeare's* Julius Caesar, pp. 3–20. © 1993 by the Center for the Philosophy of Science.

31

Rome is a man's world. No one in *Caesar* has a good word for women. Even Portia, Brutus' noble wife, is a misogynist. Even she, ashamed of her woman's heart, insists that the best human qualities neither come from nor belong to women.[2] If a woman like herself happens to show them, she does so in spite of her sex. She is "stronger than [her] sex" (II.i.296); she is manly.

That a woman must somehow overcome her nature to show the highest virtue points to the close correlation in *Caesar* between manliness and rising up or rising above the common or merely human things. Throughout the play men's activities and ambitions are repeatedly expressed in terms of standing, rising, climbing to new heights, "soar[ing] above the view of men" (I.i.74), and reaching "the upmost round" (II.i.24) while scorning everything below; and their defects and defeats expressed in the contrary terms of bending, bowing, lying, crouching, fawning, falling, sinking, kneeling, shaking, trembling, and melting.[3] The manly is associated with the firm, the brilliant, the cold, the independent, the high and the noble; the womanish, with the soft, the dull, the warm, the dependent, the low and the lowly. The manly is the outstanding; the womanish, the obscure. The manly both contains and confers distinctions. The womanish does neither. Like the body, it is the great equalizer. It tends to level all important differences.[4]

Shakespeare shows that the manly love of distinction engenders a characteristic attitude towards the world. It is one of resisting and overcoming all the things that threaten to drag a man down or overshadow him. This fundamental Roman stance is reflected in part by the great importance attached to wakefulness. Early on the ides of March, Brutus tells the other conspirators that he has been "awake all night" (II.i.88). Indeed,

> Since Cassius first did whet me against Caesar,
> I have not slept.
> (ll. 61–62)

His servant, Lucius, can "Enjoy the honey-heavy dew of slumber," because, as Brutus says, the boy has none of the "busy care[s]" that occupy "the brains of men" (ll. 230, 232). But the conspirators and Caesar alike have been kept awake by just such cares. Only those outside the political realm belong in bed. Thus Brutus sends Lucius back to bed soon after awakening him and, shortly afterwards, tells Portia, too, to "go to bed" when she complains of his having left "his wholesome bed" (ll. 237ff.). But he himself is aroused to act against Caesar by Cassius' anonymous note accusing him of sleeping and urging him to awake (ll. 46ff.); and then, arguing that they need nothing but their Roman cause to "prick" them to action, he spurs his co-conspirators on by associating "The melting spirits of women"—in contrast to "th' insuppressive mettle of our spirits"—with each man returning "to his idle bed" (ll. 114ff.).[5] It is not going too far to say that from the Roman point of view nothing very interesting ever happens in bed.[6]

Brutus and the others understand the private world to be destructive of manliness. As he indicates at Sardis shortly before the decisive battle of Philippi, to succumb to sleep is to succumb to necessity. Brutus finally puts his work aside and prepares for bed only because "nature must obey necessity" (IV.iii.226). Natural necessity, he implies, is not part of his nature. His noble nature is to oppose necessity. So while women and children "look for a time of rest" (l. 261), Brutus "will niggard" sleep with only "a little rest" (l. 227). He opposes "murd'rous slumber" (l. 266) because he opposes any form of obscurity. Men like him resist all forms of reclining because to recline is to surrender one's standing in the world. Their characteristic opposition to the earth's downward pull is well expressed by Alexander the Great's remark that, more than anything else, sleep and sex reminded him he was not a god.[7]

The specific character of manly virtue is indicated by Portia, who gashes herself in the thigh to prove that she is strong enough to keep Brutus' secret plans in confidence. The important difference between the sexes, she seems to believe, is that men are stronger than their bodies but women are not. Women are inconstant because they are weaker than bodily fears and pains.[8] One might therefore suppose that their characteristic trait is concern with necessary rather than with noble things. But Portia's subsequent actions reveal something she herself fails to see. The self-inflicted wound she calls "strong proof of my constancy" (II.i.299) turns out to be no proof at all. As soon as Brutus leaves, she is overwhelmed by anxious fears for his welfare, and her strong "patience" (l. 301) and manly endurance quickly vanish. There are evidently worse tortures for her than bodily pains and even death. Love for her husband makes her more a woman than the superiority to her body makes her a man. If, as she says, "The heart of woman" is a "weak thing" (II.iv.39–40), its weakness, her actions seem to show, stems not from fear but from affection, from loving another more than herself.

While manliness no doubt sustains a timocracy like the Roman republic, such an honor-loving regime is often praised for fostering fraternity. Its citizens, bound together by a common ancestry and upbringing, are free and equal; they respect the mutual claims to rule that only manly virtue can enforce. It is therefore fitting that only "man" is mentioned in *Caesar* more often than "love" or "friendship"[9] and the most elaborated friendship in the play is that of the leaders of the republican faction. In fact, Brutus and Cassius call each other "brother" as many as eight times[10] although Shakespeare never explains that they are brothers-in-law.[11] Shakespeare's silence is appropriately misleading. Brutus and Cassius' fraternal form of address seems entirely elective and a sign of the sort of friendship nurtured by the manly regime under which they live and which they die defending.[12] Their friendship does, I think, epitomize the republic, but not as just suggested or usually understood.

The implications of the Roman view of virtue are strikingly revealed when the tensions inherent in Brutus and Cassius' friendship surface in their ugly quarrel at Sardis late in the play. Indeed, manliness and friendship are the express themes of the quarrel. Two principal threads, closely tied, run through the scene: 1) presuming upon Cassius' expressed love, Brutus challenges his manliness and, in particular, demeans and taunts his proud anger (esp. IV.iii.38–50); and 2) he refuses to confess any love until Cassius shames himself by announcing that he utterly despairs of Brutus' contempt and will do anything to have his love (ll. 92–106). What is perhaps most telling, however, occurs not during the quarrel itself but during their apparent reconciliation (ll. 106ff.). Cassius' previous conciliatory efforts notwithstanding, Brutus still makes him solicit an explicit admission of love and forces him to plead for it, moreover, by accepting Brutus' degrading characterization of his anger as the effect of an irritable, unmanly disposition (ll. 39–50, 106–112). Thus Cassius, apologizing for having gotten angry in the first place, diffidently asks,

> Have not you love enough to bear with me,
> When that rash humour which my mother gave me
> Makes me forgetful?

And Brutus answers with only a meager "Yes," to which he quickly adds, sealing Cassius' disgrace,

> ... and from henceforth
> When you are over-earnest with your Brutus,
> He'll think your mother chides, and leave you so.
>   (ll. 118–122)

Brutus confesses only to having enough love to overlook Cassius' womanish spirit. He shall excuse his "over-earnestness" because he shall regard such fits of temper as the chiding of Cassius' mother rather than the spirited anger proper to a man.

Men such as Brutus are ambitious for love. They wish to be loved rather than to love because being loved closely resembles being honored.[13] Both are tributes of esteem. Love between such men is therefore jealous; like honor, it is ardently sought and only begrudgingly given. Unrequited "shows of love"

(I.ii.33,46) therefore amount to confessions of envy. A Roman, moreover, is a man's man. He admires manly men and seeks love from men he himself could love. The erotic Antony is disparaged by his own men in *Antony and Cleopatra* not simply because he flees battle to pursue Cleopatra but more generally because he fights bravely chiefly to impress a woman and win her love. As one of his officers complains, "so our leader's led, / And we are women's men" (*Ant.*, III.vii.69–70). The republican contest for love, however, is a contest in manliness for the love of other manly men. Moments before the quarrel, Brutus, anticipating the heart of the quarrel, contrasts true and false friends. The difference turns wholly on manly strength. Using a metaphor from war to describe what constitutes a false friend, he says,

> But hollow men, like horses hot at hand,
> Make gallant show and promise of their mettle;
> But when they should endure the bloody spur,
> They fall their crests, and like deceitful jades
> Sink in the trial.
>   (IV.ii.23–27)

False friends are hollow warriors. They lack the dauntless strength they pretend to have. The quarrel brings out the significance of this view of virtue and friendship: the manly contest for love issues finally in a struggle to crush a friend by unmanning his proud heart. Love is not an end in itself, but rather a means to win victory in the defeat and shame of a friend.[14]

Manliness is a contentious virtue. It is a "virtue" that "cannot live / Out of the teeth of emulation" (II.iii.11–12). Untempered, it is hungry, devouring, and finally self-consuming. Nothing could lower Cassius more in Brutus' esteem than his swallowing his repeated abuse and openly confessing that he is "Hated by one he loves; brav'd by his brother" (IV.iii.95). But manly love is spirited, not affectionate. It does not aim at collapsing the distance between men into intimacy but rather at expanding that distance to the point where friendship finally becomes impossible, as Caesar himself most vividly demonstrates. As manliness is displayed primarily in battle, so the combat between warriors does not stop at the city's walls. It pervades their loves as well as their enmities. Rome's civil strife seems to be Roman friendship writ large.

Antony, the major counterexample, is in many ways the exception who confirms the rule. No one can doubt that his love is spirited and has an ambitious quality. But his sought-for victory in love is altogether different from Brutus'. Just as he declares at the outset of *Antony and Cleopatra* that the "nobleness of life" is for lovers to embrace

> . . . when such a mutual pair
> And such a twain can do't, in which I bind,
> On pain of punishment, the world to weet
> We stand up peerless,
>   (I.i.36–40)

so too, when he thinks Cleopatra has killed herself for him, he wishes to end his own life so that, reunited in death, they can win even greater acknowledgment as a matchless pair:

> Eros!—I come, my queen—Eros!—Stay for me,
> Where souls do couch on flowers, we'll hand in hand
> And with our sprightly port make the ghosts gaze.
> Dido and her Aeneas shall want troops,
> And all the haunt be ours.
>   (IV.xiv.50–54)[15]

Antony wants to out-love all other great lovers and be recognized as the greatest lover the world has ever known. The achievement he imagines may imply the defeat of all other heroic lovers, but his victory would in no sense be the defeat of his own lover. He does not seek to win another's "hot" love (*JC*, IV.ii.19) while coldly withholding his own. On the contrary, his envisaged triumph is shared by Cleopatra and is, moreover, their shared glory as a singular couple. Indeed, it rests on the wished-for prospect that nothing at all, not even their bodies, will ever again separate their souls. It is the victory of the utmost devotion and intimacy between "a mutual pair."

Antony neither resents Caesar's domination like Cassius, nor seeks to dominate other men's hearts like Brutus. Yet, while having great love for Caesar, he never presumes an equality with him. His ready submission may therefore seem to foreshadow the Empire where the Emperor has no equals and all citizens are reduced to private men subject to his will.[16] But Antony loves Caesar solely for his superlative nobility and not for his favors. To him, Caesar was "the noblest man / That ever lived in the tide of times" (III.i.256–257). Antony's heart is ruled, as Cassius correctly fears, by "the ingrafted love he bears to Caesar" (II.i.184), a love which Caesar's murder turns into the most savage desire for revenge. It is not hard to see that what Antony gives to Cleopatra, or gives up for her, is meant to measure his love.[17] Not only his giving her "realms and islands" so bounteously that they are like small change "dropp'd from his pocket" (V.ii.92), but also, and even more importantly, the battles he loses or, more exactly, the losses he actively pursues, the "Kingdoms and provinces" he "kiss[es] away" (III.x.7–8), and most of all his self-inflicted death—all this is meant to measure his overflowing love.[18] The same is true of his ferocious vengeance for Caesar's assassination. However cruel and even inhuman, the vengeance is, above all, an act of giving, not of taking. Its indiscriminate savagery is intended to prove "That I did love thee, Caesar, O, 'tis true!" (III.i.194). It shows that he will spare nothing—that he will even sink to the level of a beast and scourge all human or humane feeling from the innocent as well as the guilty (III.i.254–275)—for his love. As different as they appear, Antony's terrible vengeance for Caesar is of a piece with his lavish gifts and enormous sacrifices for Cleopatra. It manifests a heart that will give up everything dear for his "strucken" "deer" (III.i.209). This "Herculean Roman" (*Ant.*, I.iii.84) is nothing if not a thoroughly immoderate lover.

In contrast to Antony, "lean and hungry" Cassius is austere and unerotic, often petty and envious, and never playful.[19] No one in *Caesar* speaks of the shame of unmanliness as much or as vehemently as he. Yet, notwithstanding his ardent wish to be entirely spirited and always manly, Cassius is the leading republican example of the tension between manliness and womanliness. If Brutus is lately "with himself at war" (I.ii.45) because of his conflicting loves for Rome and Caesar, Cassius is always at war with himself because of the conflicting sides of his mixed but unstable nature—a womanly side drawing him towards others and a manly one pulling him back or away. Although he is unquestionably shrewder than Brutus, Cassius' temper is much more volatile and his passions far less restrained. Despite his strong self-contempt for any real or imagined trace of softness, his affection is stirred as easily by sorrow as his manly resentment is provoked by envy, and he often shows solicitous care for others, even his equals. He alone shows deep feeling at the news of Cicero's murder; and in sharp contrast to Brutus, who boasts that "No man bears sorrow better" and then feigns ignorance of his wife's death to impress other men with his stoic endurance, he is willing to let others see how much he takes to heart the "insupportable and touching loss" of Portia. Cassius may have "in art" as much manly patience as Brutus to endure Portia's suicide "like a Roman," "But yet my nature," he realizes or perhaps confesses, "could not bear it so" (IV.iii.143–194). If he appears more concerned than Brutus with manliness, he does so, paradoxically, precisely because he lacks Brutus' manly constancy and reserve.

The man Cassius calls his "best friend" is his lieutenant Titinius (V.iii.35). Their friendship is probably the nearest example in *Caesar* of the sort the republic claims to foster and Brutus suggests when he describes "hearts / Of brothers' temper" as sharing "all kind love, good thoughts, and reverence" (III.i.174–176). Cassius and Titinius do indeed have mutual regard and good will. Yet their friendship is not altogether unlike Brutus and Cassius'. It too demonstrates, though in a different way, that manliness separates honor-loving men. Appropriately, the scene at Philippi depicting their friendship also presents their deaths. Each kills himself, blaming himself at least in part for the other's death. Their suicides, however, are not the same. Whereas Titinius can feel great sorrow and affection for his commander without losing pride in his Romanness (V.iii.51–90), Cassius cannot wish to die for love of another without feeling shame at his own unmanliness. During the battle, Cassius, appealing expressly to Titinius' love for him, asks him to take his (Cassius') horse and ride to where he can tell whether certain troops are friend or enemy; and, moments later, learning that Titinius has been encircled by horsemen shouting for joy, he jumps to the wrong conclusion. Deciding then to kill himself, he says in disgust,

> O, coward that I am, to live so long,
> To see my best friend ta'en before my face.
>   (V.iii.34–35)

The qualities surrounding Cassius' death are considered unmanly by all the major figures in the play. Rashness and a fatalistic despair, born of weariness and melancholic self-doubt, lead to his mistake, and his own imagined cowardice determines his act. Yet whatever else it is—and it certainly is many things[20]—Cassius' suicide is an act of friendship. Because his manliness is partly tempered by its opposite, he can wish to die for another man who soon returns the tribute in kind. But, importantly, Cassius tries to stifle his fond wish. Ashamed of all his unmanly qualities, he intends his suicide to repudiate the side of his nature that allows him to choose death thinking of anything but his honor. Ruled by his spirited heart, he kills himself, ultimately, more out of manly pride or shame than love or sorrow. The fundamentally Roman quality of his friendship with Titinius is indicated both by his suppression of his own affection and by the way each man emulates the other's brave death. But it is pointed up most of all by the more basic fact that Cassius' "best friend," though a nobleman, is not his equal. Whatever closeness there may be between them depends decisively on the distance their unmistakable inequality preserves.

As Cassius' suicide points to the limits of closeness among Roman men, so Portia's shows the limits of sharing within a Roman marriage. It marks the unattainability of the intimacy she desires from a virtuous marriage. Portia's attempt to persuade Brutus to confide in her contains the play's only expression of intimate, erotic love. Calling herself "your self, your half," she tries to "charm" him

... by my once commended beauty,
By all your vows of love, and that great vow
Which did incorporate and make us one.
    (II.i.271–274)

Love's desire or goal seems to inspire love's own special language. Lovers speak as if nothing at all separated them. Love not only makes or shows them equals, but even incorporates them and makes them indistinguishable parts of "one." Yet Portia makes this plea upon her knees. She says she would not have to kneel if Brutus were gentle. His customary gentleness, she suggests, implies or presupposes mutual respect. We see for ourselves, however, that Brutus is in fact much gentler with unequals than equals, and gentlest of all with his servant boy, Lucius. Portia nevertheless associates his recent ungentleness with his reticence and distance. "Within the bond of marriage," she continues, "tell me, Brutus,"

Is it excepted I should know no secrets
That appertain to you? Am I your self
But, as it were, in sort or limitation,
To keep with you at meals, comfort your bed,
And talk to you sometimes? Dwell I but in
    the suburbs
Of your good pleasure? If it be no more,
Portia is Brutus' harlot, not his wife.
    (ll. 280–287)

But because she is "his wife," Portia is indeed Brutus' "self / But, as it were, in sort or limitation." And her metaphor of "suburbs" as well as her subsequent self-inflicted wound tells us why. "You are my true and honourable wife," Brutus assures her,

As dear to me as are the ruddy drops
That visit my sad heart.
    (ll. 288–290)

Portia may be "dear" to him,[21] but Brutus' manly virtue rests on his valuing his heart more than his blood, his public life more than his marriage. As her own metaphor of "suburbs" ironically anticipates, Portia only "visits" Brutus' heart; she does not "dwell" there. The love of fame and honor does.

Portia wishes her conjugal plea would succeed, that Brutus would tell her what "by the right and virtue of my place / I ought to know of" (ll. 269–270). Yet, as her having already taken steps to prove herself "stronger than [her] sex" (l. 296) indicates, she never really expected it would. Recognizing that Brutus could never consider a woman his equal, she thinks she must prove herself a man to win his confidence. She realizes that, to the extent she is a woman, Brutus will never give her his trust. She fails to realize, however, that, to the extent she proves herself a man, he can no more unfold himself to her than to any other man (cf. I.ii.38–40). Since honor requires him to hide his weakness from everyone he respects and whose respect he seeks, her manly proof can succeed no better than her conjugal plea. Although Brutus at last promises to reveal his secrets, he in fact leaves home just moments later and does not return before Caesar's assassination.[22] Portia's self-inflicted wound succeeds only in shaming him to bear his troubles with greater manly patience. It inspires his prayer to be worthy of such a "noble wife" (ll. 302–303).[23]

Portia does not really understand the virtue she tries to emulate. She has too exalted a view of manliness to see its limitations. She recognizes that manliness involves the sort of strength that makes one superior to bodily pains and pleasures, but not that at the same time and for the same reason it also tends to make one superior to personal affection and sorrow. She is drawn to Brutus because of his virtue and imagines he would be drawn to her because of the same. Believing manliness the highest virtue, she also believes it supports or gives rise to every excellent human quality as well. She does not, or perhaps cannot, see that the virtue she most admires resists the sharing she desires as it strives for noble distinction, that it distances men from one another as it distances them from their own bodies. In both a literal and a figurative sense, the distance between Portia and Brutus leads to her death. Her suicide, which closely parallels her sudden loss of constancy when Brutus leaves home after her manly proof, is the piteous culmination of the madness caused by her extreme "impatience" for his return from the war and her desperate "grief" over the growing power of his Caesarian foes (IV.iii.151–155). Her touching death shows just how much her happiness and even her life depend on the closeness and well-being of the man she loves. Portia is the only character in *Caesar* to die solely for the love of another. Despite her real shame at the weakness of a woman's heart, hers is the only suicide not meant to prove manly strength.

No suicide is less like Portia's than Brutus'. Everyone understands his, quite properly, to have been a manly, death-defying act.[24] By killing himself in high Roman fashion, Brutus deprives his enemies of the honor of killing or capturing him. In another sense as well, however, "no man else hath honor by his death" (V.v.57). Brutus, like Caesar, dies tasting his unshared glory. The very last time he mentions Cassius is when he comes upon his and Titinius' corpses:

> Are yet two Romans living such as these?
> The last of all the Romans, fare thee well!
> It is impossible that ever Rome
> Should breed thy fellow. Friends, I owe more tears
> To this dead man than you shall see me pay.
> I shall find time, Cassius, I shall find time.
>   (V.iii.98–103)

Acknowledging the republican cause has been lost, Brutus praises Cassius in a way befitting what the republic had always stood for. He praises him and Titinius in the same breath. He praises them, in other words, as equals, as fellow citizens, as sons of Rome (cf. V.iii.63). For himself, however, Brutus seeks preeminent distinction, not republican equality. Just as he never again mentions Portia (even in soliloquy) after stoically bidding her farewell at Sardis (IV.iii.189–191), so he forgets Cassius entirely when, about to kill himself, he envisions the glory he shall win for his life:

> Countrymen,
> My heart doth joy that yet in all my life
> I found no man but he was true to me.
> I shall have glory by this losing day
> More than Octavius and Mark Antony
> By this vile conquest shall attain unto.
> So fare you well at once; for Brutus' tongue
> Hath almost ended his life's history.
> Night hangs upon mine eyes; my bones would rest,
> That have but labour'd to attain this hour.
>   (V.v.33–42)

Brutus' thoughts center on himself. He imagines his fame and glory as his alone, neither blurred nor obscured by any fellow Roman. More importantly and surprisingly, however, he sees his personal victory undiminished and perhaps even enhanced by his country's collapse. His "life's history" somehow stands above or apart from Rome. Brutus had of course claimed to be guided only by his country's good. "I know no personal cause to spurn at him," he had said of Caesar, "but for the general" (II.i.11–12). Indeed, Caesar's slaying, he had argued, was a personal sacrifice: "Not that I loved Caesar less, but that I loved Rome more" (III.ii.22–23). Moreover, as the sacrifice of a dear friend was proof of his fully public-spirited virtue, so too was his declared willingness to kill himself if necessary for the good of Rome: "as I slew my best lover for the good of Rome," he had pledged at Caesar's funeral, "I have the same dagger for myself, when it shall please my country to need my death" (III.ii.46–48).[25] Yet, when Brutus does finally turn his sword upon himself, Rome's welfare is absent from his thoughts. He speaks proudly of his personal "joy" and "glory," but while in effect eulogizing himself, he says not a word in praise of the republic or to lament its passing.[26] Indeed, his only allusion to Rome is that he shall have more glory than her conquerors. His personal triumph eclipses the "vile conquest" of Rome herself.[27]

Brutus sees his end as epitomizing and completing his virtuous life. He regards his death as far more than a last-ditch effort to salvage some honor from defeat, even while he understands suicide as the only honorable choice left to him (V.v.23–25; see also V.i.98–113). His end is his crowning conquest in manly love. Just as Lucilius bravely risks his own disgrace and death for the sake of defending Brutus' manly honor (V.iv.12–25; see also V.v.58–59), so, likewise, the refusal of Brutus' "poor remains of friends" to kill him when he asks them to fills his heart with joy because he understands their reluctance to spring from love (V.v.1–42).[28] Brutus believes the personal loyalty and sacrifices of his loving admirers and friends serve to show how, to the last, he is held in esteem by Rome. In more than the most obvious way, his death is Caesar's fitting revenge. For in Brutus' own eyes, the ultimate measure of his fame and glory is not his public-spirited devotion to his country but his countrymen's personal devotion to him.[29] In the end, the virtue of the "Soul of Rome" (II.i.321) shows itself as manliness, not patriotism. The Roman love of distinction, spurring him to master other men's hearts, separates Brutus finally not only from his friends and family, but even, or perhaps especially, from Rome herself.

Brutus does of course win singular praise and glory. Antony, who calls him "the noblest Roman of them all," says,

> His life was gentle, and all the elements
> So mix'd in him, that Nature might stand up
> And say to all the world, "This was a man!"
>   (V.v.69, 73–75)

In spite of Antony's generous praise, or rather precisely because of the ambiguity of "a man," the untempered affirmation of manliness seems ultimately to issue in the repudiation of one's "mix'd" nature. Even in "gentle Brutus," the Roman view of excellence encourages the desire to have all of the manly and none of the womanly qualities. Stressing hardness, distance, and assertiveness, it teaches men a willingness to risk simple cruelty and callousness in order to avoid all signs of softness, dependence, and weakness. Brutus, we saw, describes "hearts / Of brothers' temper" as sharing "all kind love, good thoughts, and reverence." But his own actions, particularly in the quarrel with his "brother" Cassius, remind us that while Rome was founded by a pair of brothers, even her own traditional accounts depict her sacred origins as lying not in fraternity but fratricide.[30] Moreover, just as Shakespeare frequently reminds us of the literal meaning of Brutus' name,[31] so he also reminds us that those same Roman accounts say Romulus was nurtured by a she-wolf.[32] Shakespeare, I think, truly admires Roman virtue. In *Caesar* he shows that such excellence does indeed involve more than human strength. But Shakespeare's appreciation of manly virtue is by no means unqualified. His portrayal of Rome, like Rome's own traditional accounts of her foundations, suggests that the Romans ultimately debase the human in order to elevate the man.

Notes

1. References are to the Arden editions of *Julius Caesar*, ed. T. S. Dorsch, and *Antony and Cleopatra*, ed. M. R. Ridley (London: Methuen, 1964).

2. II.i.292ff.; II.iv.6–9, 39–40. For the Roman patriots' disparaging their maternal origins as much as they revere their paternal origins, see I.ii.111–114, 156–159; I.iii.80–84; II.i.294–297; IV.iii.118–122; V.iii.67–71; V.iv.1–11. Note also that "ancestor(s)" always refers only to men: I.ii.111, I.iii.80–84, II.i.53–54, III.ii.51. For the fact that "virtue" derives from the Latin word for "man," see Cicero, *Tusculan Disputations*, II.43.

3. E.g., I.i.72–75; I.ii.99–136; II.i.21–27, 118, 142, 167; III.i.31–77, 122–137, 148–150, 204–210; IV.ii.23–27; IV.iii.38–50, 66–69; V.i.41–44; V.iii.57–64.

4. I.ii.268–272; I.iii.80–84; II.i.122, 292–297; IV.iv.6–10, 39–40.

5. See also I.iii.164, II.i.98–99; and cf. in context IV.iii.92ff. For Lucius, see further IV.iii.235–271. And for Caesar's estimation of "such men as sleep a-nights," see I.ii.189f. Also, note II.ii.116–117.

6. Just as the possibility of a Roman woman warrior like Antony's wife Fulvia is totally suppressed in *Caesar* (see *Ant.*, I.ii.85–91; II.i.40; II.ii.42–44, 61–66, 94–98; also I.i.20, 28–32; I.ii.101–106), so too is Caesar's erotic interest in a woman like Cleopatra (see *ibid.*, I.v.29–31, 66–75; II.ii.226–228; II.vi.64–70; III.xiii.116–117; cf. *JC*, I.ii.1–11).

7. Plutarch, *Alexander the Great*, 22.3.

8. For the importance of constancy, see Caesar's claim to divinity at III.i.31–77, esp. 58–73.

9. "Man" (including its variants) appears 148 times; "love," 51 times; "friend," 53 times. By comparison, "Rome" occurs 38, "Roman" and "Romans" together 35 times. Only Caesar's name is mentioned more often than "man."

10. IV.ii.37, 39; IV.iii.95, 211, 232, 236, 247, 303; see also II.i.70.

11. See Plutarch, *Brutus*, 6.1–2.

12. Shakespeare's silence also has the effect of concealing that Cassius is married, thus making him appear a fully spirited or public man.

13. Aristotle, *Nicomachean Ethics*, 1159a13–15.

14. See esp. IV.iii.41–50.

15. Cf. Cassius' mention of Aeneas (I.ii.111–114).

16. Paul A. Cantor, *Shakespeare's Rome* (Ithaca: Cornell Univ. Press, 1976) 129f.

17. *Ibid.*, 148–156.

18. Antony of course insists that his love is too great to be measured: "There's beggary in the love that can be reckon'd" (I.i.15).

19. See esp. I.ii.189–207. See also note 12 above.

20. Cassius' last words (V.iii.45–46), like Brutus' (V.v.50–51), acknowledge Caesar's personal victory, in the former case as a matter of revenge, in the latter as a matter of love.

21. Note that Brutus never actually says he loves Portia, though he speaks often of love.

22. Brutus cannot have returned home after II.i. When he leaves with Ligarius, he says he will reveal his plans "to thee, as we are going / To whom it must be done" (II.i.330–331); and soon afterwards they arrive together at Caesar's house to escort him to the Capitol (II.ii.108ff.). Yet there is no inconsistency in Portia's knowing in II.iv what she asks to be told in II.i. She knows as much when she asks Brutus' secret as she does later when she almost blurts it out. Whether or not she has overheard the conspirators (who leave almost immediately before she enters), it is clear from what she says and does in the earlier scene that she knows that what troubles Brutus is political and involves him in dangerous clandestine nighttime meetings. It would not require much for her to imagine the rest. Shakespeare's point, I think, is not that Portia wants to know Brutus' secret; rather, she wants him to "Tell me your counsels" (II.i.298) on the grounds that she is worthy of his trust.

23. For a contrary view of Portia and Brutus, see Mungo MacCallum, *Shakespeare's Roman Plays and Their Background* (London: Macmillan and Company, 1967) 235f., 272f., and Allan Bloom, *Shakespeare's Politics* (New York: Basic Books, 1964) 101–103. See also Jay L. Halio, "*Harmartia*, Brutus, and the Failure of Personal Confrontation," *The Personalist*, Vol. 48, No. 1 (Winter 1967) 51–52.

24. V.v.52ff.; cf. V.i.98–113, V.iv. *passim*, V.v.23–25. By contrast, only Titinius calls the dead Cassius "brave" (V.iii.80); despite everything, his death is seen by others as womanish (see V.iii.58ff.). It is perhaps not surprising that no one mentions Cassius in the last two scenes of the play.

25. See also I.ii.81–88.

26. Compare Brutus' silence here with what he says in the corresponding speech in Plutarch (*Brutus*, 52.2–3): "It rejoiceth my heart," he begins, "that not one of my friends hath failed me at my need, and I do not complain of my fortune, but only for my country's sake. . . ." *Shakespeare's Plutarch*, ed. W. W. Skeat (London: Macmillan and Company, 1875) 151.

27. The last time Brutus mentions Rome is also the last time he mentions Cassius.

28. MacCallum, 271.

29. This spirit of personalism allows Octavius to take into service those whom he says "serv'd Brutus" (V.v.60)—he does not say, "serv'd Rome under Brutus"—and who are recommended to him on the basis of their personal devotion. Note that even Massala speaks of Brutus as "my master" (V.v.52, 64–67). For a discussion of the

spirit of personalism in *Caesar*, see Jan H. Blits, "Caesarism and the End of Republican Rome," *The Journal of Politics*, Vol. 43, No. 1 (Feb. 1981) 40–55.

30. It is striking and revealing that all eight of Brutus' and Cassius' references
to each other as "brother" occur in the scene at Sardis and in the context of a contest
of wills. The first occurs literally in the opening words of their quarrel; the second
when Brutus, answering Cassius' angry charge, demands to know how he should
wrong "a brother" if he does not wrong even his enemies (IV.ii.37–39). The third
reference occurs when Cassius, "aweary of the world," despairingly shames himself
by acknowledging he is "Hated by one he loves; brav'd by his brother" (IV.iii.95);
and the fourth not long after the quarrel itself when Cassius, commanding "Hear
me, good brother" (l. 211), tries (but fails) to counter Brutus' willful overruling of
his more prudent battle plans and then is forced for the first time to defer explicitly to his will (ll. 223–224). The next two references seem, by contrast, to stress
reconciliation and even amity. Just a moment or so later, Cassius, taking leave, begs
his "dear brother" not to let "such division" ever come "'tween our souls" again; and
Brutus, assuring him that everything is well, bids "Good night, good brother" (ll.
232–236). Despite one's first impression, however, Brutus' use of "good brother"
does not reflect a restored equality or mutual respect between him and Cassius.
Coming in the general wake of their quarrel and less than a dozen lines after Cassius explicitly submits to his will, his use of the phrase springs from the generosity
of a conqueror, not the manly esteem of an equal. Brutus can afford to show Cassius greater friendliness and even praise him more highly than ever before (l. 231)
precisely because Cassius, having been forced to acknowledge the inequality in
their friendship, can no longer threaten his domination. Indeed, Brutus' valediction
"Good night, good brother" comes in direct response to Cassius' valediction "Good
night, my lord" (l. 236). At no other time does Cassius ever call anyone his "lord."
In accordance with all this, the last two references to "brother" both involve Brutus'
issuing Cassius military orders (ll. 247, 303). The only other time either man is spoken of as the other's "brother" (II.i.70) directly precedes the meeting of conspirators
when Brutus, forcing Cassius to bow to his moral domination, supplants him as the
conspiracy's leader.

31. Most esp. at III.i.77.

32. I.ii.1–11; for the connection between the Lupercal race and the story of
Romulus, see Plutarch, *Romulus* 21.3–8, and Ovid, *Fasti* II.381ff.

NICHOLAS VISSER

Plebeian Politics in Julius Caesar

At the time of the school's boycott of 1980, first-year students in the English department at Rhodes were studying *Julius Caesar*. To supplement the lectures, the department organized a showing of Joseph Mankiewicz's 1953 film of the play with James Mason as Brutus, John Gielgud as Cassius, and, famously, Marlon Brando as Antony. That same year the play was a prescribed text for the matriculation examination in DET[1] schools. Some of the boycotting students decided to attempt their final examinations as "private" students and approached various people at the university to assist them by supplying teaching materials and laying on classes. The Rhodes English department agreed to make the film available to them.

Instructive differences between the two groups emerged in their respective responses to the behaviour of the plebeian crowd in the film, especially in the scene of the speeches following the assassination of Caesar. The Rhodes students received the scene in respectful silence; for them the actions and reactions of the crowd were unexceptionable. Indeed, the scenes of crowd activity confirmed several unquestioned assumptions: crowds are easily swayed, irrational, prone to violence, prey to "mob psychology." The black matriculating students, on the other hand, as the scene progressed, began first to snigger and finally to hoot with laughter. For them there was nothing at all "realistic" about the presentation of the crowd.

From *Shakespeare in Southern Africa* 7 (1994): 22–31. © 1994 by the Shakespeare Society of Southern Africa.

These students, many of them somewhat older than the average first-year Rhodes student, were living through a formative political experience of mass meetings, demonstrations, "freedom funerals," and other forms of mass political action, all of which of course were to intensify dramatically over the next few years. Many had first-hand experience of organizational work; several were acknowledged leaders of student, youth, and community organizations. For them there was nothing irrational about the actions of political crowds, nothing fickle about their commitment to certain courses of action. The notion that a political crowd would be swayed by whomever happened to be addressing them, far from confirming prevailing "wisdom" on such matters, seemed ludicrous. It is not enough to suggest that these divergent responses merely reveal different perspectives or even different experiences. Indeed, the Rhodes students in all likelihood had no personal experience of political crowds, and could not have imagined that alternative perspectives on the matter were available. They were operating from a set of beliefs so socially and historically entrenched as to constitute a form of "knowledge." In discussions of the crowd scenes following the showing of the film, it was clear that they were drawing on what they took to be a common stock of definite information about political crowds, taking as given that fickleness and irrationality and bloodthirstiness, for instance, were recognized facts regarding such crowds. Through these strikingly different receptions, we are provided insight into how formidable an ideological signifier the crowd is, how deeply embedded in middle-class mentality are "commonsense" beliefs about the crowd, and how successfully literary and dramatic works—or, more accurately perhaps, the receptions, productions, and reproductions of literary and dramatic works—serve to codify and confirm these beliefs.

Of course critics have long debated Shakespeare's own political views, many siding with the long line of critics who have believed that Shakespeare held conservative attitudes towards the "multitude" and have differed only over whether such a view was commendable or reprehensible; others taking up more recent suggestions that he was, if not positively radical in his views, as Jonathan Dollimore and Kiernan Ryan come close to proposing but never quite do, then at the very least humanely liberal, as Annabel Patterson has argued. However much they may disagree in general about Shakespeare's views, critics have been in accord over how we are to understand the depiction of the Roman crowd in Act 3, Scene 2, of *Julius Caesar*. It is taken for granted that in that scene Shakespeare projects the view of crowd behaviour that has become established over time as a form of social knowledge. The scene, in this view, is a seminal instance of a powerful discourse of the crowd, simultaneously shaping and confirming what we know, or believe we know, about political crowds. When most playgoers first experience the scene, or when students first come upon the scene within its accompanying surround of teachers' comments, introductions, notes, and critical essays, the scene has the all-but-invariable effect of ratifying for them what they already know about crowds; and their knowledge has been formed in the first instance precisely by this scene and others like it in canonical literary and dramatic works. The African students who watched the film, on the other hand, provide a useful reminder of how partial (in both senses), how deeply ideological such social knowledge is, and how deeply implicated in the creation and circulation of such knowledge are literary works and their various forms of reproduction and dissemination, including, centrally, literary criticism.

What we glimpse in these opposed responses is the extent to which conventional notions of collective action have been shaped by what social historians call the "view from above." Those who have chiefly determined our understanding of political crowds, from classical times, through Taine and Carlyle and Arnold and other influential thinkers of the nineteenth century, and down through Gustave Le Bon, Freud, and more recent social psychologists right up to our own day, have not been among those who have participated in collective political action or endorsed popular political struggles. On the contrary, they have been drawn from and wrote in the interests of those dominant social classes and groupings which felt most directly threatened by the aspirations of people who engaged in mass political movements. Only with the work of George Rudé and other social historians who have followed his lead have we begun to gain access to a "view from below," a view that enjoins a drastic revision of prevailing conceptions of collective political action.[2] In light of their work, pronouncements today about the aptness and astuteness of Shakespeare's depiction of the plebeian crowd or of similar representations of political crowds whether in canonical literary works or social science and journalistic texts (where they flourish) are shown up for the class-based prejudice they are instead of the certain knowledge they purport to be.

Of course, Shakespeare's depiction is apt and astute only on a particular understanding of the crowd scenes. That this interpretation has become orthodox in stage and film productions as well as in critical commentaries may be less a consequence of accumulated directorial and critical wisdom than a result of directors and critics having themselves so thoroughly internalized the ideological myth of the crowd that they assume that any rendering of a crowd by the most esteemed of all writers obviously must conform to the myth. The scene will accordingly be read or produced with the "knowledge" of crowds already in place. Recent critical trends emphasizing epistemological scepticism and textual indeterminacy would naturally be a threat to such interpretative security, though more conventionally minded critics are unlikely to be moved by such notions. It might be more interesting, therefore, to ask how secure, within its own interpretative norms, the orthodox understanding of the crowd's actions is. The question we might pose, then, is whether, if we deliberately try to distance ourselves from the ideological myth and return to the scene bearing in mind the preconceptions the myth induces, we might not arrive at some other, equally plausible interpretation.

If we pause to reflect on (rather then simply endorse) some of the assertions customarily made about the scene, interesting interpretative possibilities begin to emerge. For instance, a common assertion is that the crowd shows itself to be fickle, a familiar charge against political crowds, introduced into the play by the plebeians' own tribunes in the opening scene. In relation to 3.2 the accusation arises because of the way the crowd first responds positively to Brutus' speech, then with even greater enthusiasm to Antony's. It is worth bearing a couple of things in mind here. If it is held that the scene demonstrates that crowds will be swayed by whoever happens to address them at any given moment, are we, then, to imagine, that had Brutus decided to have Antony speak first and himself after, the outcome would have been different? Can we, that is, imagine the crowd acting any differently after Antony's speech had he spoken first? (Would they, to put the question another way, even stay around to listen to anyone else?) Furthermore, the customary description of the crowd's responses to the speeches has an element of blaming the victim. Both speakers, albeit in different ways, have deliberate designs on the crowd. After Caesar's death, Brutus seeks to put aside all else "till we have appeased / The multitude" (3.1.179–80), while Antony explicitly states his intention to "let slip the dogs of war" (3.1.273) before the speeches begin.[3] The crowd does not simply spontaneously respond to Antony's speech; he *deliberately* manipulates their response toward ends of his own devising. It is not even entirely correct to say, as many critics have done, that the crowd responds more strongly to Antony than to Brutus because Antony's speech is more emotionally laden, the assumption being that crowds are inherently gullible and easily swayed by emotion. The crowd is also, and at least equally, responding to what Antony presents as evidence to refute Brutus' accusations against Caesar; that is, they are responding rationally.

The principal accusation is of course "ambition." The first thing we have to note about it is that Antony does not argue that the charge is irrelevant or meaningless; instead he energetically argues that it is untrue. The second thing to note is that while neither Brutus nor Antony links any particulars to the abstract-sounding "ambition," they clearly refer to something more than or at least other than a general character trait. With regard to the importance of the charge, it is common cause in the play that ambition is a bad thing; there is no hint of irony in Antony's concession that "If it were so, it was a grievous fault" (3.2.79). On the second point, while it is true that ambition appears to be set in opposition to the positive patrician values of honour and virtue, the repeated references in the play to ambition (fourteen times in all, counting plural and possessive usages—far more than in any other play by Shakespeare) consistently pertain to a particular ambition, the ambition to be king. What Antony is defending Caesar against is the charge that he sought to be king. Here again is a pervasive concern in the play: "king," along with "kingly" and "crown," can be found some seventeen times in the play, to which can be added frequent mentions of "tyrant" or "tyranny," "royal," "monarch," and the like. We shall return to the populace's attitudes toward monarchy; for the moment it is enough to note that only when he has offset the charge of ambition does Antony get the crowd to turn against the conspirators.

The customary response to the behaviour of the plebeian crowd in 3.2, the response of the Rhodes students, is according to orthodox views of the play, apparently emphatically confirmed in the following scene, involving Cinna the poet. Consensus may prevail in few areas of Shakespeare criticism, but critics are generally of one mind regarding what happens in 3.3 and how we are to view the depicted action: the plebeian "mob," acting according to what the ideological myth of the crowd assures us is their wont, senselessly and brutally murders Cinna. It would be difficult to find a critical commentary on the play that departs from such a view. Hence the confidence with which, for instance, the editor of the recent Oxford Shakespeare edition of the play restates as fact J. L. Styan's remark that we get in this scene a "brief glimpse of mob violence" (quoted Humphreys 188). Yet for all this rare critical unanimity, the scene is puzzling. Often cut in performance,[4] the scene has its basis in Plutarch, but with one very important departure. Plutarch has the crowd kill Cinna the poet fully believing he is Cinna the conspirator (see Spencer 129–30). There is no question, according to Plutarch, but that the crowd acts from mistaken identity. In Shakespeare's version, however, the crowd learns he is Cinna the poet, at which point the Fourth Plebeian, in an act of literary criticism the extraordinary peculiarity of which seems to have eluded the notice of critics, shouts, "Tear him for his bad verses, tear him for his bad verses" (30–31).

The scene begins with the plebeians brusquely interrogating Cinna about his name and where he is going and where he lives, but before he can answer he is further asked, with obvious comic irrelevance, whether he is married. Commanded by the citizens to answer "directly" and "briefly" and "wisely" and "truly," Cinna responds (in the tenor established by the plebeians):

> What is my name? Whither am I going? Where do I dwell? Am
> I a married man or a bachelor? Then to answer every man, directly
> and briefly, wisely and truly: wisely I say, I am a bachelor.
>
> (3.3.13–16)

The comic equivocation of his reply is significant; throughout the brief scene what passes between Cinna and the plebeians has more the character of comically aggressive interrogation and jocular raillery than deadly rage and terror. Certainly his reply to the plebeians' questions does nothing to suggest that Cinna stands trembling before a bloodthirsty mob; it does not even suggest he feels particularly anxious about his situation. We may even find in the scene, especially in the Fourth Plebeian's "Tear him for his bad verses," an indication that, far from displaying a violent crowd baying for someone's blood, Shakespeare is having a bit of rough fun with the idea of a poet being abused for writing bad poetry. Why else the change from Plutarch? And why else the similar change in 4.2, where Plutarch's Cynic philosopher is swapped for Another Poet who is berated by Cassius and Brutus for his vile rhymes and dismissed as one of "these jigging fools" (4.2.186)? At the very least it is difficult to discern in the banter exchanged by Cinna and the plebeians indications of a mindless mob intent on brutal violence. We might go even further: If we set aside the predispositions inculcated by the myth of the political crowd and examine the scene somewhat more dispassionately, it is far from certain, though critics have long taken it to be so, that in the play Cinna is actually killed by the crowd. After he repeats that he is not Cinna the conspirator, the Fourth Plebeian replies, "It is no matter, his name's Cinna. Pluck but his name out of his heart, *and turn him going*" (emphasis added), which may suggest no more than that he is to be roughed up a bit but then released. The Oxford Shakespeare edition's stage directions, like those of most editions, lend support to the idea of murder. After the Third Plebeian says, "Tear him, tear him!," the stage direction indicates, "They set upon him." After some shouting about brands and burning, the crowd exits; the stage direction reads: "Exeunt all the Plebeians, dragging off Cinna." The stage directions, neither of which, apart from the words "Exeunt all the Plebeians," has any basis in the Folio, themselves derive from and further entrench the customary interpretation of the scene. The editors who have added them obviously assume the plebeian crowd murders Cinna, but they provide no evidence that would compel us to agree. Indeed, were it not for the report of Cinna's death in the play's source, and for the assumptions embedded in the ideological myth of the crowd which critics bring to the text to begin with, one wonders if anyone would have been persuaded of his death in the play.

To be sure, critical ingenuity is hardly likely to be stymied by these remarks. An effort at recuperation might suggest, for instance, that Cinna does die and both the change from Plutarch (dropping of mistaken identity) and the perplexing tone of the scene reveal the subtlety of Shakespeare's examination of the damage (whether physical or mental) inflicted on poets and poetry under conditions of political unrest, or the vulnerability of art when it is subjected to the vagaries of public approval. That, or some similar explanation, will satisfy those critics who themselves dislike crowds and like to think Shakespeare would join them in such a view, and respond strongly to the idea of poets and poetry suffering at the hands of the *hoi polloi*. Notwithstanding such recuperations, it remains the case that the hitherto easy assumption that Cinna is the terrified victim of a frenzied mob cannot be taken for granted; the scene is, without straining against orthodox interpretative conventions, susceptible to alternative readings.

What has been said thus far about these two scenes is unlikely to persuade those who staunchly believe Shakespeare was castigating political crowds and approve his doing so. Nor, for that matter, will these remarks necessarily change the minds of those who differ from the first group only in believing such attitudes, on the part of both the critics and Shakespeare, are blameworthy. Nevertheless, the two scenes are more complicated and layered than commentaries have usually suggested, and they make possible entirely coherent and plausible interpretations which make Shakespeare's representation of the crowd in the play far less stereotypical than is usually assumed. Moreover, discussion of the plebeians in *Julius Caesar* too often fails to recognize that they have a significant role beyond these two scenes, the prominence of which in critical discussion has the effect of obscuring the wider dimension of plebeian politics in the play. After countless commentaries devoted to the political roles of Brutus and Cassius and Caesar and Antony, it is time to focus more fully on this other political dimension of the play, especially since critics, even those who set out specifically to investigate the politics of the play, almost invariably view the crowd purely as an object worked on by others, not as active agents pursuing their own political interests.[5] The plebeians in *Julius Caesar* are not the "rabblement" or "common herd" (1.2.242, 262) that Casca and generations of like-minded literary critics have alternately vilified and patronized, nor is it possible to gain a full appreciation of Shakespeare's political drama without examining their role rather more carefully than critics have in the past.

Consideration of the Roman plebeians as a political force in their own right might begin by attending to a question that is not posed in orthodox criticism. If the behaviour of the populace is invariably so irrational and fickle, so utterly beneath contempt, why does each major political figure or faction in the play apparently feel the need to seek the crowd's approval? Caesar turns to the crowd for a crown; the first thing the conspirators do after killing Caesar is rush into the streets to proclaim to the populace that "Tyranny is dead!" (3.1.78); Brutus addresses the crowd to gain support for what has been done; after him Antony turns to the crowd. All are alike in this respect, if in no other.

Why this should be is not immediately clear. The Roman plebeians, as they are represented in the play, appear to possess no independent political power. Such political representation as they have is indirect, through the tribunes, and their relations with the tribunes, as depicted at the opening of the play, reveal little in the way of solidarity or fellow-feeling. Indeed, for all that the conspirators shout to them about "Peace, freedom, and liberty!" (3.1.110), it is unclear how the plebeians may be said to enjoy these things. Nevertheless, one thing does seem clear: While the multitude may not rule in its own name, apparently no one person or social faction can rule for long without plebeian support, or, perhaps more accurately, in open opposition to their wishes.

We may begin to gain some purchase on the political role the plebeians play in Shakespeare's Rome by turning to another moment in the play that is open to misunderstanding—the off-stage action in 1.2, in which Caesar declines the crown offered by Antony before the assembled multitude. When a short while later Antony, in his speech to the crowd, seeks to exonerate Caesar of the charge of ambition, he cites variously the money derived for the state from ransoms paid for those Caesar had captured on his various campaigns, the provisions of his will (which of course Antony and his fellow triumvirs subsequently overturn), and his alleged weeping for the poor (out of character though that seems). The seemingly conclusive evidence in rebuttal concerns the crown:

> You all did see that on the Lupercal
> I thrice presented him a kingly crown,
> Which he did thrice refuse. Was this ambition?
> (3.2.95–97)

The crowd readily accepts Antony's description of Caesar's actions; the Fifth Plebeian remarks at the conclusion of the speech: "Marked ye his words? He would not take the crown; / Therefore 'tis certain he was not ambitious" (3.2.112–13).

The plebeians are not alone in accepting Antony's version of the off-stage action of 1.2. Some commentators, of a sort unlikely to believe themselves as gullible as they believe crowds to be, have been similarly confused about what goes on at this juncture. R. A. G. Carson, writing in the semi-popular journal *History Today*, confesses that he finds what goes on something of a mystery and tries to resolve it:

> If Caesar had decided on a public ceremony of coronation, his purpose would hardly be deflected by a hostile reaction from the Roman plebs: his legions, after all, were drawn up just outside the

gates of Rome. Yet this presentation and refusal are well attested. The presumption is that Caesar meant publicly to give the lie to the mounting rumours of his intention to become king.

(141)

As a description of Plutarch, this is barely plausible; as a description of Shakespeare it is not even that, though some critics and editors have seen the scene in the play much as Carson sees the incident in Plutarch. T. S. Dorsch, editor of the Arden edition of the play, takes the view more or less for granted (lvi); more recently Alan Hager goes so far as to describe Caesar's refusal of the crown as a sincere republican gesture (61).

Such interpretations, and these are just two among many, beg several questions. This is not the only crown in the play: the Senate is also to offer him one, and the prospect of that crown is enough to make him abruptly change his mind about going to the Senate on the fateful day (2.2.93–107). Now the Senate may feel itself duly empowered to offer Caesar a crown (especially one he can wear only outside Rome itself, as the play, following Plutarch, indicates at 1.3.87–88), but by what prerogative does Antony offer one? And why contrive to have it offered in the presence of the plebeian multitude? Since it is inconceivable that Antony would risk such a public ceremony without Caesar's knowledge and approval, why does Caesar decline the crown, and then fall into a fit after the third time he declines and the crowd cries out?

Casca, who in his "sour fashion" (1.2.180) is outspokenly contemptuous of both Caesar and the Roman plebeians, seems, in describing the event to Brutus and Cassius, to divine matters accurately enough. He says of Caesar's action in declining the crown, "to my thinking, he would fain have had it," and, "to my thinking, he was very loath to lay his fingers off it" (1.2.138–41). Caesar's gesture is the one we make whenever we are offered the last slice of cake: We politely decline so that the person offering will insist all the more on our accepting. In appearing to decline the crown, what Caesar desires is for the crowd to demand that he accept it. He can then do so gracefully, claiming that he did not seek it, but accepted it only because the crowd made it impossible to refuse. It is difficult to see how Carson infers from the "outcry of joy" recorded by Plutarch (Spencer, p. 83) a "hostile reaction" to Caesar. Certainly in the play it is clear from the opening scene that the populace idolises him. Indeed, they cheer him all the more for what they take to be his magnanimity in rejecting a crown. At the same time, nothing so thoroughly demonstrates that Antony is a good deal more than "but a limb of Caesar" (2.1.166), as Brutus fatefully believes him to be, than his ability to transform Caesar's momentary failure with the crowd into a device to achieve success for his own political designs. It may for once be accurate to say that the plebeians act ignorantly; however, in accepting Antony's cynical and self-serving interpretation of Caesar's gesture, they are no more ignorant that the many literary critics who have likewise misconstrued what Caesar is up to.

Caesar's unsuccessful ruse raises two questions: Why does he seek a crown from the plebeians in the first place, and why do they approve his apparent refusal so enthusiastically? In addressing the first question we return to what has already been noted about how each of the principal characters in turn appeals to the crowd at critical moments. For Caesar to seek monarchical rule is to betray the class to which he himself belongs, since achieving his goal means putting an end to their collective senatorial rule. His efforts to gain the support of the plebeians are part of that project. In their exuberant response to Caesar's triumph over the sons of Pompey at the outset of the play, the plebeians open up the possibility of providing Caesar with a counterweight to the patricians. Given popular backing, he can turn to the Senate and say, "I do not seek a crown. But these plebeians are insisting that I accept one, and owing to my immense popularity I am the only one who can control them. If you do not go along with their wishes, there could be chaos." In short, Caesar would be in a position to manipulate the dominant class's customary fear of collective action to suit his political ends. Unfortunately for Caesar, the crowd derails his plan through their unexpected failure to read the signals correctly and urge him to accept the crown despite his demurrals. This is the point when, in utter frustration, he "fell down in the market place, and foamed at the mouth, and was speechless" (1.2.250–51).

Why the plebeians would approve Caesar's gesture so enthusiastically is not immediately clear. After all, the alternative to monarchical rule in the play is not anything we would think of as fully democratic rule but rather, at least apparently, the continued dominance of the patricians. (In fact, as we shall see, the situation is not quite as either-or, monarchy or oligarchy, as this description suggests.) Since Brutus and Cassius, along with the other conspirators, act to defend the political *status quo* rather than to institute a democratic polity, a modern audience, and perhaps Shakespeare's early modern audience as well, might find something spurious in the sight of them shouting to the plebeians about freedom and enfranchisement, and something hopelessly naïve in the apparent willingness of the populace to respond favourably to such calls. It is tempting to turn here to notions of false consciousness and ideological mystification to account for the plebeians' response: The plebeians, on this reading, have sufficiently bought into republican hegemony that patricians can successfully beguile them into rejecting monarchical "tyranny" in the name of republican, or more precisely, senatorial, "liberty." The populace, such an interpretation might continue, may support such values inconsistently, displaying too eagerly their adulation for the latest conquering hero and entering too readily into personality cults, but then the actions and social practices of those whose real needs and real interests have been thoroughly mystified by hegemonic values are always typically inconsistent.[6] Although seeing the conspirators' actions and the crowd's responses as the workings of ideological mystification is at least superficially plausible, one consequence of such a view is that the plebeians are yet again reduced to mere pawns in a game shaped entirely by others. Moreover, there may be a more compelling explanation for the way the conspirators acclaim liberty and the plebeians apparently accept the acclamation.

Whatever we, or Shakespeare, or Plutarch for that matter may understand about Roman politics, there is every reason to believe that the Roman plebeians saw the mixed constitution of the Roman state, with its tribunes who were sworn to protect plebeian interests and its popular assemblies, as a guarantee of their individual and corporate rights, of their *libertas*, which C. Nicolet in his masterly study of *The World of the Citizen in Republican Rome* describes as "the supreme attribute and privilege of the citizen." *Libertas*, he writes, "is perhaps the key concept of the Roman civic and political vocabulary, invoked by everyone at all levels: by the people as a whole *vis à vis* the dominant oligarchies (patricians and senators), and by the plebs against members of the old *gentes*." It was, in other words, from "the individual's point of view . . . primarily a guarantee of equality under the law" (320). Even though we can only speculate about what Shakespeare may have known or believed regarding the politics of late republican Rome, nothing in the play contradicts such an understanding of both patrician and plebeian responses to assertions of "liberty" at the death of Caesar. Accordingly, there is nothing necessarily hypocritical in the shouts of the conspirators, nor anything necessarily naïve in the plebeians' apparently ready acceptance of such calls. And while they may fail to grasp what Caesar is actually up to when he pretends to decline a crown, the populace is in no confusion about its political preferences. As Plutarch repeatedly notes, the plebeians "could not abide the name of a king, detesting it as the utter destruction of their liberty" (Spencer, p. 187). Everything in the play pertaining to the plebeians supports that stance.[7]

Julius Caesar has suffered for too long from a critical tradition that at its best has patronized the plebeians as being no better than they should be and at its worst has abused them for being allegedly the true villains of the piece. *Libertas* provides us with a point of entry into the play that may carry us beyond such narrow and uncomprehending conceptions and enable us finally to grasp the central role they play in Shakespeare's complex depiction of the politics of late republican Rome. In so doing we must resist the temptation to compensate for the inadequacies of the critical tradition by substituting for the ideological myth of the mindless mob that sentimentalized and romanticized abstraction called "the people."There is nothing inherently progressive in the politics of the populace as Shakespeare depicts them, any more than there is in the politics of any of the major characters. Like Brutus and Cassius and the rest, the Roman plebeians seek to maintain the *status quo*, or perhaps more precisely, restore the *status quo ante*. In this there is nothing unusual; George Rudé has shown how what he calls "preindustrial" crowds (political crowds in the seventeenth and eighteenth centuries) typically acted less out of determination to shape the future than in an attempt to defend old customs, reinstate a distant (as often as not imaginary) past, and preserve or restore what they believed to be their ancient liberties (214–36). In both Plutarch and Shakespeare, the Roman crowds appear to act with similar aims. We might conclude from this that Shakespeare's crowd is more a force for political conservatism than for democratic radicalism; the more crucial point is that the crowd must be understood as a political force in its own right, possessing full political agency.

The populace of Shakespeare's Rome acts in its own perceived interests, responds to the major political figures according to its own lights and not just to whoever happens to address it, pursues its own political ends, and throughout acts not mindlessly and inhumanly but, even though it is occasionally deceived by the machinations of others, entirely consistently and rationally in light of the principal norm, *libertas*, guiding its collective political behaviour. Rudé ends his introduction to *The Crowd in History* by reiterating his conviction that the political crowd is "not an abstract formula but . . . a living and many-sided historical phenomenon" (15). We gain nothing by attributing to Shakespeare's representation of the Roman populace a less rich and inclusive apprehension of crowds and their actions.

Notes

1. Department of Education and Training: the black education authority under the Apartheid regime.

2. The most accessible survey of views of the crowd is Rudé's *The Crowd in History*. The standard work on Shakespeare's representation of crowds is Brents Stirling's, *The Populace in Shakespeare*. Politically liberal in its general impulse, Stirling's analysis nevertheless mainly recirculates conservative conceptions of popular political actions. On the history of collective political action in the period covered in the Roman plays, see Lintott.

3. All quotations are from the Oxford Shakespeare edition, edited by Arthur Humphreys.

4. Interestingly, although the scene was scripted and even shot, it was ultimately dropped from Mankiewicz's film. Jack L. Jorgens describes the deleted scene (103–4).

5. For Alexander Leggatt, for instance, the Roman crowd is purely the object of the workings of others (139–60).

6. Caesar's "silencing" of the tribunes, who could be expected to play a moderating role in the crowd scenes, removes one of the means through which the plebeians can sometimes be led to recognize their own real interests more clearly. The tribunes may be socially distant from the plebeians, as we can see in the differentiated speech forms of 1.1, but, despite Brents Stirling's groundless assertion that the tribunes are "the real villains of the Shakespearean story" (p. 42), there is nothing to suggest that they do not actively pursue what they believe to be the interests of those they are elected to represent. Preventing Caesar from becoming king is entirely consonant with their sworn duties. Furthermore, in removing the tribunes Caesar violates one of the most sacrosanct conventions of republican Rome.

7. In light of these remarks, it might be interesting to reflect on the crowd's behaviour at the conclusion of Brutus' funeral speech. In a moment critics have taken to be heavily ironical, the Third Plebeian shouts, "Let him be Caesar" (1.3.49). He does not, however, shout, "Let him be king." The difference is significant: The plebeians, who honoured Caesar and were happy for him to hold high office, signal here their willingness to have Brutus hold similarly high office.

WORKS CITED

Carson, R. A. G. "The Ides of March." *History Today* 7.3 (March 1957): 141–46.

Dollimore, Jonathan. *Radical Tragedy*. Brighton: Harvester, 1984.

Dorsch, T. S., ed. *Julius Caesar*. Arden edition. London: Methuen, 1955.

Hager, Alan., ed. *Shakespeare's Political Animal*. Newark, DE: U of Delaware P, 1990.

Jorgens, Jack L. *Shakespeare on Film*. Bloomington: Indiana U P, 1977.

Leggatt, Alexander. *Shakespeare's Political Drama*. London: Routledge, 1988.

Lintott, A. W. *Violence in Republican Rome*. Oxford: Clarendon, 1968.

Nicolet, C. *The World of the Citizen in Republican Rome*. Trans. P. S. Falla. London: Batsford, 1980.

Patterson, Annabel. *Shakespeare and the Popular Voice*. London: Blackwell, 1989.

Rudé, George. *The Crowd in History*. London: Lawrence and Wishart, 1981.

Ryan, Kiernan. *Shakespeare*. Hemel Hempstead: Harvester Wheatsheaf, 1989.

Shakespeare, William. *Julius Caesar*. Ed. Arthur Humphreys. Oxford: Oxford U P, 1984.

Spencer, T. J. B., ed. *Shakespeare's Plutarch*. Harmondsworth: Penguin, 1964.

Stirling, Brents. *The Populace in Shakespeare*. New York: Columbia U P, 1949.

R.F. FLEISSNER

The Problem of Brutus's Paternity in Julius Caesar (in Partial Relation to Hamlet)

In a recent gracious abstract[1] of an essay of mine concerning Caesar's last moments in Shakespeare's leading Roman tragedy,[2] the critic chooses to relate it relevantly to a complementary study by an Israeli scholar, Daniel E. Gershenson, appearing recently in the journal of the Folger Shakespeare Library,[3] but a turn of phrase occurs which raises now some additional concerns: "Did . . . Shakespeare deliberately *intimate* by analogy Suetonius' Greek within a Latin text by himself suddenly, and briefly, entering into Latin within an English text?" (emphasis added). The issue is that the word *intimate* was an *erratum* for *imitate*, which appears, at least on one level, closer to the original meaning.[4] For if the playwright was implying by "*Et tu, Brutè?*" that Caesar recognized Brutus as indeed his bastard son (the literal meaning of the original Greek phrase, *Kai su, teknon?* meaning *And you, son?*), as might be insinuated by "intimate," then that could make the average interpreter wonder, for example, how after all these wounds the emperor would have summoned up the utter pathos (let alone the energy) to render such a personalized exclamation.

Granted, even bringing up such a question may itself have a certain prosaic effect. In any event, the problem involved is fairly complex and worth further scrutiny. Because the dramatist must have taken seriously the rumor that Brutus was born out of wedlock and was thus kin to Caesar, in that he

From *Hamlet Studies* 19, nos. 1 and 2 (Summer and Winter 1997): 109–113. © 1997 by *Hamlet Studies*.

mentions the matter briefly in an earlier play (*2 Henry VI*, 4.1.137),[5] clearly he could have known the underlying Greek meaning. Yet, as Gershenson duly points out in his note, the noun *teknon* did not have to have the literal meaning of *son* then and so may have been a mere figure of speech (like *sonny*) in this context. In any case, the extended interpolated question, "And you, [my] son?," though perhaps providing for greater pathos and even metrical flow (accredited in the abstract to my translation but also derivative of standard sources),[6] happens to be a loose transliteration that carries little weight otherwise. So it appears plausible enough that Shakespeare did not want to get sidetracked on the further issue of Brutus's paternity in this play and thus avoided—consciously, unconsciously, or even perhaps accidentally—any specific resonance of the Greek meaning when he interpolated his own use of a foreign language in the famous last words. At least that was my original meaning in the article that was abstracted.

But now let us backtrack. To be fair, it is perfectly conceivable that the dramatist did have somewhere in the back of his mind the scandal about Brutus's paternity, specious though that account evidently was (as Gershenson fervently believes). More than likely Shakespeare simply did not have all the aspects of the hearsay and how they related to historical fact at his express command. In any case, because the account of bastardy is found in Plutarch, one of his major sources, it is likely that he picked it up there. Because he likewise referred to Brutus being a bastard in an earlier play, *2 Henry VI* (4.1.137), that could support the verdict that he was hardly beyond "echoing" the idea of Caesar referring to Brutus as a bastard later as well. Also possibly worth considering is the "bad Quarto" of *3 Henry VI*, known as *The True Tragedie of Richard Duke of Yorke* (cir. 1594), which contains the anticipatory line "Et tu, Brute, wilt thou stab *Caesar* too?" (*Julius Caesar*, ed. T.S. Dorsch, London: Methuen, Arden ed., 1955, p. 67). The interesting further point could be mentioned that Shakespeare may have been in addition "echoing" a line from a play on Caesar written in Latin, one that he may have seen or otherwise had access to at Oxford (for example at the Bodleian), but that is another matter.[7] In support of this overall variation on the theme, let us consider several related matters now with due circumspection.

First, scholarship has agreed that it was Brutus who bestowed on the dying ruler that "most unkindest cut of all" (3.2.183), and, though the exact meaning of such an exaggerated or at least unsynthesized superlative has come in for considerable debate, one fairly recent view worth mentioning is that the turn of phrase devastatingly alluded to no less than a brutal stab in the groin. Unpleasant though such a gross association may be, at least it can prompt the valid view that Brutus was somehow paying his natural father back for the 'gift' to bastardy (a terrible stigma, in Renaissance times at any rate). What other hidden significance could logically emerge? In answer, consider possibly the underlying meaning that because the son was called Brutus, his stab was therewith psychologically the most brutal as well. Or, better, these two meanings would have been conflated, enrichening the overall effect.

Now if Shakespeare wanted to suggest that Brutus, in his pagan manner, was getting due revenge on his ruler for the latter's raw act of out-of-wedlock perfidy, the implications are rather notable in terms not only of Caesar's own career, but Shakespeare's description of similar repercussions in other plays. First, apropos of Caesar's life, we are all too easily reminded of the autocrat's having also foisted such a child on Cleopatra, namely Caesarion, whereupon the tragedian then took pains to compose a pre-Baroque drama on the Egyptian queen's alliance with yet another Roman conqueror later on. Second, the spectator-reader can scarcely avoid bringing to mind as well an analogous base-born rebel, Edmund in *King Lear*, who then likewise takes revenge on his father, the Duke of Gloucester, for having made him such a low-down bastard (1.2.6–10).

Yet perhaps the most intriguing analogy of all is with *Hamlet*. There one problem that has fairly recently been posed is whether the Danish prince may plausibly entertain the possibility of his being the illegitimate son of Claudius, who, though purportedly only his uncle, does happen to call him "my son" (1.2.64), whereupon his notorious pseudo-procrastination in accomplishing his mission in righting the wrongs done his kingdom may psychologically derive from his inability to clarify for himself the exact circumstances of his paternity. In point of fact, R.W. Desai makes a provocative case for this position, presenting some solid factual points in favor of this startling argument.[8] Suffice it to say that part of the issue concerns the hero's age, whether he is truly thirty years old, as seemingly reported for our benefit in the grave-diggers' scene (5.1.152), yet this literal rendering of the figure thirty in context has certainly been challenged in print too, notably by a leading theatrically oriented critic, E.E. Stoll, as is well known.[9] Because Desai happens specifically to revert to parallels with *Julius Caesar* to support his case (the emperor and then presumably the earlier play itself being specifically cited a number of times in the Danish tragedy, as is well recognized), reintroducing the analogy now becomes particularly germane. He supports his argument by telling of the venerable tradition that Brutus was, at times, thought to have been the emperor's son born, alas, out of wedlock.

How then does this all add up? Is Shakespeare at least, if not Caesar himself, alluding to Brutus's questionable paternity in his memorable question by inadvertently harking back to the original Greek phrase? (It might be recalled in this connection that the legend of Caesar having himself reverted to a foreign language in his dying moments was as much hearsay as was the notion that Brutus was illegitimate.) For this, a succinct or obviously cogent answer is not so easy to come by. My original suggestion had been that the playwright was somehow having fun with Jonson apropos of their celebrated wit combats (hence my titular take-off, "*Et tu*, Ben?"). Then, as Hutchings puts it at the tail end of his concise abstract of my study, "Shakespeare, picking up on his own experience of a Latin play, responds to Jonson's playful attack on his limitations in the classical language." Although I would still support the value of this point as "necessarily speculative" (as Hutchings categorizes it), let us also recall that Jonson's written comment to this effect appeared only in his famous eulogy published seven years after Shakespeare's death (namely in the First Folio). The celebrated wit combats themselves, moreover, could easily have occurred somewhat later than the Roman tragedy; we can notice, for instance, a debt to the Jonsonian style of "comedy of humours" evident in *The Merry Wives* of *Windsor*, and that domestic drama is usually thought to be a few years later.

Although it does not appear requisite that the issue of Brutus's paternity is altogether relevant to the immediate context of *Julius Caesar*, this matter cannot be ruled out *in toto*. A plausible way of resolving the difficulty is to suggest that Jonson's familiar allusion to Shakespeare's "small Latine and lesse Greeke" in his eulogy actually represented, in effect, a "come-back to a come-back." In other words, Jonson was referring specifically to the switch from Greek (Shakespeare's knowledge of which was markedly "lesse") to Latin (some knowledge of which he had, albeit "small") in terms of Caesar's so-called famous last words. As R.W.B. Lewis has put it, "Shakespeare's classical knowledge was primarily Roman. He had famously even 'lesse Greeke' at his command than Latin; and where he did borrow from a Greek tradition he tended to Romanize it. In historic fact, for example, the temple of Ephesus was built in honor of Artemis; in *Pericles*, it is given over to Artemis's Roman successor, Diana."[10]

Evidently, in *Julius Caesar*, because the "upstart" from Stratford was relatively unfamiliar with the older classical language, he had felt rather more comfortable with the Latin interpolation. Yet the final point is that that explanation need scarcely have eliminated, in accompaniment, the more human problem of Brutus's paternity.

NOTES

1. William Hutchings, "*Et to Brutè* Again," *Shakespeare Newsletter*, 43 (1993), 38–40.

2. "*Et tu*, Ben? Jonson and Caesar's Last Words," *The Aligarh Journal of English Studies*, 14 (1989), 125–33.

3. "Kài ou, téKvov [Kai su, teknon]: Caesar's Last Words," *Shakespeare Quarterly*, 43 (1992), 218–19.

4. This subtlety was first brought to my attention by David George (Urbana University). The editors of *SQ* subsequently acknowledged the *erratum* (43 [1993], 58).

5. Reference to Shakespeare is to *The Complete Works*, rev. ed., gen. ed., Alfred Harbage (New York: Viking, 1977).

6. Cf. J.A.K. Thomson, *Shakespeare and the Classics* (London: Allen and Unwin, 1952): "In Suetonius' *Life of Caesar* it is stated that, according to certain persons, when Brutus attacked Caesar, the dictator cried out 'Kὰι oύ, téKvov,' thou also, my son." It may be supposed that 'Brute' was substituted for 'mi fili' because of a story that Brutus was the son of Caesar, who would then (on this supposition) be alluding to that fact in his last cry. It should have been considered that, even if Caesar did address Brutus as 'my son,' it was quite natural from an older to a younger man with whom he was on terms of intimacy" (p. 147) (also cited in brief by Gershenson). But did *Shakespeare* know of this informality? If he did not, that could be one reason behind Jonson's saying that he had "lesse Greeke." Shakespeare more than likely took *teknon* literally.

7. *Caesar Interfectus*, performed in Christ Church Hall in 1981/2. This suggestion was, to my knowledge, first put forth by Malone, though Bullough in his standard citation of Shakespeare's dramatic sources considers it as an analog only. The point is that Shakespeare may well have finished his grammar school training by the age of sixteen and so would have been eligible to be at Oxford, however briefly, at least in time for witnessing the performance at Christ Church. It is well known that the matriculation and subscription lists are incomplete; because only the extant ones do not record the playwright's name, that is little evidence to go by one way or the other. For further discussion, see my "*Et Tu*, Ben?" but also a more technical study scheduled at the time of writing to appear in *Manuscripta* (Saint Louis University).

8. R.W. Desai, "Hamlet and Paternity," *The Upstart Crow*, 3 (1980), 197–207. The essay is especially provocative in the classroom.

9. E.E. Stoll, "Not Fat or Thirty," *Shakespeare Quarterly*, 2 (1951), 295–301.

10. *R.W.B. Lewis, Literary Reflections: A Shoring of Images, 1960–1993* (Boston: Northeastern University Press, 1993), p. 34.

JOHN ROE

Julius Caesar: *Conscience and Conspiracy*

Messer Iacopo ... se n'andò alla piazza del Palagio chiamando in suo aiuto il popolo e la libertà. Ma perché l'uno era dalla fortuna e liberalità de' Medici fatto sordo, l'altra in Firenze non era cognosciuta, non gli fu risposto da alcuno.

(Machiavelli, *Istorie Fiorentine*, B 933–4; 'Giacopo ... went to the Market place of the Pallace, calling the people to aide him, and recover their libertie. But the people by the fortune and liberallitie of the *Medici* made deaffe, gave no eare to helpe him, and the Florentines had so much forgotten their libertie, as he received no aunswere at all', Bedingfield, p. 200.)

come intervenne a Roma di Cesare, che per forza si tolse quello che la ingratitudine gli negava.

(*Discorsi* 1.29; B 157; 'as happened in Rome with Caesar, who took by force what ingratitude denied him'.)

Once he had brought the *Henriad* to its triumphal conclusion, Shakespeare resumed his interest in Roman themes, as seen earlier in *Titus Andronicus* and *The Rape of Lucrece*. Both those works demonstrate the importance to him of the theme of violation, and the implications it carries for such questions as

From *Shakespeare and Machiavelli*, pp. 133–69. © 2002 by John Roe.

67

tyranny and personal freedom. *Julius Caesar* pursues similar speculations in the larger arena of political debate (involving members of the senate directly in the action) and again dramatically portrays the tension between tyranny and liberty, in particular liberty of conscience. The play may also, if only to a limited extent, raise thoughts nearer home about the relationship of monarchy to republicanism. This aspect of *Julius Caesar* in turn requires that we extend our comparison with Machiavelli beyond the *Principe* and the *Discorsi* to include his *Istorie Fiorentine*, which reflects a similar and thought-provoking conflict between republicanism and monarchy.

Critics have also remarked on similarities between Julius Caesar and Elizabeth I, both of them strong and popular, yet both of them prone to individual weaknesses, he physically infirm, she aging, and each of them wilfully precipitating a crisis in political affairs.[1] How far Shakespeare wished to pursue the analogy is difficult to say. Robert S. Miola notes one kind of parallel by identifying those Catholics who wished to assassinate Elizabeth and replace her with Mary, Queen of Scots. However, this affords an analogy with the succession crisis rather than with republicanism.[2] Depending on how fancifully one is inclined to interpret Shakespeare's intentions, it is possible to see the play (perhaps like *Richard II*, for the performing of which the company was drawn into Essex's trial) as being concerned with the possible future of the kingdom after the queen's death.[3] Since the conspirators meet an unhappy end, it might even be perceived as an atonement for the treasonable bravura of putting on the history play at the time of the Essex rebellion. On the other hand, the play might have been intended to demonstrate the impossibility of a just revolt in the England of Shakespeare's time, especially a revolt with republican aspirations. Yet a third way is to see *Julius Caesar* as a work that refuses to be bound by contemporary issues and that reflects in a more disinterested way on the conflict between political imperatives and the individual conscience.

At the end of *Henry V* the Chorus reminds the audience that 'this star of England' was succeeded by the far less fortunate Henry VI,

> Whose state so many had the managing
> That they lost France and made his England bleed,
>   (Epilogue, 11–12)

which would suggest that Shakespeare advocates undisturbed and unimpaired monarchy as an ideal form of government. Patrick Collinson reminds us that already Elizabeth's England enjoyed a form of government that corresponded sufficiently to Machiavelli's republican ideal:

    that staunch republican Machiavelli ... would have recognised in

> Elizabethan England a species of republic . . . not a kind of tyranny
> or despotism . . . but . . . a constitution which also provided for the
> rule of a single person by hereditary right.[4]

Collinson quotes from the Elizabethan Thomas Smith's work, *De Republica
Anglorum* (first printed in 1583), which offers the following description of
England as,

> a society or common doing of a multitude of free men collected
> together and united by common accord and covenauntes among
> themselves for the conservation of themselves as well in peace as
> in warre.[5]

If this is the case, then Shakespeare, along with his fellow Englishmen,
would not be especially interested in using the device of dramatic analogy to
inquire into the possibilities of replacing a monarchy wholly with a republic.
That form of republican ambition was to occur two generations later. The
crisis facing the monarch and nation turned, rather, on who was to succeed
her, and when. On the other hand, the republican concerns of *Julius Caesar* do enable Shakespeare to treat the subject of conscience in a fresh and
untrammelled way.

Whatever thoughts may lie beneath the surface of his drama, Shakespeare, for the moment, has paid his last tribute to English kingship, and
the choice of this Roman play allows him to address questions such as the
relationship of citizens to ruler with comparative immunity to the kind of
constraint that official Tudor ideology had imposed upon him. Upholding
the monarchical ideal while pursuing the narrative of English history is one
thing, but exploring the republican arguments that convince a character
such as Brutus of the rightness of assassination is another. Shakespeare represents the act of killing the king, or ruler, on more than one occasion, and
we have made such moments part of our study already, as for example in the
case of the murder of Richard II, and to a lesser extent that of Duncan. Does
Shakespeare explore Brutus's conscience in terms of remorse (as in *Macbeth*), or does he find in it comparative freedom from the shackles of guilt?
The republican themes of *Julius Caesar* make for a more open representation
of conspiracy than in either Shakespeare's tragedies or, for that matter, in
those histories which we have consulted already. Arguments in favour of
a legitimate murder are at least entertained in this play, whereas normally
such ideas cannot be countenanced at all. Republicanism, then, may provide
Shakespeare with the forum in which to debate the question of conscience
in ways that are normally closed to him. This alone brings the theme of

conspiracy close to serious Machiavellian deliberations, but as we shall see in neither Shakespeare nor Machiavelli is the outcome straightforward.

Machiavelli has a great deal to say about conspiracy, which he invariably treats in the context of republicanism. On the whole he regards conspiracy as an unwise choice of action and gives reasons for this view in a lengthy discussion of the topic in an early chapter of Book III of the *Discorsi*. Of course he approves of the *aims* of those such as Brutus and Cassius:

> *Un'altra cagione ci è, e grandissima, che fa gli uomini congiurare contro al principe, la quale è il desiderio di liberate la patria stata da quello occupata. Questa cagione mosse Bruto e Cassio contro a Cesare.*

(*Disc.*, III, 6; B 322; 'There is another reason, and a very great one, that makes men conspire against a prince, and that is the desire to liberate their country which he has taken full possession of. This is the reason for which Brutus and Cassius opposed Caesar.')

Earlier, however, he has made the point that conspirators often take action too late, when the tyrannical power they seek to overthrow has already become too strong in its effects, and that conspiracies therefore only help ruin the republic they seek to save (*Disc.*, I, 33). Caesar was stopped, but the divisions that ensued from his assassination ultimately brought Octavius Caesar to power as emperor.

In the chapter on conspiracy in *Discorsi*, III, 6 Machiavelli links the plot against Caesar to his observations on the most fascinating and extraordinary of all Florentine conspiracies, that of the Pazzi family against the Medici in 1478, which took place when he himself was a young boy. Machiavelli gives a full and vivid picture of the events and circumstances of this conspiracy in Book Eight of his *Istorie Fiorentine*, where in the course of his narrative he deliberates on the choice people are often required to make between liberty as provided by a republic and submission to the power of a prince. What he says has a bearing on the outcome of events in *Julius Caesar*, therefore, before we discuss the play's dénouement, we shall take account of his arguments in the Florentine history.

Shakespeare raises the question of conspiracy in the opening scene of Act Two of *Julius Caesar*, and deals with it at some length. As Brutus waits at his house for the other conspirators to appear, he delivers the famous soliloquy in which he determines that Caesar must be assassinated:

> It must be by his death: and for my part
> I know no personal cause to spurn at him
> But for the general. He would be crowned:

How that might change his nature, there's the question.
It is the bright day that brings forth the adder,
And that craves wary walking. Crown him that,
And then I grant we put a sting in him
That at his will he may do danger with.
    (2.1.10–17)

Scholars and critics have in general shown caution in their response to this speech, mainly because it advocates murder, at which the moral conscience naturally jibs. David Daniell speaks for many in his edition of the play when he observes sceptically, 'Brutus resolves to act only on the theoretical premise that Caesar will become tyrannical, against his own evidence of his friend'.[6] As Daniell reminds us, the speech in its musings recalls something of Hamlet's even more celebrated soliloquy in which he also contemplates a violent act, though in his case the life he thinks of taking is his own. Notwithstanding the parallel with Hamlet, Brutus's speech often fills commentators with abhorrence. If we see it merely as a piece of abstract reasoning, aloof from reality, then of course it seems no more than chilling. It may be possible, however, to understand it more from the perspective of political analysis; we must then be aware what kind of preference is being put forward. Brutus acknowledges his personal affection for Caesar but resolves that this shall not be an obstacle. Although we may oppose an action on the grounds of conscience, conscience in a pure, disinterested sense, Machiavelli reminds us that the conflict we experience as often as not lies in the opposing pull of various emotions. Not only conscience but also love stands in the way. Allegiance, loyalty (often carefully secured by bribery), and of course ties of blood, all serve to entrench a single group against the collective interest. In the political sphere love is interchangeable with hate, and both are equally resistant to conscience. Fear of the effects arising from this, rather than his indifference to conscience, explains Brutus's motives in acting as he does. He acknowledges that so far Caesar has not displayed the unstable qualities, common enough in a prince, that Machiavelli in the *Discorsi* calls '*pazzo*' or 'mad' ('unrestrained' is a more specific equivalent term).[7] Sooner or later, however, these will appear:

    But 'tis a common proof
That lowliness is young ambition's ladder
Whereto the climber upward turns his face;
But when he once attains the upmost round

He then unto the ladder turns his back,
Looks in the clouds, scorning the base degrees
By which he did ascend. So Caesar may,
Then, lest he may, prevent.
       (21–8)

We have of course heard words very much like these before; Prince Hal
utters them during his soliloquy early in his first play when he warns the
audience against identifying him too closely with the miscreants whose company he keeps. He is simply waiting for the moment to reveal himself as he
should truly be perceived:

Yet herein will I imitate the sun,
Who doth permit the base contagious clouds
To smother up his beauty from the world.
       (*1H4* 1.2.190–2)[8]

In that speech Shakespeare seems to be endorsing the prince in his declaration of his own *virtù*; in Brutus's words he is making precisely the opposite
point, that repudiating the lowly signifies desire for self-aggrandizement. It
hardly needs remarking that the word 'base' changes its meaning qualitatively from one context to the other: as applied by Hal 'base' means morally
or spiritually weak, whereas in Brutus's speech it simply denotes inferior
social status. The difference between the two speeches, in which each
character draws on identical imagery, marks a corresponding difference
in Machiavelli between his advice to the prince and his identification and
advocacy of the needs of the republic. Brutus then brings his argument to
its conclusion:

        And since the quarrel
Will bear no colour for the thing he is,
Fashion it thus: that what he is, augmented,
Would run to these and these extremities.
And therefore think him as a serpent's egg
Which hatched, would as his kind grow mischievous,
And kill him in the shell.
       (28–34)

The speech ponders the art of description (including that of redescription).
It is not that Brutus is trying to make a bad thing look good. On the contrary, he is bent on saving the republic from tyranny: his problem, then,

is rather how to ensure a good thing looks good. Hence his choice of the paradiastolic verb 'colour'. Many a principled motive has been betrayed by the public's imperfect perception of it: the representation of the murder itself eventually falls to Antony's artful redescription, as we shall see. Further, against the charge that Brutus's reasoning seems specious (i.e. he wants to find a way of justifying the unacceptable) we should observe that he has to persuade himself to overcome a personal disposition in Caesar's favour, a point which recurs immediately after the assassination when he addresses the populace:

> If there be
> any in this assembly, any dear friend of Caesar's, to him
> I say, that Brutus' love to Caesar was no less than his.
> If then that friend demand why Brutus rose against
> Caesar, this is my answer: not that I loved Caesar less,
> but that I loved Rome more.
>   (3.2.17–22)

Plutarch makes no mention of Brutus's self-communing on the eve of the conspiracy, but Machiavelli, on two occasions at least in the *Discorsi*, puts forward reasons which are substantially those Shakespeare gives to Brutus for acting against an heroic figure. The first concerns Cosimo de' Medici (the grandfather of Lorenzo), who, Machiavelli declares,

> *venne in tanta riputazione col favore che gli dette la sua prudenza e la ignoranzia degli altri cittadini, che ei cominciò a fare paura allo stato, in modo che gli altri cittadini giudicavano l'offenderlo pericoloso, ed il lasciarlo stare così, pericolosissimo.*

> (*Disc.* I, 33, B 164; 'arrived at so high a reputation by means of the credit derived from his own prudence and other citizens' ignorance, that he so greatly frightened the government as to make other citizens judge it dangerous to attack him and exceedingly dangerous to let him continue', G 265.)

The crisis was averted, or at least made less acute, by the wise, temporizing action of Niccolò da Uzzano, who understood that to move against a now powerful Cosimo would only backfire, and that any attempt to restrain him would be ruinous. The very thing Niccolò feared happened after his death: following a short banishment Cosimo was restored by his irate supporters, at great cost to the general freedom (B 265–6). Machiavelli points by analogy

to the rise of Caesar, who had outwitted Pompey and made himself too
strong for the state:

> *Questo medesimo intervenne a Roma con Cesare, ché, favorita da*
> *Pompeio e dagli altri quella sua virtù, si convertì poco dipoi quel*
> *favore in paura, di che fa testimone Cicerone, dicendo che Pompeio*
> *avava tardi cominciato a temere Cesare. La quale paura fece che*
> *pensarono ai remedi, e gli remedi che fecero accelerarono la ruina della*
> *loro republica.*

(B 164; 'The same thing happened in Rome for Caesar; his ability
was supported by Pompey and others, but a little later that support
changed into fear. Of this Cicero bears witness, saying that too late
Pompey began to fear Caesar. This fear made them think about
remedies, and the remedies they used hastened the ruin of their
republic', G 266.)

Machiavelli's advice to Brutus, as to his fellow citizens, would have been
to contain the threat, as Niccolò did, in the hope that it would gradually
be absorbed, rather than to risk exacerbating the situation to the point of
destructiveness. Cosimo eventually came back as the '*principe della republica*'
(B 164)—effectively the republic's prince. Assassination prevented Caesar
from achieving this, but the consequences of his murder produced a new
prince in Octavius.

However, in the second example Machiavelli shows a greater sympathy
for those who not only recognize, but are ready to act decisively against, the
threat posed by a man of special *virtù*. In *Discorsi*, I, 29 and 30 Machiavelli
supports the arguments put forward by Cato the Censor for denouncing
the great hero-warrior of the republic, Scipio Africanus. These did not, as
Plutarch and other historians have reported, grow out of envy of Scipio's
enormous popularity but out of a well-grounded fear that his *virtù*, feeding
his ambition, might destabilize the state—arguments closely resembling
Brutus's assessment of Caesar. A decision was taken accordingly to arraign
Scipio (following an accusation made by the tribunes of the people) and
fine him for malpractice, the specific charge being that he had accepted
bribes during the period of his administration (B 157). This was regarded
as an act of spite by Scipio and his friends, and he chose exile rather than
remain any longer in Rome; he died abroad embittered by what he had
suffered from the '*ingrata patria*'. Machiavelli, however, applauds Cato's far-
sightedness: Scipio's strength and popularity were too threatening to the
authority of the magistrates and needed to be curtailed. Clearly the action

against Scipio was much less drastic than that taken against Caesar, for the authorities still had the means of controlling him. However, we may infer from Machiavelli's account that Cato experienced the very same fears expressed by Shakespeare's Brutus, and that this—for Machiavelli—justified the magistrates in acting severely. Machiavelli does not explain to his readers how Scipio offended, and makes no mention of financial misdemeanours; he merely says:

> *E parve tanto straordinario il vivere suo, che Catone Prisco, riputato santo, fu il primo a fargli contro, e a dire che una città non si poteva chiamare libera dove era uno cittadino che fusse temuto dai magistrati.*

> (B 157–8; 'And his conduct seemed so astonishing that Cato Priscus, considered holy, was the first to act against him and to say that a city could not be called free in which there was one citizen whom the magistrates feared', G 259.)

We are not told exactly what '*straordinario il vivere suo*' might imply, for that is not what interests the author of the *Discorsi*; all we need know is that Machiavelli interpreted Cato to mean that Scipio's *virtù* was becoming intolerable to the freedom of the republic. If, turning back to *Julius Caesar*, we wish to question the sincerity of Brutus's motives in deciding to move against his friend, then we may remind ourselves that he would most likely have had the backing of Cato the Censor. Machiavelli thought that the plot against Caesar was misguided, but he condemned it only on the grounds that it was ineffectual. His discussion of the arraignment of Scipio Africanus shows that he thinks that there is every reason to anticipate what might come and, if circumstances permit, to act before it is too late. All is a matter of timing, as Brutus himself recognizes, alas, at a point when the initiative has in fact been surrendered. Machiavelli's discussion of Scipio Africanus provides a republican context into which Brutus's speech fits exactly, and which renders his motives morally more palatable.

Let us turn now to the dramatization of Brutus's encounter with the other conspirators at his house. Those who meet hugger-mugger in such an undertaking inevitably seem to smack of villainy. The word *conspiracy* too easily summons the image of the popular theatrical 'Machevil', the assassin who lurks in the dark and boasts, as in *The Jew of Malta*, of poisoning wells at midnight. Notwithstanding, the atmosphere of conspiracy in Brutus's house could hardly be less like this Marlovian example. Shakespeare establishes Brutus's difference from the popular image of conspiratorial villainy by having him stand aloof from, and even appear to reproach, his fellow conspirators

for seeming unnecessarily furtive. Until this point Brutus has not enlisted in
their number, and is able to speak with a degree of detachment:

> Let 'em enter.
> They are the faction. O conspiracy,
> Sham'st thou to show thy dangerous brow by night,
> When evils are most free? O then by day
> Where wilt thou find a cavern dark enough
> To mask thy monstrous visage? Seek none, conspiracy:
> Hide it in smiles and affability;
> For if thou path, thy native semblance on,
> Not Erebus itself were dim enough
> To hide thee from prevention.
>   (2.1.76–85)

Brutus's language is calm, measured, reflective, and judicious, which is
indeed his manner in virtually everything he says throughout the play. Conspiracy must in its operations seem furtive, or criminal, and yet this is to belie
the good intentions that accompany it. Of course, as critics and historians
have pointed out, not every conspirator's intentions may have been good, but
we are concentrating here on Brutus, for whom even his enemy is prepared
to make an exception:

> This was the noblest Roman of them all:
> All the conspirators save only he
> Did that they did in envy of great Caesar.
> He only, in a general honest thought
> And common good to all, made one of them.
>   (5.5.68–72)

'And common good to all'. Does Antony concede implicitly that the epithet
'noblest' qualitatively exceeds Caesar's 'great'? These are questions we need
to confront in the course of this chapter; for the moment let us continue with
Brutus's analysis of conspiracy. It is an unfortunate necessity, which runs
the risk of failure, because it seems shameful. Appearances are against it: it
has a 'dangerous brow' and a 'monstrous visage', and its 'native semblance'
would betray it even in the depths of the underworld. All this is appearance, however, and not essence. The truth of conspiracy appears only in
the end to which it aims, but observers cannot be relied upon to understand
this. The recommendation Brutus makes—'Hide it in smiles and affability'
(82)—sounds more rueful than confident.

Similar words occur in other contexts where acknowledged Machiavels either speak them or supply the occasion for their delivery. Gloucester (later Richard III) says, 'I can smile, and murder whiles I smile' (*3H6* 3.2.182), and Hamlet observes with reference to Claudius that 'one may smile, and smile, and be a villain' (*Ham.* 1.5.108). But Brutus is not that kind of 'Machiavel'. His conscience insists to the very end that the assassination was not murder, and despite much critical effort to prove the contrary the play provides no evidence to suspect him in this judgment—at least as far as his own intentions are concerned.[9] Not only does Gloucester enjoy his ability to disguise his intentions but he also boasts that he can murder without conscience, which sets him significantly apart from Brutus, for whom the act of killing must be answerable to conscience. However, Brutus does not grasp the Machiavellian point that circumstances too often betray intention. Incapable—for the best reasons—of keeping a distance between himself and the event, he kills Caesar openly and goes before the people for their judgment:

> With this I depart, that as I slew my best lover for the good of Rome, I have the same dagger for myself, when it shall please my country to need my death. (3.2.44–7)

Brutus's oratorical stratagem bears comparison with that of Lorenzo de' Medici following the Pazzi attempted coup, when he declares to the people of Florence:

> *né io sarei sí cattivo cittadino che io stimasse più la salute mia che i pericoli vostri; anzi volontieri spegnerei lo incendio vostro con la rovina mia.*

> (B 938; 'I am not so bad a citizen, as to preferre my private welfare, before your publique weldooing; but would willingly quench your fire, with my own destruction', Bedingfield, p. 203.)

The difference is that Lorenzo chooses the opportune moment to make this gesture of self-sacrifice. He has just survived an attempt on his life, and has the benefit of public sympathy; he knows that opinion has swung in favour of his family. Brutus as an assassin is on much trickier ground; his mistake is to assume that a situation ever arises in which candour and trust can wholly take the place of subterfuge and manipulation. Not only does he miscalculate in failing to silence Antony, as Cassius—the shrewder Machiavellian—urges, but he also errs in identifying the public good with the public's capacity to discriminate. Hovering behind Brutus's plight is the question that haunts Machiavelli in the *Istorie Fiorentine*: what value a republic whose subjects are unable, or unwilling, to pursue their true best interests? Meanwhile, the popular Machiavellian flavour of the words he uses about conspiracy does not make Brutus a Machiavel. As Machiavelli teaches in the more caustic vision of *Il Principe* (Ch. 18), it is because 'the many' do not penetrate to the truth of things, or 'see what you really are', that you must remain attentive to appearances at all times. The disingenuous man may exploit the limitations of 'the many'; the honest man is compelled to bear them in mind. Nowhere does this receive a more convincing proof than in *Julius Caesar*.

While Plutarch remains the major source for the writing of *Julius Caesar*, Shakespeare's handling of the dynamic of conspiracy reflects other kinds of thinking as well. As we have seen, Machiavelli speaks of *Julius Caesar* in several places in the *Discorsi*, as well as providing further analogues which enlarge our perspective on the situation in Shakespeare's play. His most extensive treatment of conspiracy occurs in the eighth and final book of the *Istorie Fiorentine*, where he recounts and analyses the plot instigated by the Pazzi family against the Medici in 1478. An Italian edition of the *Istorie* appeared in London in 1587, purporting to have been printed in Piacenza at the press of Gabriel Giolito de Ferrari, but as we know this was yet another venture by John Wolfe, who had already brought out surreptitious Italian editions of *Il Principe* and the *Discorsi*.[10] Shortly afterwards in 1595 it received the second of only two Elizabethan printings of works in English by Machiavelli. The first of these was the *Arte della Guerra* (or *The Arte of Warre*), translated by Peter Whitehorne, and presented to the 'new prince', Elizabeth I, in 1560 at the time of her accession. Whitehorne's description of Machiavelli, as 'this worthie Florentine and Italian', indicates the seriousness with which Englishmen could openly regard his writings before Gentillet *et al* got to work with their systematic defamation.[11] The translator of the *Istorie Fiorentine* is Thomas Bedingfield, who dates his letter of dedication to Christopher Hatton as 8 April 1588—shortly before Hatton's installation as Lord Chancellor. This is clearly a translation of the copy printed by Wolfe the year before. Bedingfield recommends the work to Hatton for its account of 'the causes of forraine and domesticall discords, the commodities and discommodities of treaties, and the *secret humours of Princes*' (my italics).[12] The last phrase carries obvious echoes of *Il Principe* as popularly understood, and Bedingfield may be enticing his reader with the prospect of cynical or brutal thinking. It is important to consider, however, that these observations (like those of Whitehorne previously) indicate a general awareness of and respect for Machiavelli's analysis of statecraft, and that the translator is offering the work to his dedicatee as Machiavelli originally offered the *Principe* to the younger Lorenzo; that is, as indispensable, practical advice. Naturally there is no knowing whether Shakespeare read the work, but its dual appearance in 1587 (in English in 1588) and 1595 tells us something of the extent of English interest in Machiavelli, as well as of the larger understanding of him. On a particular note, readers would have been comforted, especially in the year of the Armada, by these observations on the Pope, who waged war on Florence just after the plot against the Medici had failed:

> For he had not only first sent a Prelate of his to accompanye traytors, and cutthroates to commit murther in the Temple, even in the time of divine service, and at the instant of celebration of the sacrament ... but had also excommunicated them, and with his papall curses threatned and offended them. (Bedingfield, p. 203)

The experience Elizabeth had of being excommunicated finds itself anticipated by events within Italy, no doubt to the satisfaction of English readers. Machiavelli makes it clear, meanwhile, that such anti-Papal reports stem in large part from Medicean propaganda; his own narrative is more complex than the above quotation suggests. Like Shakespeare in *Julius Caesar* he conducts his argument on more than one level simultaneously.

Conspiracy in Florence, 1478

How we read the account of the Pazzi conspiracy depends on whether we feel that Machiavelli is truly celebrating the achievements of the Medici, and particularly those of Lorenzo, or whether—despite his encomia—he is critical of them. Scholars nowadays incline towards the latter position, arguing for example that while he is ostensibly writing the Medici up in positive terms his account is 'one in which those who knew Machiavelli's real views could discover a far less flattering view'.[13] Machiavelli's loyalty to the republican spirit is at odds with Lorenzo's manipulation of Florentine republican institutions, which may be regarded as similar to Augustus's manipulation of those of ancient Rome.[14] There is plenty of evidence to support such an interpretation. Humfrey Butters remarks that it takes a knowledge of *Il Principe* and the *Discorsi* fully to understand the import of the *Istorie Fiorentine*.[15] The converse is equally true: the *Istorie* shed some light on what is often, especially in *Il Principe*, cryptically or all too briefly summarized. As a family, the Pazzi were similar to the Medici but not quite so successful, the two factions having a kind of Montague-Capulet rivalry. Like the Medici, they were bankers, and one of their illustrious clients was the Pope, Sixtus IV, a fact that has bearing on the decision to make an attempt upon the lives of Lorenzo and

Giuliano de' Medici. Lorenzo was held to blame (even by his own family) for aggravating tensions with the Pazzi: he had framed the laws in such a way as to exclude his rivals from enjoying certain benefits or offices, which they felt were naturally due to them by virtue of their status. According to Machiavelli and others,[16] the city officials applied a statute passed by Lorenzo with the effect that a Pazzi daughter-in-law was deprived of her patrimony; her family held Lorenzo directly responsible.[17] Giuliano, the more cautious brother, had warned Lorenzo ('*caldo di gioventù e di potenza*')[18] that they were endangering their own fortune by excessive behaviour:

> *Giuliano de' Medici molte volte con Lorenzo suo fratello si dolse, dicendo come e' dubitava che per volere delle cose troppo che le non si perdessero tutte.*

> (B 925; '*Giuliano de' Medici* did many times lament, and complain to his brother *Lorenzo*, saying he feared lest they desiring too much, should lose all', Bedingfield, p. 196.)

Such was Lorenzo's confidence in his own abilities, and in the certainty of his family's dominance, that he gave little heed to his brother's cautions. The Pazzi felt themselves aggrieved, and their influence within the community increasingly threatened; all the same, they probably would not have moved against Lorenzo and Giuliano if the Pope had not shown his determination to lessen Medici power. It is unlikely that Machiavelli's covert disapproval of the Medici for their selfish exploitation of republican institutions meant that he rather wished the Pazzi had succeeded.[19] The latter would doubtless have played tricks similar to those of their rivals, seeking to consolidate their power by making their own head of family into the very same prince that Lorenzo, as a consequence of the plot, ironically became. This aspect of the situation was more or less the same as that which Machiavelli describes in *Discorsi*, I, 33 where he speaks of Cosimo de' Medici and Julius Caesar. As Machiavelli observes, after the half-hearted attempt against Cosimo's son Piero in 1466 had foundered, conspiracy remained ironically the only means of challenging the dominance of Medici rule—an unsuccessful method feeding on itself.[20] The Pazzi conspiracy does not provide an exact parallel with Shakespeare's account of the conspiracy against Caesar: for example, there is nothing in Machiavelli's account that equals Shakespeare's depiction of the conscience of Brutus. On the other hand, the two narratives bear an uncanny similarity in their depiction of the unfolding of events, of the alternate wresting and surrender of initiative, and above all of the responsiveness of the populace to the impact of a powerful *virtù*.

Attempt on the Medici

Giuliano and Lorenzo de' Medici were attacked by Francesco de' Pazzi and supporters of his family on Sunday morning 26th April 1478 while they celebrated mass in the cathedral church of Santa Reparata.[21] Lorenzo had already arrived for the service but Giuliano was lagging behind, and so Francesco and Bernardo Bandini, who were appointed his assassins, went with a show of friendship to his house to persuade him to come along. Machiavelli expresses his admiration at the strength of mind shown by the two conspirators:

> *È cosa veramente degna di memoria che tanto odio, tanto pensiero di tanto eccesso si potesse con tanto cuore e tanta ostinazione d'animo da Francesco e da Bernardo ricoprire.*

> (B 931; 'And truly it is a thing worthy memorie, to know how so great hatred would be so covertly kept secret in the minds of Francesco and Bernardo', Bedingfield, pp. 198–9.)[22]

Commendatory remarks on the *'tanto cuore'* of the conspirators may not have gone down well with Medici readers, but Machiavelli tempers his description by noting the *'odio'* (hatred) in those same hearts, and reminds us of the *'eccesso'* (crime) they were bent on committing. Even so, Bedingfield does less than justice to the Italian text's clear profession of respect for the courage of the assassins.[23] Machiavelli, as always in the history, aims at balance and diplomacy. Continuing his narrative, he observes,

> *e per la via e nella chiesa con motteggi e giovinili ragionamenti lo intrattennero. Né mancò Francesco, sotto colore di carezzarlo, con le mani e le braccia strignerlo per vedere se lo trovava o di corazza o d'altra simile difesa munito.*

> (B 931; 'For both by the way going to the Church, and in the Church, they entertained Giuliano with pleasant speech and youthful dalliance. Also Francesco under colour of familiar and friendly curtesie, tooke Giuliano in his armes, to feele whether he had on anie armour or garment of defence', Bedingfield, p. 199.)

This last detail is found only in Machiavelli's account of the events of the day.[24] Those *'motteggi'* and *'giovinili ragionamenti'* particularly call to mind the 'smiles and affability' of Brutus's recommendation for the appropriate conduct of conspiracy, except that Machiavelli spends less time reflecting on the moral implications of such action.[25]

Francesco and Bernardo Bandini fell on Giuliano and stabbed him several times, killing him. Francesco attacked with such fury that he managed to wound himself severely in the thigh, an injury that was to carry dire consequences. Lorenzo was attacked by far less able assailants, and despite being struck in the throat managed to escape into the sacristy and make himself safe. The failure to despatch Lorenzo proved fatal. The citizens soon rallied to the cause of the Medici, and the Pazzi found themselves without adequate support. A second stage of the plan, calculated to take place simultaneously, also foundered. Archbishop de' Salviati, who had been detailed to take an armed group to the Palazzo and assume control of the Signoria, was simply unequal to the task. The Gonfalonier of Justice, Cesare Petrucci, showing himself to be a strong man in a crisis, faced down the archbishop and arrested him and his followers. Subsequent events were horrific. The archbishop and a number of others were hanged from the windows of the Palazzo. Francesco stumbled home injured, and undressing rather pathetically 'laide himself naked in bed' (Bedingfield, p. 200), begging his elderly uncle Jacopo to take over the cause and attempt to rally public opinion to the Pazzi side. This the old man tried to do, but hardly had he left when a mob dragged Francesco from his bed and strung him up alongside the archbishop. A vengeful crowd began to hunt up and down for members of the Pazzi clan and their followers:

> Già per tutta la città si gridava il nome de' Medici, e le memore de' morti, o sopra le punte delle armi fitte o per la città strascinate si vedevano; e ciaschedun con parole piene d'ira e con fatti pieni di crudeltà i Pazzi perseguiva.

> (B 934; 'Also throughout the Citie, the name of "Medici" was proclaimed, and the members of the dead men, either carried uppon the points of swordes and launces, or drawne through the streets; morever every man, both by wordes and deedes, irefully and cruelly persecuted the Pazzi', Bedingfield, p. 200.)[26]

Lorenzo soon recovered and took charge of events, his strength now feeding on his popularity and his position growing ever more unassailable. Not least the attempt confirms the truth of Machiavelli's observation, in Chapter 19 of *Il Principe*, that the ruler should take care not to be hated by the general people because their support is his best defence against conspiracy:

> ma quando e' creda offenderlo, non piglia animo a prendere simile partito, perché le difficultà che sono dalla parte dei coniuranti sono infinite.

(B 60; 'but when [a conspirator] fears that he may offend the people he has no heart for such an enterprise, for the difficulties that conspirators face are infinite.')

This was the lesson the Pazzi had not learned, and their failure to do so resulted from their poor assessment of the affection which Lorenzo generally inspired. His personality was in large measure the key to Medici popularity. Despite Giuliano's misgivings that the family, urged on by Lorenzo, were overplaying their hand, his brother was emboldened to go as far as he did by his awareness that the populace liked him and responded to his charm. The point at which the Pazzi conspiracy truly failed can be located in the first meeting between Lorenzo and one of the Pazzi's key allies, Giovan Battista da Montesecco. It was arranged by the Pazzi in collusion with the Pope that Montesecco, an officer in the papal army, should come to Florence ostensibly to talk with the Medici concerning affairs in the Romagna, but in reality to be on hand for the conspiracy. When he met Lorenzo he was surprised to encounter a man who differed strikingly from his enemies' description of him:

> *Arrivato pertanto Giovan Batista a Firenze, parlò con Lorenzo, dal quale fu umanissimamente ricevuto e ne' consigli domandati saviamente e amorevolmente consigliato.*

> (B 927; 'Giovanbattista arrived at Florence, went unto Lorenzo, of whom he was courteously received, and in all his demaunds wisely and friendly counselled', Bedingfield, p. 197.)

Bedingfield's English hardly does justice to the fullness of Machiavelli's description of Lorenzo's behaviour; the plain style of 'courteously', 'wisely', and 'friendly' quite fails to render the languorous, polysyllabic richness of *'umanissimamente'*, *'saviamente'*, and *'amorevolmente'*, words which in turn convey the insinuating, flatteringly intimate manner with which Lorenzo practised his charm. Montesecco, an experienced soldier, had direct charge of Lorenzo's assassination. When after a number of false starts (and with time dangerously running out) the desperate decision was taken to kill the brothers in the church during mass, Montesecco cried off, protesting that the plan was sacrilegious. Machiavelli thinks that Lorenzo's affectionate overtures might have had much to do with his refusal:

> *Recusò Giovan Batista il volerlo fare, o che la familiarità aveva tenuta con Lorenzo gli avesse addolcito lo animo, o che pure altra cagione lo*

*movesse: disse che non gli basterebbe mai l'animo commettere tanto
eccesso in chiesa e accompagnare il tradimento con il sacrilegio.*

(B 930; 'Giovanbattista, refused to performe his charge, either
because the courteous usage of Lorenzo had mollified his mind, or
else for some other occasion which moved him, said, he durst not
commit so great a sinne in the Church, as to execute treason with
sacrilege', Bedingfield, p. 198.)

Machiavelli sounds sceptical of Montesecco's proffered excuse, and gives
as a prior reason (*'cagione'*, which Bedingfield translates as the similar-
looking 'occasion') Lorenzo's 'courteous usage'. Strength of personality, as
so often according to Machiavelli's analysis, exercises more influence on
human disposition than the constraints of ethics. This the Pazzi suddenly
found when faced with Montesecco's defection. Antonio da Volterra and
a priest known simply as Stefano, who was officiating at the mass, were
brought in as late substitutes for the reluctant Giovan Battista; but they
were not up to it. As Machiavelli observes, *'è assai volte veduto agli uomini
nelle arme esperti e nel sangue intrisi to animo mancare'* (B 930; 'For it hath
often been seene, that some men, used to arms and bloud, have notwithstanding in like cases, let fall their courage', Bedingfield, p. 198). The
nerve of far less hardened men is even more likely to fail at the moment
of decision.

Machiavelli's account of the dangers of conspiracy inevitably brings
up the question of the tone he deploys for various narrative details. On the
whole this is level and objective, sometimes disconcertingly so; details that
may well horrify the reader appear not to horrify the author. But then, the
man who composed the *Istorie Fiorentine* also wrote *Il Principe*. One of
his modern editors notes that Machiavelli limits himself to blaming the
'imprudenza' (or poor tactics) of choosing priests for the task, without making much of the fact that these same priests undertook to do the killing
in the cathedral and at the supreme moment of the mass: *'lascia the la cosa
parla da sé'* ('he lets the thing speak for itself').[27] As it happens, Machiavelli
lays not so much stress on the Pazzi's *'imprudenza'* as on their misfortune
in losing their key assassin to Lorenzo's charm. (Montesecco was later executed for his part in the conspiracy; his unwillingness to perform the deed
cut no ice with an intransigent, unforgiving Lorenzo.) Does a thing ever
speak for itself? Silence over the event may be interpreted variously. The
Istorie Fiorentine is remarkably free of the rhetoric of denunciation, which
Machiavelli could so easily have drawn upon in order to ingratiate himself with the current lords of Florence, and particularly the Medicean pope

(a son of Giuliano, to boot) for whom he is writing.[28] Machiavelli makes no show of pity for Giuliano, expresses no concern over the manner of his death; in short, supplies nothing that the family could take comfort in. Possibly the cruelty of the incident reminded him of his own sufferings at their hands when they administered the *strappado*. His style remains resolutely impartial; as we shall see in a moment, Machiavelli was content to leave the show of rhetoric to Lorenzo. This does not mean, however, that he will not undermine Lorenzo's rhetoric with his own.

Although an unwilling partner in the enterprise, Jacopo de' Pazzi did as the wretched Francesco requested of him, and made a last attempt to stir up anti-Medici feeling with cries of '*libertà*' and '*popolo*':

> *Ma perché l'uno era dalla fortuna e liberalità de' Medici fatta sordo, l'altra in Firenze non era cognosciuta, non gli fu risposto da alcuno* (see heading to this chapter).

Jacopo's brother-in-law, Giovanni Serristori, persuaded him to give up and return home, assuring him that '*il popolo e la libertà era a cuore agli altri cittadini come a lui*' (B 934; 'the welfare of the people, and the libertie, touched other Citizens aswel as him', Bedingfield, p. 200).[29] But Machiavelli has made it sufficiently clear that the Medici were offering '*liberalità*' rather than '*libertà*'; and that this offer was good enough to succeed. As Butters remarks, the underlying warnings of the *Istorie Fiorentine* emerge more clearly in earlier works such as *Il Principe*,[30] especially with regard to liberality, the example once again being Julius Caesar:

> Cesare era uno di quelli che voleva pervenire al principato di Roma; ma se, poi che vi fu venuto, fusse sopravissuto e non si fussi temperato da quelle spese, arebbe destrutto quello imperio.
>
> (*Il Principe*, Ch. 16, B 52; 'Caesar was one of those who wanted to become prince of Rome; but if he had achieved this, and gone on living and not become more moderate in his expenditure, he would have destroyed his position as ruler.')

Allan Gilbert points out, in his translation of *Il Principe* (Ch. 17), that Machiavelli tactfully advised Giovanni de' Medici in 1512, when the family returned and once again took control of Florence, not to try and recover property they had lost at the time of their expulsion in 1494 (G 63). Their profligacy had several times brought them near to bankruptcy, and the 'liberality' which they made so much use of threatened to incur

the consequences Machiavelli warns against in the *Principe* (Ch. 16),
when he says that premature lavishness in time necessitates an unpopular
parsimony. The *Istorie Fiorentine* is a text which exemplifies the lessons
of the earlier book. The question of Florentine liberty always runs up
against the Medici's practice of purchasing support through their generosity—a tactic which in different ways imposed a strain on both the
family and the city.

With the internal phase of the conspiracy at an end, Florence entered
into a war with the Pope and the King of Naples, who had supported the
Pazzi in the hope of dislodging the Medici. In Machiavelli's narrative Lorenzo
speaks to the city on the eve of hostilities, justifying his family's actions and
appealing for continued assistance:

> *E veramente quelle autoritadi meritono di essere odiate che gli uomini
> si usurpano, non quelle che gli uomini per liberalità, umanità, e
> munificenza si guadagnano.*

> (B 938; 'For surely those authorities deserve hate, which men
> usurpe, not those which with curtesie, liberallitie, and magnificence
> be gained', Bedingfield, p. 202.)

Of course 'liberallitie' has already been shown to be compromised in
Machiavelli's comment on the futile attempt of Jacopo de' Pazzi to fill the
Florentines with a sense of their endangered liberty (a reasonable reminder
in Machiavelli's view, whatever Jacopo's motives). Otherwise, Machiavelli
allows Lorenzo 'to speak for himself' without comment, except to report
the impact Lorenzo makes on his audience, who tearfully pledge their support (B 939). Lorenzo's rhetoric, as Machiavelli demonstrates, wins over the
citizens, who are moved to furnish further propaganda, arguing for example
that the Pope had shown himself to be more of a wolf than a pastor, and that
not wishing to be devoured by him as guilty parties, they are determined
to set the record straight for the benefit of the rest of Italy: *'con tutti quelli
modi potevono la causa loro giustificavano'* (B 939; 'by all possible meanes
they iustified their cause', Bedingfield, p. 203). At this point, and only as a
demonstration of Medici-inspired rhetoric, does Machiavelli introduce the
observation that earlier seemed, surprisingly, to hold no interest for him:

> *il papa . . . aveva mandato quegli che alle prime prelature aveva tratti,
> in compagnia di traditori e parricidi, a commettere tanto tradimento
> in nel tempio, nel mezzo del divino officio, nella celebrazione del
> Sacramento.*

(B 939; 'he had . . . sent a Prelate of his to accompanye traytors, and cutthroates to commit murther in the Temple, even in the time of divine service, and at the instant of celebration of the sacrament', Bedingfield, p. 203.)

As for the Pope, we would not normally expect Machiavelli to show much interest in what be may have to say in his defence, yet in the *Istorie Fiorentine* that is precisely what he does:

Non mancavano ancora al papa ragioni di giustificare la causa sua; e perciò allegava appartenersi a uno pontifice spegnere le tirannide, opprimere i cattivi, esaltare i buoni: le quali cose ei debbe con ogni opportuno rimedio fare, ma che non è già l'ufficio de' principi seculari detenere i cardinali, impiccare i vescovi, ammazzare, smembrare e strascinare i sacerdoti, gli innocenti e i nocenti sanza alcuna differenzia uccidere.

(B 940; 'On the other side, the Pope wanted not reasons to iustifie his cause: and therefore alleaged it was the office of a chief Bishop, to remove tyrants, oppresse the wicked, and advaunce the good. All which things, it behoved him by all waies to procure. For it was not the office of secular Princes to imprison Cardinals, hang up Bishops, to kill, cut in peeces, and drawe the Priests through the streets, murthering both guiltie and unguiltie people, without respect', Bedingfield, p. 203.)

The Pope in his rhetorical denunciation of the Florentines refers to the execution of Archbishop de' Salviati, hanged from the window of the Palazzo della Signoria. The vendetta against the Pazzi claimed a total of three hundred persons, apparently indiscriminately slaughtered.[31] Significantly, as this section of the eighth book closes, the Pope is accorded the last word in the game of mutual accusations. Machiavelli may give the impression of wishing to present a balanced, impersonal account of events and actions; but the nature of this balance is itself revealing. His silence over the ethics of the attack in the cathedral (he merely quotes Medicean condemnation of it), coupled with his prominent siting of the Pope's rejoinder, would indicate that he is reluctant to make more than a perfunctory gesture on behalf of the Medici cause. What emerges is a characteristic Machiavellian (and para-diastolic) attitude to truth: a thing matters less in itself than in the impact it makes and the manner in which it is perceived. While observing this phenomenon on the one hand, Machiavelli is not slow to make use of it on the other. All is rhetoric: in the course of his narrative Machiavelli shapes the arguments of his historical personages to his own design.

Julius Caesar

While Shakespeare may not have read the *Istorie Fiorentine* (despite its availability in both the Italian printing by John Wolfe and the Bedingfield translation), his play none the less throws up some interesting parallels with the eighth book of Machiavelli's narrative. The competition for supremacy, whether moral or practical, assumes rhetorical expression. Machiavelli shows that this competition takes place between the historian himself and representatives of the victorious Medici family, principally Lorenzo. Does Shakespeare insinuate himself into the dialogue in the same way? His play is rhetorical at every turn, but its debates seem to involve its characters exclusively. Two contrasts stand out in each half of the drama: that between Brutus and Caesar in the first part, and between Brutus and Antony in the second. For both Shakespeare and Machiavelli the populace is the single most important audience for such rhetoric. In both works the rhetoric focuses especially on the act of killing, which makes it impossible to give a simple, straightforward reading of the assassinations of either Julius Caesar or Giuliano de' Medici. Shakespeare, in particular, makes a great deal of the imagery of blood, a word which occurs nine times in the first scene of Act Three and four in the second. Caesar introduces the word, then Brutus, and subsequently Antony, appropriates it: each makes it integral to his argument, Antony most effectively but, as we shall see, least ingenuously.

What distinguishes Machiavelli from Shakespeare is the difference they make of their shared topic of republicanism. For Machiavelli republicanism is a desired end. For Shakespeare it is more a means of exploring conscience, and the degree to which conscience can ever be truly free. Machiavelli is the true republican of his own text. The Pazzi may invoke republican principles against the Medici, as old Jacopo desperately tries to do, but there is no indication that had they triumphed, they would have been any better than their opponents in this respect. The conflict between the two families rather resembles the earlier one that is acted out between Caesar and Pompey, two members of an uneasy triumvirate, the latter in turn repeated in the triumvirate of Antony, Octavius, and Lepidus. The republic is the battleground which finds itself inexorably reshaped into empire. Machiavelli meditates on the possibilities of achieving, and sustaining, republican government in a number of texts which, as we have seen, comment upon each other: not only the *Istorie Fiorentine* but also *Il Principe* and the *Discorsi*. He, more than any spokesman whose words or deeds he quotes, reminds his readers of the republican principles to which they avowedly aspire, but to which they more often than not pay mere lip service.

In *Julius Caesar*, Shakespeare identifies republican principle especially—one is tempted to say exclusively—with Brutus, as no other character shows quite such disinterested commitment to it. For himself, Shakespeare probably does not pursue republicanism with any special determination. If we accept Collinson's argument (see above), England had already achieved a desirable form of republican monarchy, one that Machiavelli himself would have found acceptable. There is no doubt that Shakespeare observes the classical opposition between tyranny and republicanism on more than one occasion. In *The Rape of Lucrece* Lucius Junius Brutus's action in turning public opinion against the Tarquins, and thus ending the tyranny of monarchy, reflects the Machiavelli of the *Discorsi* and, discreetly, of the *Istorie Fiorentine*. Robert S. Miola argues that in *Julius Caesar*, 'Shakespeare appropriates the famous story not to illustrate the evils of tyranny, rebellion, or both, but to give his audience a look at a pivotal moment in Roman history'.[32] This may indeed have been one of Shakespeare's intentions, and in the course of his chapter Miola demonstrates effectively just how thoroughly Shakespeare absorbed Roman detail, but it remains debatable whether it is the Roman theme as such that occupies Shakespeare or whether he does not have in mind issues of a later culture. Shakespeare would certainly have regarded Rome as a locus for constitutional transitions; notwithstanding, he does not appear to be furthering the cause of republicanism all that much. Reading between the lines does not give the impression that he is wishing monarchy away. At the same time, in *Julius Caesar* he invests monarchy with something less than that idea of the sacred that it carries in the histories, or in a tragedy such as *Macbeth*. What the republican context manages more than anything else, then, is to define issues of conscience as they operate in the sphere of the political. The play posits notions of freedom while expressing reserve over the prospect of its being truly exercised—a conclusion not unlike that which Machiavelli reaches in the *Istorie Fiorentine*.

Julius Caesar is fundamentally (not superficially) Machiavellian in the degree to which it can contemplate the act of killing without imposing the usual moral perspective, whereby homicide necessarily defines itself as murder. As I have argued with respect to Brutus's soliloquy at the beginning of the second act, concern for liberty sufficiently guarantees that the action is moral in intention. Brutus is drawn into the conspiracy partly by subterfuge and persuasion (initially he shows himself reluctant, a kind of Jacopo de' Pazzi, the most likeable—or perhaps least objectionable—of all the Florentine conspirators), but once he has entered into the design, his motives prove honourable. If, therefore, the rhetoric of assassination offers a contrast of interpretation, then this lies not so much within the play (notwithstanding the important conflict between Brutus and Antony) as between this play and another: *Macbeth*. Antony does his best to depict Brutus as a murderer, or 'butcher'—a word used to effect in both plays.[33] What the interpretative contrasts within *Julius Caesar* show is how powerfully Antony imposes, on both the audience and the populace, a vision of Brutus as bloody tyrant, when in fact Brutus has acted against tyranny, which is already stained with blood. According to Plutarch Pompey's statue bleeds in approval of the killing of Caesar:

> whereupon Pompeys image stoode, which ranne all of a goare bloude, till he was slaine. Thus it seemed, that the image tooke just revenge of Pompeys enemie, being throwen downe on the ground at his feete, and yelding up his ghost there. (Bullough, V, 86)

Brutus's own paradiastolic attempt to redefine the act of bloodshed along the lines of sacrifice is doomed to failure. Unlike his fellow conspirators, who concern themselves only with the practicalities of assassination, Brutus feels the need to square the killing of Caesar with the demands of conscience, but only succeeds in weakening his strategic position. He shows anxiety about the enterprise relatively early when he opposes Cassius's sensible wish that Antony should be killed along with Caesar (there is no doubt whose opinion the author of *Il Principe* would prefer), and tries valiantly, yet vainly, to separate the nobility of the intention from its savage physical appearance. Brutus shows his own wariness of the word 'butcher' as he cautions against excessive violence:

CASSIUS.
  Let Antony and Caesar fall together.
BRUTUS.
  Our course will seem too bloody, Caius Cassius,
  To cut the head off and then hack the limbs—
  Like wrath in death and envy afterwards—
  For Antony is but a limb of Caesar.
  Let's be sacrificers but not butchers, Caius.
  We all stand up against the spirit of Caesar,
  And in the spirit of men there is no blood.
  O that we then could come by Caesar's spirit
  And not dismember Caesar! But, alas,
  Caesar must bleed for it. And, gentle friends,
  Let's kill him boldly, but not wrathfully:
  Let's carve him as a dish fit for the gods,
  Not hew him as a carcass fit for hounds.
  And let our hearts, as subtle masters do,

> Stir up their servants to an act of rage
> And after seem to chide 'em. This shall make
> Our purpose necessary and not envious,
> Which so appearing in the common eyes,
> We shall be called purgers, not murderers.
> (2.1.160–79)

This speech contains rather more in the way of motivation than its source in Plutarch, who (Machiavellian *avant la lettre*) limits the debate about Antony to a point subsequent to the assassination, and then, commenting in a tone that avoids moral censure, blames Brutus purely for his practical misjudgment:

> For the first fault he did was, when he would not consent to his fellow conspirators, that Antonius should be slayne: and therefore was he justly accused, that thereby he had saved and strengthened a stronge and grievous enemy of the conspiracy. (Bullough, V, 104)

Those, and there are many of them, who see fit to judge Brutus according to Antony's version of him, might consider how strong and attractive a conscience he reveals by such deliberations which, as both Plutarch and Machiavelli demonstrate, merely interfere with the basic business of conspiracy.

Through Brutus Shakespeare raises one of the major problems of Renaissance ethics: the relationship of body to soul. In *The Rape of Lucrece*, that other work with republican dimensions, Shakespeare has Lucrece express horror at the violation of her soul through her body, and then depicts her attempt to find redemption through her bodily destruction. As is well known, St. Augustine, insisting on the separateness of the two, condemned the historical Lucretia for her action.[34] Shakespeare, well aware of this threat to Lucrece's reputation, ensured that she died with sufficient pathos for it to be difficult for his readership to condemn her action without feeling callous. The enormity of her rape by Tarquin keeps our doubts in check as to whether she was right to kill herself. Brutus as aggressor rather than victim gains the benefit of no such moral 'luck'. However, he resembles Lucrece closely in his anxiety over the act of killing and how it will be morally perceived, and demonstrates the obverse of her concern (to release her pure soul from its infected body) by wishing he could only terminate a corrupt soul without injuring the body:

> We all stand up against the spirit of Caesar,
> And in the spirit of men there is no blood.
> O that we then could come by Caesar's spirit

And not dismember Caesar! But, alas,
Caesar must bleed for it.
    (167–71)

The comparison with Lucrece should help us form an estimate of Brutus, especially with regard to Shakespeare's conception of him. Critics who look for a fatal flaw in his arguments find something specious in passages such as the one just quoted. Notwithstanding, Brutus wrestles with a dilemma every bit as serious as that facing Lucrece. The soul's inability to escape the body means that intentions are necessarily prey to the actions that accompany them. Lucrece kills herself as the only means of preserving her reputation; but commentators have questioned whether she was justified in doing so. Brutus would kill the spirit of tyranny in Caesar, leaving the man whom it has possessed to live on. In so far as Roman spiritual conventions will allow, he is advocating a kind of exorcism. However, he recognizes that Caesar's blood must be shed if the less tangible element of tyranny is to be arrested. There can unfortunately be no mere dealing in abstractions and principles.

Despite the different emphasis each of them brings to the dilemma, an identical element runs through both Brutus's and Lucrece's deliberations. Body and spirit coexist uneasily, and the different texts before us reveal their speakers either labouring under the weight of the problem they confront, or finding ingenious ways of resolving it. Contemporaries would therefore be less inclined to detect suspicious flaws in Brutus's reasoning—flaws that call into question his bona fides—and would see him rather as struggling heroically, if desperately, with a familiar ethical question. *Julius Caesar* brings into focus through its republicanism-vs.-tyranny debate an issue that recurs in several Shakespearean texts.

Brutus's chief adversary understands much more clearly than he does that the blood-spirit debate can never be resolved satisfactorily, and that it inevitably lends itself to strategic or opportunistic interpretation. In this respect, Antony also recognizes that 'blood' is the key word, and he begins using it to effect from the moment he encounters the conspirators following the assassination:

BRUTUS.
  But here comes Antony. Welcome, Mark Antony.
ANTONY.
  O mighty Caesar! Dost thou lie so low?
  Are all thy conquests, glories, triumphs, spoils,
  Shrunk to this little measure? Fare thee well.
  I know not, gentlemen, what you intend,

Who else must be let *blood*, who else is rank.
If I myself, there is no hour so fit
As Caesar's death's hour, nor no instrument
Of half that worth as those your swords, made rich
With the most noble *blood* of all this world.
    (3.1.147–56)

He continues with similar, insidious expressions: 'whilst your purple
hands do reek and smoke, / Fulfil your pleasure' (158–9), and 'Caesar, by you
cut off, / The choice and master spirits of this age' (162–3). Antony's tactic in
representing the assassination as a piece of horrific blood-letting unworthy
of 'gentlemen' (ironically used) hardly requires comment; nor does his trick
in suggesting that the assassination acquires nobility from the blood of the
victim and not from the blows struck in defence of liberty, as Brutus sup-
poses. Antony—who in this recalls the Machiavelli of the *Principe*—knows
that rhetoric does not deal in truth but in various and competing versions of
events or actions. He speaks somewhat defensively, sensing that the likes of
Cassius and Casca would just as soon run him through with the same blades
that killed Caesar as stop and parley; but he knows too that he will find safety
in the conscience of Brutus. His awareness of his vulnerability shows up in
his choice of deferential words such as 'purple' (i.e. denoting patrician) to
describe the conspirators' hands, but such vulnerability and deference skil-
fully invoke the tradition of the martyr confronting his murderers ('purple'
hands are none the less bloody). Simultaneously he undermines their moral
status by associating verbs like 'reek' and 'smoke'—just on the acceptable side
of the 'sacrificial' (and recalling Brutus's attempt at defining Caesar's slaying)—with their actions. 'Smoke' has a long association with lust, either for
sex or blood.[35] Meanwhile, Brutus persists vainly in attempting to distinguish
outer appearance from inner motive:

O Antony, beg not your death of us:
Though now we must appear bloody and cruel,
As by our hands and this our present act
You see we do, yet see you but our hands
And this the bleeding business they have done:
Our hearts you see not. They are pitiful,
And pity to the general wrong of Rome—
As fire drives out fire, so pity pity—
Hath done this deed on Caesar. For your part,
To you our swords have leaden points, Mark Antony.
Our arms in strength of malice, and our hearts

Of brothers' temper, do receive you in,
With all kind love, good thoughts and reverence.
(164–76)

This overture is quite untypical of what Shakespeare has previously registered in his portrayal of conflicting parties in such plays as the histories, where opponents invariably dispute each other's claims to truth, and where proffered blandishments are almost always false. Here, there is no denying Brutus's sincerity: after all, he has had to talk his friends into sparing Antony's life. Antony does not exactly demur, but he is cagey in his acceptance of Brutus's offer. For the moment of course he has little choice except to go along with it; more significantly, however, he is reluctant to embrace the republican cause. Why? Antony's personal motives are never clear, either to the conspirators or to the audience. Does he think that the 'butchering' of Caesar impugns the reasons for it irreparably? If so, he never raises this objection as such, but limits himself to deploring Caesar's death and blaming the hands of those who have occasioned it. When faced with the conspirators, Antony is in no position to speak freely, a situation that happens to be to his advantage. They regard him as Caesar's friend, and so do not require understanding or agreement from him, merely compliance. Antony is allowed to keep his counsel. What, then, does he really think? Antony either cannot see beyond the act to the principle motivating it or, for reasons undisclosed, he chooses not to. He certainly pays no heed to the arguments so painfully and conscientiously articulated by Brutus. When left alone with the corpse of Caesar, he speaks as a traditional revenge figure, expressing horror at the bloodiness of his friend's death and avowing retribution. Brutus's attempt to justify assassination on the grounds of republican principle is ignored utterly, as Antony shows himself to be gripped by the passion of personal loyalty, an example of the 'personal cause' that, as Brutus had earlier (2.1.11) recognized, threatens any attempt to view situations disinterestedly. Almost immediately, Antony looks for ways of incriminating the conspirators, implicitly if not overtly describing the assassination as murder. Twice he refers to the gesture of shaking hands: 'Let each man render me his bloody hand' (184), and 'Shaking the bloody fingers of thy foes' (198).

Also, in the sentence in which this latter phrase occurs, Antony deftly adopts Brutus's distinction between blood and spirit:

If then thy spirit look upon us now,
Shall it not grieve thee dearer than thy death
To see thy Antony making his peace,
Shaking the bloody fingers of thy foes?
(195–8)

Antony continues, steering a careful line between permissible homage to Caesar (after all, Brutus regrets his death) and accusation of his slayers, and concludes with a 'neutral', time-honoured image of the deer hunt:

> Pardon me, Julius! Here was thou bayed, brave hart.
> Here didst thou fall. And here thy hunters stand
> Signed in thy spoil and crimsoned in thy lethe.
> O world, thou wast the forest to this hart,
> And this indeed, O world, the heart of thee.
> How like a deer, stricken by many princes,
> Dost thou here lie?
>   (204–210)

Antony plays a version of the 'stricken deer' gambit. Representing the assassination in terms of the traditional image of hunting, frequently used as a symbol in love poetry, he manages to continue speaking of aggression and cruelty while not pointing the finger of blame in any apparent sense. The lover in such poetry is often depicted as a 'hart' receiving his wound from the unpitying lady; at the same time the allegory, as well as expressing emotional torment, may reflect something that is taking place in the real world, as it does here. Cassius, aware of the game, cautions Antony, who tactfully retreats. Shakespeare, almost at the same time as he wrote *Julius Caesar*, made satirical use of the deer image in *As You Like It*, where he has Jaques reportedly 'moralize this spectacle' of the hunt and its victim:

> 'Ay,' quoth Jaques,
> 'Sweep on, you fat and greasy citizens;
> 'Tis just the fashion. Wherefore do you look
> Upon that poor and broken bankrupt there?'
> Thus most invectively he pierceth through
> The body of the country, city, court,
> Yea, and of this our life; swearing that we
> Are mere usurpers, tyrants, and what's worse,
> To fright the animals and to kill them up
> In their assign'd and native dwelling-place.
>   (*AYLI* 2.1.54–63)

Jaques speaks in accents that Antony would approve of, likening the huntsmen, who are 'princes' in Antony's speech, to the very tyrants whom the conspirators in *Julius Caesar* would oppose. Shakespeare well knows that the language of allegory can be enlisted in the practice of redefining things as their opposites (virtues as vices, and so forth). Those who have acted against tyranny in killing Caesar Antony tries, and indeed successfully, to represent as tyrannical in their own nature. Does Antony's use of 'princes' have a pointedly Machiavellian echo, making capital out of the fact that for many readers of *Il Principe* the terms 'prince' and 'tyrant' were indistinguishable? This would be a case of the Machiavel Antony accusing his enemies of his own practice, as he does later in his speeches to the crowd.

Jaques's casual dismissal of those 'fat and greasy citizens' who ignore the plight of the hunted similarly introduces the theme, of much greater moment in *Julius Caesar*, of the people and their role as arbiters. Jaques has in mind well-fed, unappealing burghers whom we have already seen Machiavelli describe as '*tristi*': motivated almost exclusively by self-interest, and incapable of responding to appeals to principle, as Brutus ultimately discovers. The citizens in *Julius Caesar* are less well-nourished than in Jaques's image of them, and indeed more resemble Caesar's view of the conspirators in being 'hungry'. Antony understands that success will lie with those who know how and what to feed them. After Brutus's speech, where he explains his motives to the crowd, the response he receives from them betrays their sizeable lack of conceptual awareness:

> Had you rather Caesar were living, and die all slaves, than
> that Caesar were dead to live all freemen?
> (3.2.22–4)

Within moments of his saying this, the plebeians show themselves ready to create another tyrant in place of the one who has just been suppressed:

> 1 PLEBEIAN.
>   Bring him with triumph home unto his house.
> 2 PLEBEIAN.
>   Give him a statue with his ancestors.
> 3 PLEBEIAN.
>   Let him be Caesar.
> 4 PLEBEIAN.
>   Caesar's better parts
>   Shall be crowned in Brutus.
>   (49–52)

Brutus's own perception of his ancestors' significance is rather different. Earlier he has said:

Shall Rome stand under one man's awe? What Rome?
My ancestors did from the streets of Rome
The Tarquin drive when he was called a king.
     (2.1.252–4)

The inclination of the crowd to reimprison themselves in the very cap-tivity from which, as Brutus explains, he has just sought to release them, is ominous enough. It is all the cue Antony needs. The underlying debate probably turns less on whether Shakespeare is contemplating an England free from monarchy than on a general human tendency to repeat the errors of the past even when these have been exposed with the utmost clarity. Machiavelli expresses similar thoughts in his account of the Pazzi conspir-acy when he describes the failure of Jacopo de' Pazzi to rouse the *popolo* to thoughts of true liberty (see chapter head note). His brother-in-law's bland assurance that liberty is safe and sound thinly disguises the reality that the Medici have secured their own position not with liberty but with liberality (as we have seen, Machiavelli contrasts the two words pointedly). Within moments the terrible slaughter begins in Florence. As Antony contemplates the body of Caesar, which he addresses as 'thou bleeding piece of earth', it is hard to determine whether he is speaking out of genuine love (of which the text of the play has so far shown little evidence) or opportunistically. He is probably acting out of both. In the key speech, which I have already anal-ysed ('It must be by his death'), Brutus warns against the dangers emanating from personal involvement, whether of allegiance or grievance, which dis-turb clarity and objectivity and confuse reason with passion. Certainly, the large-scale bloodshed which Antony 'prophesies' occurs mainly as a result of his own efforts at whipping up the mob to a frenzy. Robert S. Miola comments:

> Antony turns the original argument for the assassination against
> the conspirators. In his view this attempt to restore Rome to
> civilized order has brought about only bestial violence.[36]

'In his view'? We might counter this relaxed interpretation of Antony's motives by saying that the bestiality issues directly and exclusively from his incitement of the mob. If he had kept quiet perhaps republicanism would have been made safe by the death of Caesar alone. On the other hand, civil war in one form or another would almost inevitably have broken out; but that would have been as a result of the usual scramble for power, rather than out of any concern to avenge Caesar. Shakespeare gives Antony a speech straight out of the revenge tradition, one that looks back partly to Kyd, while looking forward to *Macbeth*. The lines,

> Their infants quartered with the hands of war:
> All pity choked with custom of fell deeds,
>   (3.1.267–8)

evoke parts of Macbeth's speech when he contemplates what may be the awesome consequences of Duncan's 'taking-off':

> And pity, like a naked new-born babe,
> Striding the blast, or heaven's cherubin hors'd
> Upon the sightless couriers of the air,
> Shall blow the horrid deed in every eye,
> That tears shall drown the wind.
>   (1.7.21–5)

The two speakers select similar images, in particular those of infants and pity, which are often aligned in the common understanding. Interestingly, they apply these ideas, which function in each case in terms of prophecy, in an opposite sense. Macbeth's 'naked new-born babe' embodies the spirit of compassion which, outraged by Duncan's death, will protest the deed and make it public for universal condemnation. Antony, by contrast, looks forward to the grisly slaughter of innocent young ones, which will proceed on such a scale as to induce callousness even in the dead infants' mothers (unlikely as that seems). Such indeed proves to be the eventual conduct and state of mind of Macbeth himself, but at this point he shrinks from it in horror. Antony seems to welcome the very thing that terrifies Macbeth, and for the obvious reason that he presents it as a scourge on the land rather than as an emblem of his own conscience. Antony brings his speech to a conclusion similar to that of Macbeth's in its prophecy of dreadful consequence, except instead of tears drowning the wind, blood will soak the land:

> And Caesar's spirit, ranging for revenge,
> With Ate by his side come hot from hell,
> Shall in these confines, with a monarch's voice,
> Cry havoc and let slip the dogs of war,
> That this foul deed shall smell above the earth
> With carrion men, groaning for burial.
>   (270–5)

As a pragmatic kind of Machiavellian, Antony knows instinctively that blood is the element in which to find and exploit advantage. Whatever protest he makes at the horror of Caesar's murder must yield, in our evaluation, to the use he makes of it, just as in *The Rape of Lucrece* the dispassionate Lucius Junius Brutus seized the occasion of the protagonist's death, and the anger emanating from it, to turn the people against the Tarquins.

However, complicating our reception of Antony's lines is their echo of other works of Shakespeare besides *Macbeth*. One feels in listening to Antony that his words, rather than proceeding from the immediate situation, would carry greater logical conviction if applied to another context. (He never, for example, pauses to assess the validity of the republican cause; nor does he stop to consider the unreasonableness of ascribing Brutus's well-judged argument to no other motive than that of 'butchery'.) Along with the confused and intermittent *Macbeth* echoes, Antony's speech takes on something of King Henry's threat to the citizens of Harfleur:

> The gates of mercy shall be all shut up,
> And the flesh'd soldier, rough and hard of heart,
> In liberty of bloody hand shall range
> With conscience wide as hell, mowing like grass
> Your fresh fair virgins and your flow'ring infants.
> What is it then to me if impious war,
> Array'd in flames, like to the prince of fiends,
> Do, with his smirch'd complexion, all fell feats
> Enlink'd to waste and desolation?
> (*H5* 3.3.10–18)

Henry's apocalyptic threat works; the city gates are opened, so the 'gates of mercy' need not be 'shut up'. Since Henry is deploying a vision of the horrors of war for strategic purposes, and furthermore succeeds in his objective without recourse to violence on private citizens and their women and children, then his words need not lie on his conscience. Antony contemplates rather a vision of civil war that comes to pass. Furthermore, he could be said to have incited personally the ensuing violence. He dismisses his own powers of oratory ('For I have neither wit, nor words, nor worth, / Action, nor utterance, nor the power of speech', 3.2.214–5) only to 'stir men's blood' (216) to such a degree that, following his departure, the mob tears Cinna the Poet to pieces 'for his bad verses' (3.3.30), in a scene reminiscent of the savage dismemberment enacted in Florence in Machiavelli's description. What Macbeth dreads Antony wills, and like Macbeth, therefore, Antony cannot disengage himself from the consequences that follow. If Antony, along with those critics who find him plausible, is right to describe the assassination of Caesar as butchery, then what words will suffice for the mob slaying of Cinna? David Daniell would simply equate the two acts of killing with each other as both mindless, even while allowing the assassins some motive: 'there are in the play two frenzied gang-attacks. The first killed Caesar, who was said to have had some guilt; the second victim is innocent'.[37] Nobody can claim with certainty how the killing of Caesar will be perceived, as that depends on the effect individual productions aim at, but Brutus's prior argument for a principled, 'sacrificial' killing cannot be ignored. More to the point, however, is that the language of the play differs markedly from one scene to the other. During Caesar's assassination, Casca declares, 'Speak hands for me'; Caesar pronounces the famous words, '*Et tu, Brute?*—Then fall, Caesar'; and Cinna (the conspirator) cries, 'Liberty! Freedom! Tyranny is dead!' (3.1.76–78). However the motivation is construed, the tone and temper of these exchanges find only the most grotesquely distorted of echoes in, 'tear him for his bad verses'.

Although the conspirators commit the initial act of violence, responsibility for the subsequent flow of blood falls on Antony. Many commentators, as we have seen, do not want to accept this. Miola, for example, in analysing Brutus's speech (2.1.162 ff.) where he contemplates the manner of killing Caesar, detects echoes of Lucius's speech in *Titus Andronicus*:

> Give us the proudest prisoner of the Goths,
> That we may hew his limbs, and on a pile
> *Ad manes fratrum* sacrifice his flesh,
> (1.1.96–8)

and goes on to liken Brutus's 'use of blunt, vivid verbs—"cut," "hack," "kill", and especially "hew"', to those used by Lucius.[38] The echoes may indeed be heard. Yet the vengeful enthusiasm for killing that Lucius's words express could not be further removed from the mood of Brutus's speech, despite the fact that the two statements draw upon similar diction and imagery. Brutus tries his best to purge the act of vindictiveness. Whether one considers his choice of words to be successful or not, he determines to give Caesar his dignity:

> Let's kill him boldly, but not wrathfully:
> Let's carve him as a dish fit for the gods,
> Not hew him as a carcass fit for hounds.
> (2.1.171–3)

Caesar's death must be honourable and according to his status (Brutus seems even to be endorsing Caesar's Olympian aspirations as expressed in his

remark just prior to the assassination—'Hence! Wilt thou lift up Olympus?',
3.1.74). Brutus's language is much more measured and temperate than that of
the eager Lucius in the extract just quoted. Note, in contrast to Miola's analysis, that Brutus expressly repudiates the word 'hew' ('*Not* hew him as a carcass', etc.). Similarly, he denounces all that those 'blunt' verbs imply, when he
pleads with Cassius not to kill Antony. Yet herein lies his problem. Brutus's
flaw is not (*pace* his critics) that he succumbs involuntarily to savagery but, on
the contrary, that *he is not savage enough*. His very next words show that he is
holding a Machiavellian card which he does not know how to play:

> And let our hearts, as subtle masters do,
> Stir up their servants to an act of rage
> And after seem to chide 'em. This shall make
> Our purpose necessary and not envious,
> Which so appearing to the common eyes,
> We shall be called purgers, not murderers.
>   (174–9)

The first part of the passage carries a fairly obvious echo of the notorious
Remirro de Orco anecdote in *Il Principe*, where the deputy's 'acts of rage'
performed in bringing the Romagna under subjection are, so to speak,
cancelled or 'chided' by his own grisly execution. Cesare Borgia does not,
as part of the appeasement, give back the ground won for him by Remirro;
on the contrary, the threat of further blood hangs over those very citizens
whose pleas have been answered (in part) by the 'sacrifice' of his hench-
man. Savagery, far from being removed by Remirro's grim fate, remains in
force—indeed is emphasized by the nature of the punishment. Brutus, in
his perpetual desire to distinguish bloody action from abstract principle,
attempts to internalize the example of Remirro (his heart will remonstrate
with his hand); and therefore loses sight of the Machiavellian truth that
the bloodier the action the more likely that principle will be served. The
bloodier action, in this case, would have been to kill Antony as well as Caesar. Only then would the conspirators have earned the right to 'be called
purgers, not murderers', when the people had had the leisure to enjoy liberty
under a republic.

Antony knows all of this by intuition. Blood is the optimum rhetoric in
the circumstances: working on the people's capacity for anger will best serve
his purpose. A grim irony resides in the fact that even as he reads the will in
which Caesar has bequeathed to the citizens the parks and walks and places
of recreation 'this side Tiber' (3.2.240), his rhetoric produces in them an urge
to practise uncontrolled vandalism:

2 PLEBEIAN.

 Go fetch fire.

3 PLEBEIAN.

 Pluck down benches.

4 PLEBEIAN.

 Pluck down forms, windows, anything.

 Exit Plebeians (with the body)

ANTONY.

 Now let it work. Mischief, thou art afoot:

 Take thou what course thou wilt.

  (3.2.248–52)

All could go horribly wrong—indeed, it does so anyway—and Antony's readiness to put the city at risk will rebound seriously upon him should the conspirators regain the initiative. We might observe, in passing, the degree of irresponsibility with which he relishes opening the door to 'Mischief', rather as one might open Pandora's box. But he senses correctly that a dangerous calculation of this sort, one that gambles on the volatile mood of the people, is worth taking in the present circumstances. Brutus's logic is unassailable in republican terms: it can only be countered by shifting the argument on to a plane where reason gives way to emotion. (Brutus scrupulously denies himself any advantage deriving from emotional appeal, a rhetorical strategy which undoes him.)[39] Antony, then, whether or not he acknowledges as much to himself, is bent on winning Rome back for the conditions of monarchy. He certainly makes no admission of this to the audience, let alone to the crowd, to whom, other than expressing his anger at the assassination, he issues an invitation that will appeal to their self-interest, and reads out Caesar's will. Nor does he remind them of the price they would have paid for Caesar's generosity, or of the price they will pay once the conspirators have been overthrown. The relevant pages of the *Istorie Fiorentine* afford a comparable example of astutely applied *liberalità*. Shakespeare's play and Machiavelli's history cast doubts on the feasibility of republicanism, even though Machiavelli holds it up as an attainable ideal throughout the pages of the *Discorsi*. Perhaps a measure of republicanism, as Collinson implies, is the most that could be attained. Even so, the malleability of the public, the ease with which they succumb to blatant bribery, and above all their quickness to embrace heedless violence suggest a wariness on Shakespeare's part about going further in the cause of popular government.

 It is in the climactic pages of the twenty-fifth chapter of *Il Principe* that we find the appropriate analogue for Antony's behaviour. Machiavelli commends the decisive, risk-taking conduct of Pope Julius II who managed to wrest the initiative from his more cautious rivals:

Papa Iulio II procedé in ogni sua cosa impetuosamente, e trovò tanto
e tempi e le cose conforme a quello suo modo di procedere che sempre
sortì felice fine. Considerate la prima impresa che fe' di Bologna ... E
Viniziani non se ne contentavano: el re di Spagna quel medesimo; con
Francia aveva ragionamenti di tale impresa; e nondimanco con la sua
ferocia e impeto si mosse personalmente a quella espedizione. La quale
mossa fece stare sospesi e fermi Spagna e Viniziani.

(B 81–2; 'Pope Julius II proceeded impetuously in all his
undertakings, and found that times and circumstances so conformed
to his methods that he always came out on top. Consider the first
expedition he made against Bologna ... The Venetians were against
it, and so was the King of Spain; and there were discussions too
with France about such an enterprise. Nonetheless, he undertook
the expedition personally with his usual strength and ferocity; and
such was his momentum that he left both Spain and the Venetians
standing.')

It is tempting to identify Antony's tactics with those which Machiavelli
ascribes to the fox, in his famous Chapter 18 of *Il Principe* (*'Bisogna adunque*
essere golpe a conoscere e lacci', pp. 56–7), but the strength of purpose he shows,
even to the point of 'ferocity', and his readiness to put all to chance ('Mischief
.../ Take thou what course thou wilt') makes him resemble more the portrait
of Pope Julius above. As Wayne A. Rebhorn observes, 'The word [Machia-
velli] has chosen [*virtù*] suggests that however important the cleverness and
prudence of the confidence man may be, the toughness, resolution, and dar-
ing of the hero are more basic'.[40] One sees Machiavelli himself succumbing to this side of the equation in the enthusiasm with which he takes up
the examples of *virtù* in the *Principe*. Chapter 25 ends with the particularly
ruthless depiction of Fortune as a woman who responds most willingly to
those who are prepared to use her roughly. This is how Machiavelli accounts
for Julius's amazing success, and it is how Shakespeare seems to account for
Antony's successful seizure of the initiative from the more deeply reflective
Brutus. Charisma plays its part in securing success for any action undertaken
by a figure of *'ferocia e impeto'*, as the example of Julius indicates, and as that
of Cesare Borgia confirms more emphatically. Shakespeare in turn demonstrates this point by making Antony a more charismatic figure than Brutus—
or more precisely by giving the actor playing Antony a greater opportunity
to make Antony charismatic in his appeal to the crowd. Yet charisma is dis-
quieting. While I disagree with those who argue that Henry V is depicted as
untrustworthy and 'beguiling' (see Chapter 3), I have no difficulty in seeing

this as the response that Shakespeare is aiming for in creating Antony. The vandalism and murderous mayhem that his speech kindles sufficiently make the point.

As for acting him, an effective way to play the famous 'Friends, Romans, Countrymen' scene is for 'Antony' to include the audience in his address as if they were fellow Romans along with the actors. Theatrical conditions vary today, so as to make the enterprise more or less difficult depending on the venue. Smaller, intimate theatres are clearly much better fitted for the task than Grand Opera Houses. In the Globe the freedom of movement of the crowd in the yard, unfettered by seating arrangements, made for conditions that challenged the performer on the one hand and that he could exploit on the other. (This is something that can be tested today, though within limits, in the restored Globe.) An audience already on its feet is in a position to dissent more vociferously than one that is seated; at the same time such an audience can be swayed more easily than one that enjoys the circum-spection that comes with sitting. Naturally a theatre audience as *crowd* will be different in quite complex respects from other kinds of crowd, but the point nevertheless seems worth making.[41] The playing of the crucial scene in *Julius Caesar* is *live* in the important sense that if the actor cannot convert the crowd (audience) from its feelings of sympathy with Brutus, then not only the production but the moment of history which it enacts fails. For their part, the gentry in the Globe (i.e. those who were in fact seated) were afforded the dubious pleasure of reliving for themselves the experience of their Florentine counterparts (the '*ottimi*'), who were in a position, to one side of events, where they could witness the power exerted on the people by a powerful orator, be it a prince or a demagogue.

It is not only, then, that Shakespeare wishes us to observe differences of characterization in Brutus and Antony, but that he also shows how *opportunity* performs differently for each character according to his understanding of the changing flow of circumstances. Brutus's insight into the necessity of seizing the moment ('There is a tide in the affairs of men', 4.3.216) comes too late to enable him to regain the initiative that he has lost in ceding so much ground to Antony in the period immediately following Caesar's death. As with all of Brutus's understanding it comes introspectively and with limited capacity to take effect, whereas Antony, whose more reflective speeches tend to disintegrate upon analysis, carries the situation by acting upon instinct.

The republican framework of *Julius Caesar* gives Shakespeare certain freedoms that he does not have—or not to this degree—elsewhere (certainly not in the histories, and perhaps not in the tragedies either) to explore in a precise, political way what Bacon, applying the Machiavelli of the *Discorsi* rather than of the *Principe*, might have described as, 'what happens to men, not what ought to happen to them'. The histories in particular show a concern to make things come out right, in accordance with providential will. In the tragedies, the moral sanction against killing, especially the killing of a monarch, determines how we should interpret the action of a play such as *Macbeth*. The effect of this, in the latter example, is to locate the play deep in Macbeth's conscience. In *Julius Caesar*, I have argued, the matter of conscience preoccupies Shakespeare altogether differently. We should not think the less of Brutus when he registers no guilt over the killing of Caesar, for he is under no obligation to do so. Like Lucrece before him (who insists that her self-murder reflects her purity of mind), he has made every effort to square assassination with conscience, even though this proves to be a forlorn endeavour. Not guilt but circumstances, especially as exploited by Antony, betray him. When, therefore, Caesar's ghost accosts him in the military camp in 4.3, he replies with comparative equanimity, and with nothing like the terror, anguish, and remorse of either Macbeth when confronted with the ghost of Banquo or Richard III when visited by several spirits on the eve of Bosworth. Rallying himself Brutus says, 'Now I have taken heart thou vanishest' (4.3.285), a line which Daniell interprets as meaning, 'momentarily Brutus tries to persuade himself it was imagination', but which surely means that a ghost, even a *real* ghost, has no power over strength of mind. Brutus never denies the reality of the visit, but only interprets it later (5.5.17), when all is lost, to mean that the gods were ill disposed towards him. The visitation need be no more than a sign that things are changing, that he has miscalculated, and that fate is delivering its judgment.

The world Shakespeare depicts in *Julius Caesar* is a world without absolutes. Brutus makes the fatal miscalculation, though an appealing one, of maintaining that they exist, when it would be clearly in his interests to assume otherwise. This misjudgment leads to his downfall: he does not behave ruthlessly enough to command *fortuna* (*Il Principe*, Ch. 25). However, as Machiavelli makes clear in his two great texts, it is easier to behave decisively as a prince than as a republican, for whom obtaining overall assent is of vital importance. His mistake regarding Antony is the only weakness of Brutus's that matters. Everything else merely supplies the play with its tempo. Cassius's guileful 'seduction' of Brutus to make him join the conspiracy (1.2), Brutus's troubled relations with his wife and his restlessness before the assassination (2.1), the bickering between Brutus and Cassius followed by the ghostly appearance of Caesar to Brutus on the eve of Philippi (4.3): all this is secondary to the plot and occurs merely to provide the dramatic colouring that any play of ideas requires if it is not to stultify its audience.

The impression that all is relative appears often in Shakespearean drama: in the tragedies he voices the possibility that actions and feelings have no root in moral value, but he tends to dispel such sceptical intimations by means of a strong, final counter-movement in the dénouement. Here he contemplates fully, for the first time, something that Machiavelli had always assumed. In this world the act of killing need not involve the operations of conscience; on the contrary, conscience is a disadvantage. As Shakespeare depicts him, Brutus is a man not without conscience, but with too much of it for his own good. In this, more than any other character, he resembles Lucrece, whose conscience would not allow her to live. Lucius Junius Brutus seized the opportunity her suicide provided to overthrow the tyranny of the Tarquin family. Marcus Junius Brutus, in consulting his conscience, makes no presumption of guilt: he is only concerned that people should understand that his reasons for killing Caesar were good ones. The answer to this, as he finds out, is not that there are no good reasons for killing, but that its action is too dangerous to be left to others to interpret. The killing of Caesar is appropriated and reinterpreted by Antony, leading to the establishment of a new tyranny. The man of *virtù* triumphs over the man of good (or the man who has the much greater claim to good); and so effectively that even today commentators are more often swayed by Antony's emotive arguments than by Brutus's rational appeal, which is dismissed, interestingly, as bloodless.[42]

NOTES

1. David Daniell (*Julius Caesar*, 1998), pp. 25–9. References are to this edition.

2. See '*Julius Caesar* and the "Tyrannicide Debate"', p. 272.

3. Despite various arguments to the contrary, it is most likely Shakespeare's play rather than another that the company performed. The deposition scene (4.1) was suppressed in editions of the play published during Elizabeth's lifetime. See Gurr, pp. 6–10.

4. 'The Monarchical Republic of Queen Elizabeth', p. 400. Collinson finds support for this in Skinner (*Foundations* I, p. 229).

5. Collinson, p. 400. See Dewar, p. 57. The book's title changed to *The Commonwealth of England* in 1589.

6. Daniell, p. 197.

7. See the argument regarding the comparative wisdom and stability of the populace *vis-à-vis* the prince (*Discorsi*, I, 58). Machiavelli says, '*un principe che può fare ciò ch'ei vuole è pazzo*' (B 213; 'a prince who can do what he wants to is crazy', G 317).

8. See above, Ch. 3, p. 70.

9. Daniell (pp. 57–8) pursues a Bradleyan investigation into Brutus's motives, even picking up the hint in Plutarch that he was Caesar's illegitimate son. Shakespeare makes no use of this detail in *Julius Caesar*, though he perhaps alludes to it in *Henry VI, Part Two*: 'Brutus' bastard hand / Stabb'd Julius Caesar' (4.1.136–7). Daniell also thinks that in his weakness Brutus was 'seduced' by Cassius into the murder.

10. See above, Chapter 1.

11. *The Arte of Warre* (Cust, I, p. 9).

12. *The Florentine Historie*, Sig. Aii[r].

13. Humfrey Butters, 'Lorenzo and Machiavelli' (Mallett and Mann, p. 275).

14. Butters, 'Lorenzo and Machiavelli', p. 277. Alison Brown, citing a number of anti-Lorenzo writings, observes: 'Others wrote dialogues or Thucydidean histories in which criticism could be concealed in fictitious speeches—as Machiavelli helpfully explains . . . There are, for example, two occasions in his *Florentine Histories* when Machiavelli alerts us to criticism of Lorenzo through speeches, one during the Pazzi War, and the other concerning Lorenzo's harsh handling of the Volterra revolt in 1472'. See her 'Lorenzo and Public Opinion', p. 67. A more favourable view is given by Harold Acton, who complains that it is 'modish to denigrate this remarkable family at present' (*The Pazzi Conspiracy*, p. 7).

15. 'Lorenzo and Machiavelli', p. 275.

16. Machiavelli is of course one of several chroniclers, the majority of whom are sympathetic to republicanism, and who regard the Medici with varying degrees of animosity. Guicciardini, for example, lamented the outcome of the conspiracy, especially since the death of Giuliano made it all the easier for Lorenzo to become, as Machiavelli would describe it, *'un principe della republica'*. See Mark Phillips (*Francesco Guicciardini*, pp. 23–4). This unchecked consolidation of power by the Medici bears little resemblance to government by a constitutional monarch presiding over a 'species of republic', as described by Collinson (above).

17. B 925.

18. B 925: 'flushed with youth and power'.

19. See Najemy, 'Machiavelli and the Medici', p. 572.

20. Machiavelli makes the point at the opening of Book Eight of the *Istorie Fiorentine*, specifically on the Pazzi conspiracy. See also Brown, 'Lorenzo and Public Opinion', p. 63 n.

21. The church is so named according to Machiavelli's account. Santa Reparata was the name of the church which formerly stood on the site where the Duomo was built. Although the new cathedral had been completed earlier in the fifteenth century Machiavelli continues to call the church by its original name.

22. Plutarch notes in the margin, 'the wonderful constancy of the conspirators in killing Caesar' (Bullough, V, 99). Shakespeare may have been influenced by Plutarch or by Machiavelli or by both.

23. Allan Gilbert translates as follows: 'could with such rare courage and such firmness of mind be kept hidden by Francesco and Bernardo' (G 1390).

24. According to Gaeta (ed.), *Istorie Fiorentine*, p. 518.

25. Similarly, 'colour' (as noun) recalls Brutus's use of the word as a verb (2.1.29). Here it means pretext or disguise, whereas Brutus uses it in the more reflective and interpretative sense of representation.

26. Machiavelli narrates substantially the course and events of the crisis, though he is necessarily subject to diplomatic bias in favour of the Medici, notwithstanding the fact that we observe an underlying criticism of them throughout his argument. De Grazia gives a colourful account of the fates of various members of the Pazzi family, who managed to escape from Florence, in the opening chapter of *Machiavelli in Hell*. For an overall consideration of the conspiracy see Acton.

27. B 930 n.

28. He delivered the eight books to Clement VII, formerly Giulio de' Medici, in 1525. This Pope, the illegitimate and last child of Giuliano, was born in 1478, a few months after his father's death.

29. Following a futile attempt to escape, Jacopo was brought to trial and executed. His body was taken from the family tomb, dragged naked around the city, and finally flung into the Arno. Lorenzo continued to feed and exploit popular anger at the Pazzi.

30. 'Lorenzo and Machiavelli', p. 275.

31. B 940 n.

32. *Shakespeare's Rome*, pp. 76–7.

33. See *Macbeth* 5.8.68, 'this dead butcher and his fiend-like queen', and *JC* 3.1.254–5: 'O pardon me thou bleeding piece of earth / That I am meek and gentle with these butchers'.

34. *City of God*, I, 19.

35. Consider the description of lust as pillage in *Venus and Adonis*: 'With blindfold fury she begins to forage; / Her face doth *reek and smoke*, her blood doth boil' (554–5).

36. *Shakespeare's Rome*, p. 105.

37. Daniell (1998), p. 269.

38. *Shakespeare's Rome*, p. 93.

39. Against Brutus, Daniell cites Vickers's analysis of his use of a 'spurious enthymeme' in his speech of justification (Vickers [1968], p. 243, and Daniell [1998], p. 55). Vickers's argument owes something to Sister Miriam Joseph (*Shakespeare's Use of the Arts of Language*, p. 179).

40. *Foxes and Lions*, p. 148.

41. See Emrys Jones citing Gustave Le Bon's *The Psychology of Crowds* (*Scenic Form*, pp. 132–3).

42. Compare Vickers, *The Artistry of Shakespeare's Prose*, pp. 241–8. Vickers demonstrates why Antony is a better orator than Brutus, but does not pursue the darker implications of his emotional appeal.

BIBLIOGRAPHY

The Bibliography lists all the works cited in the text plus a number of others of relevant interest.

Acton, Harold. *The Pazzi Conspiracy: The Plot Against the Medici*. London: Thames & Hudson, 1979.

Adelman, Janet. *The Common Liar: An Essay on Antony and Cleopatra*. New Haven and London: Yale UP, 1973.

Alvis, John E. and Thomas G. West (edd.). *Shakespeare as Political Thinker*. Wilmington: ISI Books, 2000 (2nd revised ed.).

Anglo, Sydney. *Machiavelli: A Dissection*. London: Gollancz, 1969.

Armstrong, William A. 'The Influence of Seneca and Machiavelli on the English Tyrant', *RES* 24 (1948): 19–35.

Ascoli, A. R. and V. Kahn (edd.). *Machiavelli and the Discourse of Literature*. Ithaca & London: Cornell UP, 1993.

Atkinson, James B. and David Sices (transl. and edd.). *Machiavelli and his Friends: Their Personal Correspondence*, Dekalb, Illinois: Northern Illinois UP, 1996.

Augustine, Saint. *The City of God Against the Pagans*. Ed. and transl. R. W. Dyson. Cambridge: CUP, 1998.

Aulis, Joseph and Vickie Sullivan (edd.). *Shakespeare's Political Pageant. Essays in Politics and Literature*. Lanham, Md.: Rowman & Littlefield, 1996.

Barton, Anne. *Essays, Mainly Shakespearean*. Cambridge: CUP, 1994.

Bawcutt, N. W. 'Some Elizabethan Allusions to Machiavelli'. *English Miscellany* 20 (1969): 53–74.

———. 'Machiavelli and Marlowe's *The Jew of Malta*'. *Renaissance Drama*, NS 3 (1970): 3–49.

———. '"Policy," Machiavellianism, and the Earlier Tudor Drama'. *ELR* 1 (1971): 195–209.

———. 'Barnabe Barnes's Ownership of Machiavelli's *Discorsi*'. *N&Q* 227 (Oct. 1982): 411.

Berlin, Isaiah. 'The Originality of Machiavelli' (in Gilmore, pp. 147–206).

———. 'The Question of Machiavelli' (in A 206–36).

Bishop, Morris (tr. and ed.). *Letters from Petrarch*. Bloomington, Ind. & London: Indiana UP, 1966.

Bleznick, Donald W. 'Spanish Reaction to Machiavelli in the Sixteenth and Seventeenth Centuries'. *JHI* 19 (1958), 542–50.

Boose, Lynda E. 'The 1959 Bishops' Ban, Elizabethan Pornography, and the Sexualisation of the Jacobean Stage' (in Burt, pp. 185–200).

Boughner, Daniel C. *The Devil's Disciple: Ben Johnson's Debt to Machiavelli*. New York: Philosophical Library, 1968.

Brown, Alison. 'Lorenzo and Public Opinion' (in Garfagnini, pp. 61–85).

Bullough, Geoffrey, *Narrative and Dramatic Sources of Shakespeare*. 8 vols. London: RKP, 1957–75.

Burt, Richard and John Michael Archer (edd.) *Enclosure Acts: Sexuality, Property, and Culture in Early Modern England*. Ithaca & London: Cornell UP, 1994.

Butterfield, Herbert. *The Statecraft of Machiavelli*. London: Bell, 1940.

Butters, Humfrey. 'Lorenzo and Machiavelli' (in Mallett, pp. 275–80).

Campbell, O. J. (ed.), *The Living Shakespeare*. London & New York: Macmillan, 1949.

Carroll, D. Allen (ed.). *Greene's Groatsworth of wit: bought with a million of repentance (1592); attributed to Henry Chettle and Robert Greene*. Binghamton, NY: MRTS, 1994.

Castiglione, Baldassare. *The Book of the Courtier (1528)*. Tr. Thomas Hoby (1561). Ed. J. H. Whitfield. London: Dent, 1974.

Chambers, E. K. *William Shakespeare: A Study of Facts and Problems*. 2 vols. Oxford: Clarendon Press, 1930.

Champion, Larry S. 'The Function of Mowbray: Shakespeare's Maturing Artistry in *Richard II*'. *ShQ* (26 (1975): 3–7.

———. *'The Noise of Threatening Drum': Dramatic Strategy and Political Ideology in Shakespeare and the English Chronicle Plays*. Newark, N.J.: U of Delaware P, 1990.

Chaudhuri, Sukanta. 'The New Machiavelli: Shakespeare in the Henriad', in *Literature East and West: Essays presented to R. V. Dasgupta*. Edited G. R. Taneja and V. Sena. New Delhi: Allied Publishers Ltd, 1995.

Cicero, M. Tullius. *De Officiis*. Tr. Walter Miller. Cambridge, Ma.: Harvard UP (Loeb Classical Library), 1913.

Coby, J. Patrick. *Machiavelli's Romans: Liberty and Greatness in the Discourse on Livy*. Lanham, Md: Lexington Books, 1999.

Coleridge, Samuel T. *Shakespearean Criticism*. Ed. T. G. Raysor. *2 vols*. London: Dent, 1960.

Colish, Marcia L. 'The Idea of Liberty in Machiavelli', *JHI* 32 (1971): 323–50.

———. 'Cicero's *De Officiis* and Machiavelli's *Prince*'. *Sixteenth Century Journal* 9/4 (1978): 81–93.

Collinson, Patrick. 'The Monarchical Republic of Queen Elizabeth'. *BJRL* 69 (1987): 394–424. (Also in Guy, pp. 110–34).

Coyle, Martin (ed.). *Niccolò Machiavelli's The Prince: New Interdisciplinary Essays*. Manchester: MUP, 1995.

Craig, Hardin (ed.). *Machiavelli's The Prince: an Elizabethan Translation*. Chapel Hill, NC: U of North Carolina P, 1944.

Curren-Aquino, Deborah T. (ed.), *King John: New Perspectives*. Newark, N.J.: U of Delaware P, 1989.

Danby, John F. *Shakespeare's Doctrine of Nature*. London: Faber, 1949.

D'Andrea, Antonio. 'Studies on Machiavelli in the Sixteenth Century'. *JMRS* 5 (1961): 214–48.

———. 'Machiavelli, Satan and the Gospel'. *Yearbook of Italian Studies*, 1 (1971): 156–77.

Daniel, Samuel. *Samuel Daniel: The Civil Wars*. Ed. Laurence Michel. New Haven: Yale UP, 1958.

Dean, Paul. 'Shakespeare's Historical Imagination'. *RenSt* 11 (1997): 27–40.

De Grazia, Sebastian. *Machiavelli in Hell*. Princeton: Princeton UP, 1989.

Dewar, Mary (ed.). *De Republica Anglorum by Sir Thomas Smith*. Cambridge: CUP, 1982.

Dollimore, Jonathan. *Radical Tragedy: Religion, Ideology, and Power in the Drama of Shakespeare and His Contemporaries*. Brighton: Harvester Press, 1984.

Donaldson, Peter S. *Machiavelli and Mystery of State*. Cambridge: CUP, 1988.

Empson, William. *Essays on Shakespeare*. Ed. D. B. Pirie. Cambridge: CUP, 1986.

Flanagan, T. 'The Concept of *Fortuna* in Machiavelli' (in Parel, 1972), pp. 127–56.

Froissart, Jean. *The Chronicles of Froissart Translated out of French by Sir John Bourchiers Lord Berniers*. 6 vols. 1523–25. The Tudor Translations, no. 27. Ed. W. E. Henley. London, 1903.

Gardiner, Stephen. *A Machiavellian Treatise*. Ed. and tr. [from the Italian] by Peter S. Donaldson. Cambridge: CUP, 1975.

Garfagnini, G. C. (ed.). *Lorenzo il Magnifico e il suo mondo*. Florence: Olschki, 1994.

Gentili, Alberico. *De legationibus libri tres*. London, 1585.

Gentillet, Innocent. *Discours contre Machiavel* (1577). Ed. A. D'Andrea and P. D. Stewart. Florence: Casalini, 1974.

———. *A Discourse upon the Meanes of Wel Governing . . . Against Nicholas Machiavell the Florentine*. Tr. Simon Patericke (1602). Amsterdam-New York: Da Capo, 1969.

Gilman, Ernest B. *The Curious Perspective: Literary and Pictorial Wit in the Seventeenth Century*. New Haven and London: Yale UP, 1978.

Gilmore, Myron P. (ed.). *Studies on Machiavelli*. Florence: Sansoni, 1972.

Gohory, Jacques. *Le Prince de Nicholas Machiavel secretaire et citoyen florentin, dedié au magnifique Laurens fils de Pierre de Médicis. Traduit d'italien en françois avec la vie de l'autheur mesme, par Jacques Gohory*. Paris, 1571.

Gordon, D. J. *The Renaissance Imagination: Essays and Lectures*. Collected and edited by Stephen Orgel. Berkeley: U of California P, 1975.

Guy, John (ed.). *The Tudor Monarch*. London: Arnold, 1997.

Hager, Alan. *Shakespeare's Political Animal: Schema and Schemata in the Canon*. Newark, N.J.: U of Delaware P, 1990.

Hayward, John (ed.). *John Donne: Complete Poetry and Selected Prose*. London: Nonesuch Press, 1929 (rpt 1972).

Hexter, J. H. *The Vision of Politics on the Eve of the Reformation: More, Machiavelli, and Seyssel*. New York: Basic Books, 1973.

Hoenslaars, A. J. 'The Politics of Prose and Drama: The Case of Machiavelli's "Belfagor"' (in Marrapodi, 1998).

Holinshed, Raphael. *Chronicles of England, Scotland, and Ireland* (1587). 6 vols. London, 1807.

Holland, Norman N. *'Measure for Measure*. The Duke and the Prince'. *CL* 11 (1959): 16–20.

Horace [Quintus Horatius Flaccus]. *The Odes of Horace*. Transl. James Michie. New York: Washington Square Press-Orion Press, 1965.

Ingman, Heather. *Machiavelli in Sixteenth-Century French Fiction*. New York: Peter Lang, 1988.

Jones, Emrys. *Scenic Form in Shakespeare*. Oxford: Clarendon P, 1971.

Kahn, Victoria. *Machiavellian Rhetoric: From the Counter-Reformation to Milton*. Princeton: Princeton UP, 1994.

———. *'Virtù* and the Example of Agathocles in Machiavelli's *Prince'* (in Ascoli, pp. 195–217).

Lewis, Wyndham. *The Lion and the Fox: The Role of the Hero in the Plays of Shakespeare*. London: Grant Richard Ltd, 1927; rpt Methuen, 1955.

McPherson, David C. 'Aretino and the Harvey-Nashe Quarrel'. *PMLA* 84 (1969): 1551–8.

Machiavelli, Niccolò. *Opere*, Vols I–IV. Turin: UTET, 1984–89.

———. *Opere*. Ed. Mario Bonfantini. Milan-Naples: Ricciardi, 1954.

———. *Machiavelli: The Chief Works and Others*. Transl. Allan Gilbert. Durham & London: Duke UP, 1989.

———. *The Arte of Warre*. Transl. Peter Whitehorne. London, 1560. In *Machiavelli*. Ed. Henry Cust. 2 vols. London: D. Nutt, 1905.

———. *I discorsi di Nicolo Machiavell* [John Wolfe, London, 1584].

———. *Discorsi sopra la prima deco di Tito Livio*. Ed. Corrado Vivanti. Turin: Einaudi, 2000.

———. *The Florentine Historie. Written in the Italian tongue, by Niccolò Machiavelli, Citizen and Secretarie of Florence. And translated into English, by T.B.* [Thomas Bedingfield] *Esquire*. London, 1595.

———. *Istorie Fiorentine*. Ed. F. Gaeta. Milan: Feltrinelli, 1962.

———. *Lasino Doro di Nicolo Machiavelli, Con Tutte Laltre Sue Operette* [John Wolfe, London, 1588].

———. *Legazioni e commissarie*. 3 vols. Ed. Sergio Bertelli. Milan: Feltrinelli, 1964.

———. *Il Principe* [John Wolfe, London, 1584].

———. *Il Principe*. Ed. L. A. Burd. Oxford: Clarendon Press, 1891 (rpt 1968).

———. *Il Principe*. Ed. Giorgio Inglese. Turin: Einaudi, 1995.

———. *The Prince*. Transl. Edward Dacres, 1640.

———. *The Prince and the Discourses*. Tr. Max Lerner. New York: Modern Library, 1940.

———. *The Prince*. Transl. and ed. Quentin Skinner and Russell Price. Cambridge: CUP, 1988.

———. *The Prince*. Transl. and ed. Robert M. Adams. 2nd ed. New York and London: Norton, 1992.

Mallett, M. and N. Mann (edd.). *Lorenzo the Magnificent: Culture and Politics*. London: Warburg, 1994.

Manheim, Michael. 'The Four Voices of the Bastard' (in Curren-Aquino, pp. 126–35).

———. *The Weak King Dilemma in the Shakespearean History Play*. Syracuse, NY: Syracuse UP, 1973.

Marlowe, Christopher. *The Complete Works*. Ed. Roma Gill and others. 5 vols. Oxford: OUP, 1987–98.

Marrapodi, Michele and others (edd.). *Shakespeare's Italy: Functions of Italian Locations in Renaissance Drama*. Manchester: MUP, 1993.

——— (ed.). *The Italian World of Renaissance Drama*. Newark, N.J.: U of Delaware P, 1998.

Mattingley, Garrett. 'Machiavelli' (in Plumb, pp. 19–35).

Maus, Katharine Eisaman. *Inwardness and Theater in the English Renaissance*. Chicago: U of Chicago P, 1995.

Meyer, Edward. *Machiavelli and the Elizabethan Drama*. Weimar, 1897; rpt New York: Burt Franklin, 1969.

Miles, Geoffrey. *Shakespeare and the Constant Romans*. Oxford: Clarendon P, 1996.

Miola, Robert S. *Shakespeare's Rome*. Cambridge: CUP, 1983.

———. '*Julius Caesar* and the "Tyrannicide Debate"'. *RenQ* 38 (1985), 271–89.

Morey, James H. 'The Death of King John in Shakespeare and Bale'. *ShQ* 45 (1994), 327–31.

Najemy, John M. *Between Friends: Discourses of Power and Desire in the Machiavelli–Vettori Letters of 1513–1515*. Princeton: Princeton UP, 1993.

———. 'Language and *The Prince*' (in Coyle, pp. 89–114).

———. 'Machiavelli and the Medici: The Lessons of Florentine History'. *RenQ* 35 (1982): 551–76.

Nashe, Thomas. *Works*. Ed. R. B. McKerrow (rev. F. P. Wilson). 5 vols. Oxford: Clarendon P, 1958.

Ornstein, Robert. *A Kingdom for a Stage*. Cambridge, Ma.: Harvard UP, 1972.

Orsini, Napoleone. 'Elizabethan Manuscript Translations of Machiavelli's *Prince*'. *JWCI* 1 (1937): 166–9.

———. '"Policy" or the Language of Elizabethan Machiavellianism'. *JWCI* 9 (1946): 122–34.

Parel, Anthony (ed.). *The Political Calculus*. Toronto: U of Toronto P, 1972.

———. *The Machiavellian Cosmos*. New Haven: Yale UP, 1992.

Parker, Patricia and David Quint (edd.). *Literary Theory/Renaissance Texts*. Baltimore: Johns Hopkins UP, 1986.

Petrarca, Francesco. *Canzoniere*. Ed. G. Contini. Turin: Einaudi, 1968.

Phillips, Mark. *Francesco Guicciardini: The Historian's Craft*. Toronto: U of Toronto P, 1976.

Pitkin, Hanna Fenichel. *Fortune Is a Woman: Gender and Politics in the Thought of Niccolò Machiavelli*. Berkeley: U of California P, 1984.

Plumb, J. H. (ed.). *Renaissance Profiles*. New York: Harper, 1965.

Pocock, J. G. A. *The Machiavellian Moment: Florentine Political Thought and the Atlantic Republican Tradition*. Princeton: Princeton UP, 1975.

Praz, Mario. 'Machiavelli and the Elizabethans', in *The Flaming Heart*. New York: Doubleday, 1958.

Price, Russell. 'The Senses of *Virtù* in Machiavelli'. *European Studies Review* 3 (1973): 315–45.

———. 'Gloria in Machiavelli'. *RenQ* 30 (1977): 588–631.

———. 'Ambizione in Machiavelli's Thought'. *History of Political Thought* 3 (1982): 382–445.

Prior, Moody E. *The Drama of Power: Studies in Shakespeare's History Plays*. Evanston: Northwestern UP, 1973.

Puttenham, George. *The Arte of English Poesie*. Ed. G. D. Willcock and Alice Walker. Cambridge: CUP, 1936 (rpt 1970).

Raab, Felix. *The English Face of Machiavelli: A Changing Interpretation 1500–1700*. London: RKP, 1965.

Rabelais, François. *Gargantua and Pantagruel*. Tr. J. M. Cohen. Harmondsworth: Penguin, 1955.

Rebhorn, Wayne A. *Foxes and Lions: Machiavelli's Confidence Men*. Ithaca and London: Cornell UP, 1988.

Reese, M. M. *The Cease of Majesty. A Study of Shakespeare's History Plays*. London: Arnold, 1961.

Ribner, Irving. *The English History Play in the Age of Shakespeare*. Princeton: Princeton UP, 1957.

———. 'The Significance of Gentillet's *Contre-Machiavel*'. *MLQ* 10 (1949): 153–7.

Ridolfi, Roberto. *The Life of Niccolò Machiavelli*. Transl. Cecil Grayson. London: RKP, 1963.

Riebling, Barbara. 'Virtue's Sacrifice: A Machiavellian Reading of *Macbeth*'. *SEL* 31 (1991): 273–86.

Rossiter, A. P. *Angel with Horns and Other Shakespeare Lectures*. London: Longmans, 1961.

Sanders, Wilbur. *The Dramatist and the Received Idea: Studies in the Plays of Marlowe and Shakespeare*. London: CUP, 1968.

Schaefer, David Lewis. *The Political Philosophy of Montaigne*. Ithaca, N.Y.: Cornell UP, 1990.

Scott, Margaret. 'Machiavelli and the Machiavel'. *RenD* 15 (1984): 147–74.

Sellers, Harry. 'Italian Books Printed in England Before 1640'. *The Library*, 4th Series, 5, no. 2 (Sept. 1924): 105–28.

Shakespeare, William. *The Complete Works*. Ed. Peter Alexander. London & Glasgow: Collins, 1951.

———. *Antony and Cleopatra*. Ed. David Bevington. Cambridge: CUP, 1990.

———. *Antony and Cleopatra*. Ed. Emrys Jones. Harmondsworth: New Penguin, 1977; rpt, 1997.

———. *Hamlet*. Ed. Philip Edwards. Cambridge: CUP, 1985.

———. *Henry V*. Ed. J. Dover Wilson. Cambridge: CUP, 1947.

———. *Henry V*. Ed. T. W. Craik. London: Routledge, 1995.

———. *Henry V*. Ed. Gary Taylor. Oxford: OUP, 1982.

———. *Julius Caesar*. Ed. David Daniell. Walton-on-Thames: Nelson, 1998.

———. *King John*. Ed. L. A. Beaurline. Cambridge: CUP, 1990.

———. *King John*. Ed. J. Dover Wilson. Cambridge: CUP, 1936.

———. *King John*. Ed. E. A. J. Honigmann. London: Methuen, 1954.

———. *King John*. Ed. R. L. Smallwood. Harmondsworth: Penguin, 1974.

———. *King Richard II*. Ed. Andrew Gurr. Cambridge: CUP, 1984.

———. *King Richard II*. Ed. Peter Ure. London: Methuen, 1956.

———. *King Richard II*. Ed. J. Dover Wilson. Cambridge: CUP, 1939.

———. *King Richard III*. Ed. Anthony Hammond. London: Methuen, 1981.

———. *The Life and Death of King John*. Ed. A. R. Braunmuller. Oxford: OUP, 1989.

Shaw, George Bernard. *The Bodley Head Bernard Shaw*. Ed. supervisor Dan H. Laurence. 7 vols. London: Mac Reinhardt, 1970–74.

Sidney, Sir Philip. *An Apology for Poetry*, ed. Geoffrey Shepherd. London: Nelson, 1965.

Sister Miriam Joseph. *Shakespeare's Use of the Arts of Language*. New York: Columbia UP, 1947.

Skinner, Quentin. *The Foundations of Modern Political Thought*. 2 vols. Cambridge: CUP, 1978.

———. *Machiavelli*. Oxford: OUP, 1981.

———. 'Thomas Hobbes: Rhetoric and the Construction of Morality'. *PBA* 76 (1991), 1–61.

———. *Reason and Rhetoric in the Philosophy of Thomas Hobbes*. Cambridge: CUP, 1996.

Smith, Sir Thomas. *De Republica Anglorum* (1583). (See Dewar.)

Spenser, Edmund. *The Faerie Queene*. Ed. A. C. Hamilton. London: Longman, 2001.

Spivack, Bernard. *Shakespeare and the Allegory of Evil*. New York: Columbia UP, 1958.

Strauss, Leo. *Thoughts on Machiavelli*. Chicago: U of Chicago P, 1958 (rpt 1978).

Struever, Nancy. *Theory as Practice: Ethical Inquiry in the Renaissance*. Chicago and London: U of Chicago P, 1992.

Sullivan, Vickie. 'Princes to Act: Henry V as the Machiavellian Prince of Appearance' (in Aulis, pp. 125–52).

Tillyard, E. M. W. *Shakespeare's History Plays*. London: Chatto & Windus, 1944.

Tinkler, John F. 'Praise and Advice: Rhetorical Approaches in More's *Utopia* and Machiavelli's *The Prince*'. *Sixteenth Century Journal* 19/2 (1988): 187–207.

Vaughan, Virginia Mason. 'Between Tetralogies: *King John* as Transition'. *ShQ* 35 (1984): 407–20.

Vickers, Brian. *The Artistry of Shakespeare's Prose*. London: Methuen, 1968.

———. 'Machiavelli and Marvell's *Horatian Ode*'. *N&Q* New series 36 (March 1989): 32–8.

Whigham, Frank. *Ambition and Privilege: The Social Tropes of Elizabethan Courtesy Theory*. Berkeley: U of California P, 1984.

Whitfield, J. H. *Discourses on Machiavelli*. Cambridge: Heffer, 1969.

Williams, Benjamin (tr. and ed.). *Chronicle of the Betrayal and Death of Richard King of England*. London: Publications of the English Poetry Society, 1846.

Wimsatt, W. K. (ed.). *Dr Johnson on Shakespeare*. Harmondsworth: Penguin, 1969.

Yeats, W. B. *The Poems: A New Edition*. Ed. Richard J. Finneran. London: Macmillan, 1984.

LLOYD DAVIS

Embodied Masculinity in
Shakespeare's Julius Caesar

Amid the famous historical figures and events of *Julius Caesar* a complex
question about gender identity recurs—what is masculinity's perfect form?
Antony's famous eulogy on Brutus invokes ideal manhood: "This was the
noblest Roman of them all . . . nature might stand up / And say to all the
world 'This was a man'" (5.5.67–74).[1] He says that Brutus acted not out of
envy but out of honest conviction for the good of all. His ally, Octavius sums
up these noble principles by the important word, "virtue" (5.5.75), which,
from the Latin *virtus*, signified "an ideal of manhood" for many English
Renaissance writers.[2] The final speeches receive the imprimatur of dramatic closure; yet traces of certain ambiguity are not entirely effaced by the
climactic tone. For those who celebrate Brutus are those who have defeated
him; simply put, they can afford to be generous. Their praise is earnest and
expedient, and it is also carefully qualified—confining Brutus's nobility to
the past, while suggesting that for all his valour Brutus was not as great a
figure as the victors. The tribute uses Brutus to celebrate true masculinity
but subtly directs it away from him. The closing scene thus captures the
way that masculinity is idealised in conflicting terms throughout the play.
It remains a singular virtue, prized by men of all social ranks. It is also com-
peted for, since its social and political value is sharply appreciated. Everyone
(that is, every man), regardless of rank, thinks he might be able to claim it,

From *EnterText* 3, no. 1 (Spring 2003): 161–82. © 2003 by Brunel University.

either for himself or to attribute it to another—the tribunes lionise Pompey, the populace Caesar, Brutus and Cassius try to claim it for themselves. There are many men but one ideal. Whose version of masculinity is the real thing? How is the distinction to be made? Which criterion is right?

Antony claims that nature ultimately states who man is. It is a powerful way to put things, since it appears not only to support what is said (Brutus is a man) and how (Antony quotes nature), but also to guarantee the speech's premise—man is the pre-eminent natural ideal. The proof of man's perfection is the body—"the elements / So mixed in him" (5.5.72–73)—a seemingly unique attribute, given at birth yet also a man's own to mould and use. No matter that, as happens constantly through the play, men's bodies are always being re-formed verbally, visually, and physically by people and events around them. This ongoing process can be ignored as long as the elemental man-body-nature complex seems to hold together in the eyes of others. Repeatedly in *Julius Caesar*, the naturalness of the body and the perfection of man are shown to depend on their representational impact.

Shakespeare's drama at once unveils and conceals the dominance of the aristocratic male body. In staging the production of the masculine ideal, the play suggests that it is never natural. Yet true to the historical tradition it invokes, the action does not move towards depicting a world not defined in terms of the aristocratic male body. This perspective is affirmed even though the play's title figure is not pre-eminent, and hence, for some commentators, the play fails to conform to a "great man" approach to history. In 1712 John Dennis criticised the playwright's ignorance of ancient works, which led him to portray Caesar as "but a Fourth-rate Actor in his own Tragedy."[3] Twenty years earlier, Thomas Rymer had maintained that Shakespeare misrepresented not simply the protagonist but all the major characters: he "sins ... against the most known History and the memory of the noblest Romans."[4] Rymer specially condemned the depiction of Brutus, picking his speech as entirely inappropriate, "unless from some son of the Shambles, or some natural offspring of the Butchery."[5] He alludes to Shakespeare's connection to the cattle industry through his father's early work as a glover, which John Aubrey embellished as follows: "his father was a butcher, and I have been told heretofore by some of the neighbours, that when he was a boy he exercised his father's trade, but when he kill'd a calf, he would do it in high style, and make a speech."[6] In contrast to the biographical panegyric that is soon to begin with Nicholas Rowe's *Some Account of the Life &c. of Mr. William Shakespear* (1709), and notwithstanding Aubrey's image of the proto-tragedian, Rymer insinuates that Shakespeare's yeoman background prevents him from characterising heroic masculinity. Despite their different tones, from sarcasm to panegyric, the writers readily assume more or less direct connections between Shakespeare as a man, his lineage, and the kind of plays he can write.

For Rymer and Dennis, the gap between history, genre, and Shakespeare's characterisation threatens to expose and undermine if not historical tradition, then certainly traditional masculinity: if the near-legendary Caesar and Brutus come across as ordinary or inferior, where does that leave all other male figures? Some other early commentators did, however, take a different view. It is in his departures from the sources that Margaret Cavendish locates the success of Shakespeare's characters: "certainly *Julius Caesar*, *Augustus Caesar*, and *Antonius*, did never Really Act their parts Better, if so Well, as he hath Described them, and I believe that *Antonius* and *Brutus* did not Speak Better to the People, than he hath Feign'd them."[7] She praises an imaginative response that improves on historical accounts. Antony's eulogy to Brutus exemplifies this enhancing effect. It reaffirms a masculine order of things that has been disturbed not overturned, tested but reinforced. *Julius Caesar* reveals the capacity that masculinity, like all ideologically compelling concepts, has to be reinvented and reasserted: "let's away / To part the glories of this happy day" (5.5.79–80), the new man concludes. Though civil order seems on the verge of implosion and the public imagination is flooded with irreconcilable ideals, the play does not develop a radical or critical perspective on masculine mythology. Rather, the effects it dramatises run parallel to those traditionally played in western discourse by an idealised masculine body: "a corporeal 'universal' [that] has in fact functioned as a veiled representation and projection of a masculine which takes itself as the unquestioned norm, the ideal representative without any idea of the violence that this representational positioning does to its others."[8] Despite the emulous rivalries played out between characters, and the potential demystification of heroic male figures that offended Rymer and Dennis, an embodied masculine norm remains intact. In a sense, it needs to be threatened to be able to re-emerge and be celebrated. Ultimately *Julius Caesar* maintains, in Elizabeth Montagu's words, "Roman character and sentiments,"[9] by staging the potent capacity of culturally dominant masculinity to recreate and perpetuate itself.

The weaknesses and contradictions of man's body often figure as a sobering trope for moral discourse in the period when Shakespeare was writing. In Caesar's disabilities and Brutus's self-doubts, at times *Julius Caesar* echoes the ambivalent tone of such writers as Thomas Wilson: "Let us see him what he is: Is his bodie any thing els, but a lumpe of earth, made together in such forme as we doe see? A fraile vessel, a weake carion subiect to miserie, cast downe with euery light disease, a man to day, to morowe none." Wilson grounds man's identity in a mortal, material body.[10] Perhaps because of these overt failings, man is preoccupied with his physical state: "Trueth it is," Wilson claims, "we are more fleshly then spirituall, soner feeling the ache of our body, then the greefe of our soule: more studious with care to be healthful in car-kasse, then seeking with praier, to bee pure in spirite."[11] The emotions too appear most significant on account of their physical consequence, the "diuers effectes" on the body of the "passions of the minde:" "like as ioye comforteth the heart, nourisheth bloud, and quickeneth the whole bodie: So heauinesse and care hinder digestion, ingender euill humours, waste the principal partes, and with time consume the whole bodie."[12] Wilson's moralising shares the anatomical premise that recurs through the sixteenth and seventeenth centu-ries: examining man's body reveals his true nature. Yet it is not only corporeal detail that is uncovered on early modern dissecting tables. Various notions of man's identity are supported through anatomical discourse, be they in terms of the Christian ethic that Wilson offers, or of a solidly individualised and gendered selfhood, or of a more sceptical and equivocal sense of masculine ethos, as has been recently suggested.[13]

For Wilson, the body starkly denotes man's origin, emotions, and death. Its vivid meanings exemplify the body's potential to act as a paradigmatic personal and cultural sign; as Mary Douglas has influentially put it, "Just as it is true that everything symbolises the body, so it is true ... that the body symbolises everything else."[14] Hence those who can define and interpret its meaning and stage its appearance are likely to influence and control others. In *Julius Caesar* Shakespeare dramatises these issues through a series of confron-tations between characters over the meanings of the male body as an idea and symbol, as a site where identity is asserted and imposed, and as a means of achieving social goals. Where Wilson uses man's body to underscore physical and spiritual dilemmas, Shakespeare uses it to explore the ethics and poli-tics of masculine identity. Douglas notes generally that the body can "stand for any bounded system"—a nation, a class, a faction, a gender, even that of individuality itself. But she adds that the body is especially suitable to repre-sent "threatened or precarious" boundaries.[15] *Julius Caesar* is set at a time of huge transition in Roman politics and society, and it contributes to an analo-gously liminal phase in early modern England, as Elizabeth I's reign drew to a close.[16] In these terms, the play participates in an "unmasking of the politics of representation per se, in a detailed anatomy of the body politic," by staging critical episodes, past and present.[17] More specific to my concerns, as part of its wide-ranging political interest, the play represents an ideological struggle over the way the male body looks and is looked at, acts and is acted upon, and speaks and is spoken about.

Hence in addition to its relevance to early modern notions of power, rep-resentation, and discourse, *Julius Caesar* offers a view of some of the important conceptions of masculinity and male relations in Shakespeare's time and after.

The play presents a society publicly dominated by and symbolically fixated on men. Commentators often note that both female characters, Portia and Calpurnia, are confined to a private domain, their concerns brushed aside (as in Calpurnia's case) unless they try to assume a conspicuous masculine persona, as does Portia through repeated self-wounding.[18] Sidelining the female characters to this degree leaves what is basically a one-gender world where homosocial bonds are acted out through fervent comradeship and enmity in politics and war. Even among allies there exists a "routine intensity of competition central to the definition of Romans as men."[19] Shakespeare depicts a somewhat similar world in *Coriolanus*, but both there and to a still greater extent in *Antony and Cleopatra* he develops the psychological, erotic, social, and political impacts that women can have, notwithstanding (perhaps more on account of) the limitations and pressures brought to bear upon them. With an unwavering focus on men, *Julius Caesar* contrasts to both of these plays, and to Shakespeare's other works with classical settings, including *Troilus and Cressida*, *The Rape of Lucrece*, and *Titus Andronicus*, where female figures are objects of, but also influential, perhaps uncontrolled, factors in relations between men. (Nonetheless, there remains little sense through most of these works that women are able to relate to themselves or each other outside patriarchal codes. Female characters such as Lavinia and Tamora, Lucrece, Cressida and Helen are forcibly isolated among males). Mario DiGangi has noted that it might be critically and historically unsound to consider Shakespeare's depictions of men's relationships as "culturally 'representative'" on any broad scale.[20] Acknowledging his point, we can think of *Julius Caesar* as offering a sharp perspective on one particular code of aristocratic male conduct, shaped by Shakespeare's reading of both Plutarch and the society around him. While the play includes many different types of men and relationships, it does assume that, despite some crucial contradictions, the aristocratic code with its specific kinds of male figures and notions of masculinity is extremely influential in determining the course of wider social events and people's lives.

The action opens in the midst of a political conflict being waged through many kinds of male conduct, from out-and-out warfare to orchestrated public appearances. The tribunes, Flavius and Murellus, attack the plebeians for celebrating Caesar's recent victory over Roman rivals. They criticise "poor men of your sort" (1.1.56) for wearing their "best apparel" and celebrating one who "comes in triumph over Pompey's blood" (1.1.1–50). The workers are commanded to return home and "fall upon your knees." They "vanish tongue-tied," and the tribunes separate to "Disrobe the images" of Caesar and to curb his ambition (1.1.51–74). It is immediately apparent that men's bodies are being constantly observed and talked about. They are treated as visual and rhetorical signs whose meanings are judged and fought over. The way they dress signifies political allegiance and social rank; their bearing connotes submission or resistance. (As has been observed, disputed Elizabethan sumptuary codes and puritan-led debates over attitudes to self-discipline increase these stakes).[21] The drive to monitor and regulate men's costume and posture locates their bodies in a "politics of visibility,"[22] all the more urgent because amid escalating political tension, the codes and meanings of body language have become equivocal and could intimate existing and perhaps potential support, conflict, or rivalry.

Various kinds of uncertainty immediately come into play. Caesar's retinue enters to participate in the celebration of Lupercalia, through which Calphurnia might "shake off [her] sterile curse" (1.2.11). The link between Caesar and sterility, despite being ascribed to his wife, unsettles the pomp of the "titular hero's" entrance.[23] It intimates other physical and personal failings soon to be revealed. Foreboding is reinforced by the soothsayer's warning of the Ides of March. Ever the theatre professional, Shakespeare plays upon the audience's knowledge of Caesar's end. The well-known outcome increases rather than reduces suspense—every gesture seems a possible index to when the killing will occur. Like many of the characters, who sense that something is going to happen in light of constant omens, military and political manoeuvring, the audience is encouraged to fasten on any portent. Cassius's ensuing dialogue with Brutus exemplifies the continually motivated and ambivalent gaze that all the characters practise, modelling audience scrutiny. Every man is looking at each other but tries to hide the fact or conceal his response. Cassius claims that Brutus has been looking at but not seeing him: "Brutus, I do observe you now of late: / I have not from your eyes that gentleness / And show of love as I was wont to have" (1.2.34–36). In reply, Brutus admits that his attention has been turned in rather than out: "If I have veil'd my look, / I turn the trouble of my countenance / Merely upon myself" (1.2.39–41). The reflexivity of sight is underlined. Though looking at and being perceived by the other, one regards the self. It sounds as though the gaze is rendered harmless to others, since it is always self-referential. But such reflexivity might allow greater scrutiny of the other: what I may discern in him is already within. This double vision is at work in Caesar's view of Cassius later in the scene. He is troubled by the other's appearance because he knows what it means when a man looks that way: "Yon Cassius has a lean and hungry look. . . . Such men as he be never at heart's ease / Whiles they behold a greater than themselves, / And therefore are they very dangerous" (1.2.195, 209–10).[24] Emulous rivalry and knowledge make the aristocrats' versions of one another, "fashioned through violent competition" and seeking the goals of power and identity through superior insight and at the expense of others.[25] Yet if each man is a version of the self, his demise is incipiently one's own. In viewing the other the self foresees, without necessarily recognizing, its own grim prospects.

Hence the reflexivity of the gaze is repressed as it is exercised. The aristocrats try to deny or foreclose the self-interest and reference of male vision, and instead presuppose its objective truthfulness. In this way, focusing on others might work to confirm and insulate rather than threaten the observer's identity. After he surveys Cassius, Caesar disavows any personal concern and asserts an eternal presence: "I rather tell thee what is to be fear'd / Than what I fear; for always I am Caesar" (1.2.212–13). Cassius's critical account of Caesar would affirm his own probity through narrative: "honour is the subject of my story. . . . He had a fever when he was in Spain / . . . I did mark / How he did shake. 'Tis true, this god did shake" (1.2.94, 1.2.121–23). Having had his self-perceptions mirrored and endorsed by Cassius (1.2.69–72), Brutus can concede that Caesar's probable ascent justifies his decision to strike for "no personal cause . . . But for the general . . . So Caesar may. / Then lest he may, prevent" (2.1.11–12, 27–28). Only Cicero willingly admits to men's personal investment in what they perceive: "men may construe things, after their fashion, / Clean from the purpose of the things themselves" (1.3.34–35). This admission of subjective understanding is later undercut by the blunt literalness with which Cicero's own death is imposed and confirmed: "Ay, Cicero is dead, / And by that order of proscription" (4.2.231–32). The performative violence of the Latinate "proscription" obliterates Cicero's relativism and rhetorical subtlety. The death of the poet Cinna in Act Three scene three offers a similarly forbidding version of the capacity of language and reason to withstand sheer aggression. Like the proscription that condemns Cicero, the plebeians' words are marked by destructive performativity: "Pluck but his name out of his heart. . . . Tear him, tear him!" (3.2.32–34). They enact a kind of violent anatomy that annihilates language and identity.

Relentlessly scrutinising one another, the men compel themselves to follow a course of crafty self-presentation that will, in turn, be more and more closely dissected and defined. These practices are exemplified in Act Two, scene two when various characters try to display and interpret a series of bodily images. Each man reads others and is read by them; each tries to impose his version of self-realisation on others, while adjusting his identity in response to theirs. The affirmation which they all seek often blinds them to risks of their own misreading and to the motivated readings of others. Before he ventures to the Senate, Caesar calls for an augury over sacrificial entrails to confirm his course of action (2.2.5–6). The custom implies a belief in definite physical meaning and interpretation. The previous night Calpurnia had dreamt of danger, with Caesar's statue running "pure blood" from a hundred spouts (2.2.77–78). In contrast to Calpurnia, Caesar and the conspirator Decius Brutus interpret her dream positively, as urging him to bravery and patronage, but each does so for entirely different reasons (2.2.83–91). In the next act, when things proceed from dreams to action, Caesar's body and blood are graphically objectified. Yet even their manifestly physical presence cannot restrict differently motivated meanings and conflicting interpretations. After the stabbing, Brutus insists that the killers "bathe" and "besmear" their arms and knives in the blood to proclaim peace, freedom, and liberty visually (3.1.106–11). When Antony grasps the bloody hands of the killers, declaring "Friends, I am with you all, and love you all" (3.1.222), Brutus accepts the gesture at face value, though as Cassius suspects and we soon hear, the moment seals Antony's antagonism, "Woe to the hand that shed this costly blood!" (3.1.261).[26]

The ambiguous handshaking near the end of Act Three suggests that characters' reading and misreading of the male body focus sharply on its actions and gestures. The men play important physical roles in various political rituals. The male body is often the object of ceremonies and attention, but it also acts to score political and social points. The key example of the latter occurs, suspensefully offstage, when Caesar thrice rejects a crown presented to him by Antony before a vast public audience. Casca contemptuously reports the manipulated emotions of the crowd, which equally celebrates the offering and refusal of sovereignty (1.2.235–70). The episode underscores the importance of public performance in winning and maintaining political power and provides "a model of authoritarian populism" that both Brutus and Antony later vie to effect.[27] However, Caesar's actions also reveal the risks that can be involved in this kind of display. The power of performance is always potentially double-edged: "a formal occasion cannot ignore or terminate what it is that is designated the official focus of attention. It follows that every celebration of a person gives power to that person to misbehave unmanageably."[28] In succumbing to "the falling sickness" (1.2.252), Caesar loses control of his body; it takes over and conveys mixed signals about his fitness to rule. Indeed, throughout the first half of the play, Caesar's body is an equivocal political factor, liability and asset. Its lameness and deafness undercut his imperial claims, while its colossal status riles as much as it overshadows his peers, who are ready to conceive it as "monstrously grotesque and structurally disruptive."[29] He is trapped, to his benefit and loss, by the power his body signifies. Although conditions such as epilepsy, deafness, and sterility may bolster Caesar's position with some—charismatically revealing a person beneath the role, one whose apparent weaknesses do not undermine his status—they also expose him to attack for aspiring to a power beyond his capacity.[30] Cassius images this power as the imposition of physical submission: "And this man / Is now become a god, and Cassius is / A wretched creature, and must bend his body / If Caesar carelessly but nod on him" (1.2.116–20). Ironically, the conspirators use such bowing and scraping to distract Caesar before the stabbing (3.1.34–76); Antony later charges them with doing just so (5.1.42–45). Caesar's fall is thus ironically preceded by physical expressions that seem to verify his dominance, just as his offstage *coup de théâtre* is simultaneously being framed by the beginnings of conspiracy.

Cassius's words angrily exaggerate the process of submission, but the image he uses registers sharp sensitivity to the two bodies' relative status, bearing, and control. The apparent absence of intention and minimal movement in Caesar's careless nod magnify his mastery. Such bodily power is a scarce commodity: not everyone can have it, and it seems to concentrate in one man at the expense of others. Physical power tends to be exclusive. In this same society, however, there is one type of bodily agency that cannot be taken away from any individual. It remains a fundamental prerogative: the potential to wound or kill oneself. In such a case the body acts and is acted upon; it is both agent and object. Cassius dwells obsessively on this trope of identity, which preserves selfhood by destroying or damaging it: "I had as lief not be, as live to be / In awe of such a thing as I myself" (1.2.97–98); "I know where I will wear this dagger then; I Cassius from bondage will deliver Cassius … That part of tyranny that I do bear / I can shake off at pleasure" (1.3.88–89, 1.3.98–99); "Cassius or Caesar never shall turn back, / For I will slay myself" (3.1.21–22). Brutus invokes suicide as the supreme sign of patriotism at the end of his oration to the people (3.2.42–43). Portia declares that her self-wounding testifies to a "constancy" beyond female measure (2.1.290–301), and embraces it as her own "honorifically gendered, purgative, voluntary wound."[31] The contrast between Portia's idea of suicide and Lucrece, who retains a sense of female agency despite her rape—"I am the mistress of my fate," she avers[32]—is another mark of the thoroughly masculinised society that is staged in *Julius Caesar*.

The ways in which links between self-wounding and masculine identity can be read as destructive rather than constructive are reinforced in the play's closing scenes. The men want to believe that suicide defines a final control over selfhood, or at least deprives others of the renown of killing them: "For Brutus only overcame himself, / And no man else hath honour by his death" (5.5.56–57). Killing oneself and others earns honour which, like other social values, seems to be conceived quantitatively, or perhaps economically, as something that adds up or diminishes ("Ambition's debt is paid," Brutus remarks after Caesar's death [3.1.82]). Yet the circumstances of death in the last scenes challenge the image of quantifiable control and honour. While Titinius actually does kill himself, Cassius and Brutus have to persuade others to assist them. The extra involvement diminishes the gesture of absolute agency: Cassius orders a servant to help and thereby win his freedom; Brutus must ask four soldiers before finding one who will hold the sword. These situations suggest that not everyone holds the same view of suicide; Clitus replies earnestly to Brutus's request but his words border on grotesque humour, "I'll rather kill myself" (5.5.7). Cassius dies having confused Titinius's reception by friends as capture: "O coward that I am, to live so long, / To see my best friend ta'en before my face!" (5.3.34–35). His mistake later moves Titinius to kill himself anyway, with Cassius's own sword. Brutus dies having earlier suggested that he considers suicide "cowardly and vile, / For fear of what might fall so to prevent / The time of life" (5.1.103–5). Finally, Cassius and Brutus both expire with Caesar's name on their lips, forced to acknowledge his victory over themselves, as they die by the same blades used to kill him.

The pattern of suicides verges on the mock-heroic, suggesting contradictions in the aristocratic code of valour and honour (a possibility Shakespeare again raises in Antony's unsuccessful suicide attempt in *Antony and Cleopatra*—a final act of self-mastery which ends up leaving him all the more dependent on others: "I have done my work ill, friends. O, make an end / Of what I have begun!" [4.15.105–6]). Total physical control over the body seems to be the same as loss of control. The paradox of the suicides is that they render the male body its own self-defeating site. The attempt to reify identity seems to undermine the ethical system that promotes selfhood in these terms. For integrity, at once a moral and bodily principle, is of the highest value for the males, as exemplified in the dispute between Brutus and Cassius over money and honour. Each is willing to sacrifice his heart to verify his character: Brutus would "rather coin my heart, / And drop my blood for drachmas" than "wring" money from peasants (4.2.127–29); Cassius offers Brutus his dagger, "I, that denied thee gold, will give my heart" (4.2.158). Ironically, the acts they would undertake to prove their integrity would rupture masculine wholeness, reproducing the wounds fatal to Caesar's majesty on themselves.

The belligerence of Brutus and Cassius's words is soon balanced by their reconciliation. The scene concentrates the play's threats to masculine identity and relationships, both of which are for the moment restored. Eighteenth-century critics often distinguished the duo's reunion as having a special poignancy. Richard Steele praised the scene in *The Tatler*: it was "an Incident which moves the Soul in all its Sentiments." Characters and audience share the experience, as "something of a plain and simple Nature … breaks in upon our Souls by that Sympathy."[33] Writing in 1743, William Smith, classical scholar and translator of Longinus, saw the encounter as exemplifying Shakespearean sublimity: "The Heart is melted in an instant, and Tears will start at once in any Audience that has Generosity to be moved or is capable of Sorrow and Pity."[34] Lewis Theobald found much "Beauty" in the scene. He contrasts John Fletcher's inability to equal it in the exchanges between Melantius and Amintor in *The Maid's Tragedy*: "Honour and Friendship, the

Violation of each and the Desire of recementing them are the Topicks of this Action. The Passions are strong and vehement, but conducted more according to the luxuriant Fancy of the Poet than any Standard in Nature."[35] For these commentators, the scene reflects Shakespeare's insight into brave, passionate manhood and his ability to induce a similar ethos in spectators and readers. It registers an enduring bond between Roman, Shakespearean, and eighteenth-century masculinity. Steele also singled out Act Two, scene one—the meeting in Brutus's orchard—as presenting "that great Soul debating upon the Subject of Life and Death with his intimate Friends."[36] The later scene expands the circle of male intimates to include the audience. Where Fletcher's version is idiosyncratic and excessive, Shakespeare's captures the capacity of manliness to be fortified by a preceding breach.

Just as man's individual integrity is ambivalently symbolised by threats and acts of bodily violence, so is the broader system of aristocratic unity and equality. In this code, physical violence works to destroy the bonds it celebrates; yet as in the individual case, destruction is central to the ultimate celebration. Emulous rivalry "makes for class disintegration as well as class cohesion."[37] The dead body is a synecdochic ideal, the central trope in a rhetoric of masculinity envoiced solemnly by all characters (there is no Thersites as in *Troilus and Cressida* to parody the trope). The sequence of eulogies through the play most clearly reveals the way this rhetoric works. While the appearance and actions of the body are significant, the manner in which corpses are spoken about, and in a sense speak, most vividly depicts the body's social value and function. The play is structured around a series of eulogies, beginning with Murellus's words on Pompey and ending with Antony and Octavius's comments on Brutus. In between come the well-known orations on Caesar by Brutus and Antony, as well as Brutus's and Cassius's remarks on Portia, and Brutus's on Cassius and Titinius. Each of these speeches not only commemorates the dead but also strives to establish the body's "true" meaning in order to shore up and control the intertwined system of violence and honour. The eulogists do not disagree on the worth of the system but on which faction has the right to speak for it and claim it as their own.

The key motif in Murellus's speech is Pompey's decline from the star of triumphal processions to mere matter over which a new victor rides: "do you now strew flowers in his way, / That comes in triumph over Pompey's blood" (1.1.49–50). The refusal to name Caesar, along with using the depersonalised pronoun "That," attempts to deny his position and restore Pompey's. But where bodily integrity, "the intact ideal maleness of the classical body,"[38] is considered all-important, the loss of bodily control, in battle or as a victim, reduces men's social stature in life and death; Pompey's status cannot be retrieved. The people do, however, comply with the tribune's words which, for the time being, grant him considerable power. This effect recurs through the play. A charismatic quality adheres to the eulogist, as if he alone were able to control the equivocal meanings connoted by the corpse. A similar kind of aura radiates from Brutus in his responses to news of Portia's death, strengthening his leadership over Cassius, Titinius, and Messala, "Even so great men great losses should endure," they concur (4.2.245). Unlike the unsettling reflexivity that can arise from looking at the deceased or weakened other, and which might disturb one's self-image or presage one's demise, speaking of the dead can reinforce one's status and authority.

Such is the case for Brutus with his speech to the people after Caesar's death. It is the first move in "a battle for the interpretation of Caesar's murder," waged between the two parties.[39] Despite being daubed with Caesar's blood, Brutus tries to suppress the materiality of death. His speech uses logical analogies, Socratic-like questioning, and flattering appeals to the hearers' wisdom and speaker's honour to position the audience to agree. In contrast, Antony speaks through Caesar's body. An impression of physical and verbal fusion with the corpse charges his words and overpowers the audience. His mouth and the stab wounds supplement each other to speak: "thy wounds ... like dumb mouths do ope their ruby lips, / To beg the voice and utterance of my tongue" (3.1.262–64); "I ... / Show you sweet Caesar's wounds, poor poor dumb mouths, / And bid them speak for me" (3.2.215–17). At the same time, Antony manoeuvres the corpse like a stage prop, carrying it out but then withholding it from the crowd, gradually moving it closer to them, finally revealing it beneath the torn and stained mantle. As his own emotions fluctuate, Antony professes union with the dead body, "Bear with me. / My heart is in the coffin there with Caesar" (3.2.102–3). He adapts the orthodox rhetoric of blood and body, by overturning its emphasis on integrity and control. Through playing upon the corpse's visceral presence, he induces the people to stage a carnivalesque uprising. For a liminal period, social hierarchy is undone. The people seize Caesar's body, drive the aristocrats from the city, and subvert linguistic order. The rhetoric of the body politic is fragmented.

The end of the play sees the restoration of social and political order, with a newly dominant faction under Octavius's leadership. The final eulogies reinstate an orthodox rhetoric of the male body, suppressing its materiality to reassert the body politic's symbolic integrity. Before his death, Brutus sets the recuperative process in train with his words on Cassius and Titinius: "Are yet two Romans living such as these? / The last of all the Romans, fare thee well!" (5.3.97–98). The ethos of "Romanness" is salvaged even though he mourns its loss. The victors then celebrate that ethos and imply its persistence. Antony commemorates the fallen Brutus as proof of Roman masculinity. Octavius reinstitutes a controlled decorum around the body, removing

Brutus's corpse from sight. In contrast to the highly public function of Caesar's body—"Produce[d] . . . to the market place" (3.1.230), as a kind of rhetorical and political prop that continues Caesar's own politically expedient theatricality—Brutus's body is used to uphold a restricted code of aristocratic masculinity, an icon around which those values are solemnly consolidated: "According to his virtue let us use him, / With all respect and rites of burial. / Within my tent his bones tonight shall lie, / Most like a soldier, ordered honourably" (5.5.75–78). By stressing its symbolic value, the new leader erases the masculine body's physical limits. The decline that Thomas Wilson saw as intrinsic to that physical materiality is for the moment also suspended, and a future for the masculine body politic is invoked. It is at most an equivocal future, as the fate of Lepidus and Antony will show.

Cynthia Marshall has suggested that in the move from Plutarch's tales to Shakespeare's plays, "relationships to the past are theorized on textual and characterological levels."[40] In many respects, *Julius Caesar* exemplifies this sort of complex response to classical narrative. It dramatizes the problematic effects of a world controlled by aristocratic men. They experience the failures and triumphs of their own dominance, both subject to and the subjects of the power they embody. Their submission to the system they command is the paradox that allows a culture of male authority to continue even though powerful individuals fall. Shakespeare's drama unravels the costs of the system for masculine selfhood but stops short of staging in much detail its consequences for those outside the focal group, including women and men from different classes. Critical perspective is circumscribed by theatrical, historical, and contemporary attraction to the powerful, aristocratic male. Though questioning aspects of this figure's charismatic sway, *Julius Caesar* reproduces what is perhaps the chief means through which it gains and maintains power—a naturalised, bodily rhetoric of superior masculinity whose universal acceptance is assumed. That assumption is complicated and tested by Shakespeare in other plays; yet its early modern cultural and theatrical preeminence provides a major pretext for critical responses to Shakespeare through the seventeenth century and beyond.

Notes

1. All references to Shakespeare's work are to the *Norton Shakespeare*, eds., Stephen Greenblatt, Jean E. Howard, Walter Cohen, and Katharine Eisaman Maus (New York: Norton, 1997). References are included in the text.

2. Robin Headlam Wells, *Shakespeare on Masculinity* (Cambridge: Cambridge University Press, 2000), 2; cf. Coppélia Kahn's discussion of *virtus* in *Roman Shakespeare: Warriors, Wounds, and Women* (London: Routledge, 1997), 11–15.

3. John Dennis, *On the Genius and Writings of Shakespear* (1712), in D. Nichol Smith, ed., *Eighteenth Century Essays on Shakespeare* (2nd ed., Oxford: Clarendon Press, 1963), 32.

4. Thomas Rymer, *A Short View of Tragedy* (1693), in Brian Vickers, ed., *Shakespeare: The Critical Heritage*, 6 vols. (London: Routledge & Kegan Paul, 1974–81), 2.55.

5. Ibid., 2.56.

6. John Aubrey, *Brief Lives*, ed. Richard Barber (Woodbridge: Boydell, 1982), 286. Katherine Duncan-Jones' explanation of the technical differences between glovers and butchers confirms Rymer's rancorous tone; see *Ungentle Shakespeare: Scenes from His Life* (London: Arden, 2001), 15.

7. Letter CXXII, in *CCXI Sociable Letters* (1664), in Ann Thompson and Sasha Roberts, eds., *Women Reading Shakespeare 1660–1900: An Anthology of Criticism* (Manchester: Manchester University Press, 1997), 13.

8. Elizabeth Grosz, *Volatile Bodies: Toward a Corporeal Feminism* (Sydney: Allen and Unwin, 1994), 188.

9. Elizabeth Montagu, *An Essay on the Writings and Genius of Shakespear* (1769), in *Women Reading Shakespeare*, 26.

10. Thomas Wilson, *The Arte of Rhetorique* (1560), ed. G. H. Mair (Oxford: Clarendon, 1909), 83.

11. Ibid., 71.

12. Ibid., 67.

13. On anatomy and individualised selfhood, see Francis Barker, *The Tremulous Private Body: Essays in Subjection* (London: Methuen, 1984), and David Hillman, "Visceral Knowledge: Shakespeare, Skepticism, and the Interior of the Early Modern Body," in David Hillman and Carla Mazzio, eds., *The Body in Parts: Fantasies of Corporeality in Early Modern Europe* (New York: Routledge, 1997), 81–105; on the link between anatomy and self-knowledge, see Jonathan Sawday, "The Fate of Marsyas: Dissecting the Renaissance Body," in Lucy Gent and Nigel Llewellyn, eds., *Renaissance Bodies: The Human Figure in English Culture c. 1540–1660* (London: Reaktion, 1990), 111–35, and Gail Kern Paster, "Nervous Tension: Networks of Blood and Spirit in the Early Modern Body," in Hillman and Mazzio, 107–25; and on the connection between anatomy and gender, see Valerie Traub, "Gendering mortality in early modern anatomies," in Valerie Traub, M. Lindsay Kaplan, and Dympna Callaghan, eds., *Feminist Readings of Early Modern Culture* (Cambridge: Cambridge University Press, 1996), 44–92, and Katharine Park, "The Rediscovery of the Clitoris: French Medicine and the Tribade, 1570–1620," in Hillman and Mazzio, 171–93.

14. Mary Douglas, *Purity and Danger: An Analysis of Concepts of Pollution and Taboo* (London: Routledge and Kegan Paul, 1966), 122.

15. Ibid., 115.

16. For discussions of various kinds of "boundary" threats in the play see: René Girard, "Collective Violence and Sacrifice in Shakespeare's *Julius Caesar*," *Salmagundi* 88/89 (1990–91), 399–419, on the body politic; Wayne A. Rebhorn, "The Crisis of the Aristocracy in *Julius Caesar*," *Renaissance Quarterly* 43 (1990), 75–111, on the aristocracy; Gail Kern Paster, "'In the spirit of men there is no blood:' Blood as Trope of Gender in *Julius Caesar*," *Shakespeare Quarterly* 40 (1989), 284–98, on gender; Sharon O'Dair, "Social Role and the Making of Identity in *Julius Caesar*," *Studies in English Literature 1500–1900* 33 (1993), 289–307, and Gary B. Miles, "How Roman Are Shakespeare's Romans?" *Shakespeare Quarterly* 40 (1989), 257–83, on identity. In "Conjuring Caesar: Ceremony, History, and Authority in 1599," *English Literary Renaissance* 19 (1989), 291–304, Mark Rose sums up the historical and cultural relevance of such issues at the end of Elizabeth I's reign.

17. John Drakakis, "'Fashion it thus:' *Julius Caesar* and the Politics of Theatrical Representation," *Shakespeare Survey* 44 (1991), 72. The notion of a material and rhetorical "body politic" is adapted from Michel Foucault's influential gloss of the term as "a set of material elements and techniques that serve as weapons, relays, communication routes and supports for the power and knowledge relations that invest human bodies and subjugate them:" from *Discipline and Punish: The Birth of the Prison*, trans. Alan Sheridan (New York: Vintage, 1979), 28.

18. In her introduction to the play in the *Norton Shakespeare*, Katharine Eisaman Maus helpfully sums up this position (1529–30). Portia's actions might also be related to a more critical perspective on male conduct that is considered below.

19. Kahn, 85.

20. Mario DiGangi, *The Homoerotics of Early Modern Drama* (Cambridge: Cambridge University Press, 1997), 12.

21. On these contextual Elizabethan issues, cf. Richard Wilson, "'Is this a holiday?' Shakespeare's Roman Carnival," *English Literature History* 54 (1987), 31–44, and Rose, "Conjuring Caesar," *passim*.

22. Peter Stallybrass, "Reading the Body: *The Revenger's Tragedy* and the Jacobean Theater of Consumption," *Renaissance Drama* n.s. 18 (1987), 122.

23. T. S. Dorsch, Introduction, *Julius Caesar*, Arden edition (London: Methuen, 1979), xxvii.

24. Cf. Antony's later comment on the military tactics of Brutus and Cassius: "I am in their bosoms, and I know / Wherefore they do it" (5.1.7–8). Being able to see other men in terms of one's own knowledge and emotion is conceived as crucial to dominance.

25. Rebhorn, 85; cf. Girard: "Caesar is a threat . . . but whoever eliminates him, *ipso facto*, becomes another Caesar" (400).

26. Brutus is far more attuned to deceptive signs when he has something to hide, as his aside before the murder suggests: "every like is not the same, O Caesar" (2.2.128).

27. Wilson, 36.

28. Erving Goffman, *Frame Analysis: An Essay on the Organization of Experience* (Boston: Northeastern University Press, 1986), 431.

29. Paster, 291.

30. Note Goffman's remark that "a sense of the humanity of a performer is somehow generated by a discrepancy between role and character" (294); cf. the impact on the crowd of Antony's tears, which interrupt his oration over Caesar's corpse (3.2.102–14).

31. Paster, 294; cf. Kahn, 101.

32. *Rape of Lucrece*, line 1069.

33. Richard Steele, *The Tatler* 68 (14 September 1709), in *Critical Heritage*, 2.206–7.

34. William Smith, "On Shakespeare and the Sublime," in *Critical Heritage*, 3.96.

35. Lewis Theobald, *Censor* 70 (2 April 1717), in *Critical Heritage*, 2.310.

36. Steele, *The Tatler* 53 (10 August 1709), in *Critical Heritage*, 2.205.

37. Rebhorn, 95.

38. Paster, 298.

39. Girard, 413; cf. Paster, 286, 298.

40. Cynthia Marshall, "Shakespeare, Crossing the Rubicon," *Shakespeare Survey* 53 (2000), 74.

BARBARA J. BAINES

"That every like is not the same": The Vicissitudes of Language in Julius Caesar

Language is, of course, extremely important in all of Shakespeare's plays; often the action turns on a single word—"nothing" in *King Lear*, "indeed" in *Othello*, "done" in *Macbeth*, "boy" in *Coriolanus*, and "if" in *As You Like It*, for example. But in *Julius Caesar*, language is *the central concern*, the play's subject, more so than in any other play of the canon. Much of the criticism on this play demonstrates its concern specifically with the art of rhetoric and the way rhetoric determines politics in the Roman world of *Julius Caesar*. Most recently Richard Burt has illustrated what he calls "the Discursive Determinism of Cultural Politics" that constitutes "a dangerous Rome."[1] The play declares its focus on rhetoric with the cameo appearance of Cicero, whom Anne Barton describes as the "acknowledged grand master of the art of persuasion, the greatest orator and rhetorician of the ancient world."[2] Barton also observes that Shakespeare's Rome is a city "of orators and rhetoricians: a place where the art of persuasion was cultivated, for better or for worse, to an extent unparalleled in any other society."[3] For worse, the play's negative perspective on the art of rhetoric echoes Montaigne's in his essay "On the Vanitie of Words."[4] In what I consider the finest essay on this play, Gayle Greene shows that the play reflects not only Montaigne's but also Bacon's deep distrust of rhetoric. Greene states: "In the Rome of *Julius Caesar*, language is power and characters rise or fall on the basis of their ability

From *Julius Caesar: New Critical Essays*, edited by Horst Zander, pp. 139–53. © 2005 by Routledge.

131

to wield words . . . rhetoric . . . is integral to characterization, culture, and to the central political and epistemological concerns."[5]

As Shakespeare dramatizes "the power of speech/To stir men's blood" (3.2.215–16), he also delineates the instability and potential for misconception that is inherent in the nature of language. In what is virtually a thesis for the play, Cicero voices the anxiety of the skeptic and the nominalist: "Indeed it is a strange-disposed time. / But men may construe things after their fashion / Clean from the purpose of the things themselves" (1.3.33–35). The play's action demonstrates a skepticism even deeper than Cicero's, for men not only *may* but inevitably *do* "construe things after their fashion," that is, according to their subjective perspectives and motives. Furthermore, contrary to Cicero's pronouncement, the play calls into question the ability to know "the purpose of the things themselves." In a relativism that signifies his feigned and real madness, Hamlet declares, "there is nothing either good or bad but thinking makes it so" (2.2.250). In *Julius Caesar*, nothing is but speaking makes it so. Caesar, himself, is that which is most frequently construed and whose truth is never known. What I hope to show in this chapter is the power and the failure of words, both of which derive from their instability, from the inevitable slippage between words and referents. This instability enables the performativity of language, as well as the self-reflective theatrical performances that determine the political reality of Rome.

Although Stanley Fish has shown that *Coriolanus* is "a speech-act play," that is to say, "it is *about* what the theory is 'about,'"[6] no play shows better how to, and how not to, do things with words than *Julius Caesar*. In fact, the play illustrates what Fish describes as the undoing or "self-consuming" tendency of J.L. Austin's theory on performative language.[7] Austin begins *How to Do Things with Words* with a distinction between constative utterances and performative utterances. Constatives merely describe a state, condition, or event and may, therefore, be considered true or false; whereas performatives are utterances that perform an action.[8] Fish claims that, by the end of *How to Do Things with Words*, Austin has discovered "that all utterances are performative—produced and understood within the assumption of some socially conceived dimension of assessment—and that therefore all facts are institutional, are facts only by virtue of the prior institution of some such dimension."[9] In their descriptions of individuals, events, and the state of affairs in Rome, Cassius, Brutus, and Antony demonstrate the performative nature of the constative and the ways in which all utterances in this play are self-reflexive performances. The theatricality of the political, in fact, accounts for the conspicuous metadramatic quality of *Julius Caesar*.

What the characters do with words manifests itself first in what they do with names. Using Marvin Spevack's concordance, Madeleine Doran notes that the name of Caesar appears 216 times in the play and that of Brutus 137 times.[10] Each name is a sign, the combination of signifier (arbitrary sound-images) and signified (a concept or construction), a combination that allows for the disassociation of the one from the other and for various forms of symbolic divestment and investment. Cassius's power, in fact, resides in his understanding of the work that names do—that, as R.A. Foakes explains, they are important in themselves as "marks of the lineage and standing of a character, and indicating the qualities and virtues the character ought to have, though not necessarily those he actually possesses."[11] Cassius's strategy, therefore, is first to sever the name of Caesar, the signifier, from the concept of greatness which it has come to signify. It is the name that bestrides the world like a colossus, but it is the man whom he rescued in the swimming contest and who in Spain suffered a fever and cried for drink as "a sick girl" (1.2.128) and even now suffers from the falling sickness. It is the spirit of Caesar that resides in the signifier of his name, the spirit that Brutus would kill, without killing the man. To enlist Brutus in the conspiracy, Cassius must not only separate the name from the man but transfer the power invested in the name of Caesar to the name of Brutus:

> 'Brutus' and 'Caesar': what should be in that 'Caesar'?
> Why should that name be sounded more than yours?
> Write them together: yours is as fair a name:
> Sound them, it doth become the mouth as well.
> Weigh them, it is as heavy: conjure with 'em,
> 'Brutus' will start a spirit as soon as 'Caesar'. (1.2.141–46)

Cassius also invokes the concept of Roman republicanism and liberation from tyranny signified in the name of Brutus's ancestor, Lucius Junius Brutus (1.2.158–60), a name to conjure Brutus into the conspiracy. Brutus is won by Cassius' construction of "the great opinion / That Rome holds of *his name*" (1.2.317–18; emphasis added).

Honor is the concept that Brutus would have his name signify; he loves "the name of honour" more than he fears death (1.2.88–89). But in that declaration of his identity as honor is a slippage between name and thing: to love *the name* or reputation of honor is not necessarily to love honor itself, as Antony demonstrates in his deconstruction of the conspirators as "honourable men." The concept of "Caesar"—what the name signifies—for Caesar, on the other hand, *is* Caesar: "for always I am Caesar" (1.2.211). As God in Exodus 3:14 declares, "I am that I am," so Caesar is Caesar. Reflecting Caesar's self-perception, Cassius is correct when he says, "this man / Is now become a god" (1.2.115–16). Antony contributes to the elevation by defining Caesar's word as the Logos: "When Caesar says 'Do this', it is performed" (1.2.10); whatever Caesar says is an illocutionary act.[12] Again, in his funeral oration, Antony claims, "But yesterday *the word* of Caesar might / Have stood against the world" (3.2.119–20; emphasis added).

John Velz observes that Caesar is the only important character that does not play the orator. His language is "not persuasive but declarative, not manipulative but pontifical."[13] The words he spoke in banishing Publius Cimber become the act that cannot be revised. The performative nature of his words, unlike the "sweet words" of persuasion, defines his divine status as one who is "constant as the northern star"; to alter his word would be to "lift up Olympus" (3.1.60; 74). For his insistence upon the performative nature of his utterances, he will die by the hands of the rhetoricians; that is to say, the elevation of Caesar through his performative language results in his assassination as the conspirators realize that for them words alone do not perform in the same way they do for Caesar. Words, for the conspirators, are means of persuasion, ways of knowing, conceptual systems—most conspicuously, metaphors, the vehicles of which govern the tenors. For the conspirators, language requires the supplement of action; the deed must then be suited to the word. With the first blow, Casca cries, "Speak hands for me!" (3.1.76). Swords replace words. As Kyd's Lorenzo of *The Spanish Tragedy* says, "Where words prevail not, violence prevails" (2.1.108).[14] In *Julius Caesar* the work that words do—whether the Olympian performative utterance of Caesar or the linguistic fashioning of Cassius, Brutus, and Antony—is finally to precipitate violence.

For Brutus, the ultimate performative utterance would be the exorcizing of the spirit of Caesar in lieu of killing the man. Because such a verbal enactment is so devoutly to be wished, Brutus is seduced by Cassius's suggestion that "Brutus" is a name to conjure with, that "'Brutus' will start a spirit as soon as 'Caesar'." Mark Rose asks the crucial question: "Is Brutus an exorcist or a conjurer, Rome's doctor or the means by which the spirit of Caesar is permanently established in the state?" Rose concludes that the play's action is "an attempt at exorcism that turns into a conjuration."[15] Ironically the only truly performative utterance, in Austin's terms, that Brutus offers is in response to the forged letters Cassius provides in the name of "the general" (the citizens of Rome) urging Brutus to "Speak, strike, redress" (2.1.47; 55). To this imperative, Brutus utters the promise to which he is bound: "O Rome, I make thee promise, / If the redress will follow, thou receivest / Thy full petition at the hand of Brutus" (2.1.56–58). Much virtue in "if," as Touchstone says, for the assassination, the act intended to "redress" or rectify a wrong, will first be dressed in the metaphors of Brutus only to be redressed or reclothed in the language and theatrical performance of Antony.

In the sense of construing or fashioning, Brutus is quite good at doing things with words, but in the process, he and his fellow conspirators are "done in" by them, specifically by their metaphors. The little but important book by George Lakoff and Mark Johnson, *Metaphors We Live By*, makes clear that metaphors are inescapable, for they govern the conceptual system in our everyday lives.[16] What the play illustrates is that the reign of metaphor over our conceptual system is frequently dangerous—perhaps best described as a tyranny rather than a reign—when the action contemplated is both momentous and suspect. Metaphors constitute rather than simply contain, and they hide as well as highlight.[17] What they hide returns as "a phantasma or a hideous dream" (2.1.65). The play of metaphor becomes conspicuous in the soliloquy Brutus speaks in the orchard before the arrival of his fellow conspirators. The soliloquy is not Brutus's effort to decide whether to join the conspiracy; the first line, "It must be by his death" (2.1.10), makes clear that the decision has already been made. Rather, the soliloquy presents his efforts to justify or rationalize the commitment that will shortly become the speech act of his promise to Rome (2.1.56–58). That justification is constructed not by logical reasoning but through metaphor and the conditional mode based upon the hypothetical. He begins by acknowledging that the justification for the murder is weak: "for my part / I know no personal cause to spurn at him / But for the general. He would be crowned" (2.1.10–12). The phrase "for my part" suggests a distinction between his perspective and that of others, particularly Cassius's—a distinction that he must overcome in order to proceed. The phrase "for the general" is usually glossed "for the common, collective good" as in the new Arden Edition, but the phrase could as easily mean "for the general" cause that "he would be crowned." In the latter meaning, "the common, collective good" or what Antony in his funeral oration for Brutus will call the "common good to all" (5.5.72) for which Brutus joined the conspiracy is lost; and what remains is the idea that it is only Caesar's desire to be crowned, whatever the effect of that desire, that becomes the cause of his assassination.

Brutus fashions the malevolent potential of that desire through the extended adder and ladder metaphors; the latter (the ladder) is conjured in Brutus's imagination by its rhyme with the former. Once he seizes upon the adder metaphor—perhaps it is more accurate to say that once it seizes upon him—he can extend it by equating Caesar's possession of the crown with the sting of the serpent (2.1.14–17). His mind next tries to free itself from the tyranny of this vehicle by acknowledging that

> Th'abuse of greatness is when it disjoins
> Remorse from power; and to speak truth of Caesar

I have not known when his affections swayed
More than his reason. (2.1.18–21)

Then suddenly, as if to hide the truth of his own constative utterance, the second metaphor, "lowliness is young ambition's ladder" (2.1.22), emerges. As Greene notes, in this metaphor the vehicle suits the tenor even less than in the adder metaphor because Caesar is not at the beginning of his career but at its apex—hardly, that is, "in the shell" (2.1.34).[18] Brutus later acknowledges that the conspirators "struck the foremost man of all this world" (4.3.22). Unlike Shakespeare's Henry IV at the beginning of Part 1, Caesar has not in his rise to power turned his back unto the ladder; he has not cut himself off from his fellow patricians, a point that is made in his communion with the conspirators on the morning of the assassination: "Good friends, go in, and taste some wine with me, / And we, like friends, will straightway go together" (2.2.126–27). In this Renaissance representation of Rome, male friendship is predicated upon equality. Although Brutus can, in an aside, respond, "That every like is not the same" (2.2.128), he cannot face the duplicity of his own metaphors, revealed in the disparity between tenor and vehicle. The "like," a form of metaphor, is not the same as that which it claims to be.

Brutus is not seduced so much by Cassius as by his own metaphors. Once he begins to "Fashion it thus" with them (2.1.30), they do his thinking for him. Freeing him from logic, they become the content and the container of his thought. First in the opening soliloquy and then in the resolve of the conspirators, the long, crucial first scene of the second act presents the words that will fashion Caesar's wounds. The scene culminates, appropriately, with a wound that will fashion words. The voluntary wound in Portia's thigh elicits from Brutus a full verbal disclosure. He tells her,

... thy bosom shall partake
The secrets of my heart.
All my engagements I will construe to thee,
All the charactery of my sad brows. (2.1.304–7)

Men "construe" even in their most private narratives and most personal relationships.

Cassius also suffers the tyranny of Brutus's metaphors as his good advice that Antony should die with Caesar is negated by Brutus's assertion that Antony is but "a limb of Caesar" that can do no harm "when Caesar's head is off" (2.1.164; 182). Fashioning the assassination through his metaphors, Brutus claims that the conspirators will "be sacrificers but not butchers," and will carve

Caesar "as a dish fit for the gods, / Not hew him as a carcass fit for hounds."
They will thus be called "purgers, not murderers" (2.1.165; 172–73; 179). Cassius's plain language and logic cannot contend with the transformative power of
Brutus's metaphors. His better judgment will again be subjugated by the power
of Brutus's metaphor in the decision to meet the forces of Antony and Octavius
at Philippi. Cassius is, in effect, drowned in that "tide in the affairs of men /
Which, taken at the flood, leads on to fortune" (4.3.216–17). As Brutus's language shapes the assassination, it has the power to swell the number of the conspirators, as well as lead them to destruction. Of Caius Ligarius he says, "Send
him but hither and I'll fashion him" (2.1.219). Ironically, it is Ligarius who
fashions Brutus in precisely the language (1.2.141–46) of Cassius's seduction:

> . . . Soul of Rome,
> Brave son, derived from honourable loins,
> Thou like an exorcist hast conjured up
> My mortified spirit. (2.1.320–23)

These lines are particularly ironic following Brutus's wish to conjure and kill
the spirit of Caesar:

> We all stand up against the spirit of Caesar,
> And in the spirit of men there is no blood.
> O that we then could come by Caesar's spirit
> And not dismember Caesar! . . . (2.1.166–69)

Brutus does, indeed, encounter the spirit of Caesar but only by shedding his
blood. To Volumnius, Brutus acknowledges:

> The ghost of Caesar hath appeared to me
> Two several times by night: at Sardis once,
> And this last night, here in Philippi fields:
> I know my hour is come. (5.5.17–20)

With his last words, Cassius directly addresses the spirit of Caesar that
ranges for revenge: "Caesar, thou art revenged / Even with the sword that
killed thee" (5.3.45–46). In the suicides of Cassius and Titinius, Brutus likewise acknowledges the spirit of Caesar that the assassination has not killed
but set free: "O Julius Caesar, thou art mighty yet. / Thy spirit walks abroad
and turns our swords / In our own proper entrails" (5.3.94–96).

  Although the assassination releases the spirit from the flesh, it is Antony, not Brutus, who conjures "Caesar's spirit, ranging for revenge" through

his curse and prophecy (3.1.254–75). His saying, in the soliloquy spoken over the corpse of Caesar, seems to make it so, in Austin's terms.[19] But Antony's utterances, like Brutus's, are primarily transformative rather than illocutionary; he construes with words "to stir men's blood." The "red weapons" that the conspirators wave over their heads as they cry "Peace, Freedom and Liberty" (3.1.110) become in Antony's words the "swords, made rich / With the most noble blood of all this world" (3.1.155–56). Names again become significant (literally signifying) as Antony takes the bloody hand of each conspirator and speaks his name. This act of naming not only ends anonymity and community among the conspirators in the ritualized murder but also establishes their names as signifiers of the bloody deed. Cinna, the Poet, discovers what is in a name. What Brutus fashions as a ritual sacrifice becomes through Antony's refashioning the "savage spectacle" (3.1.223) that Brutus tries unsuccessfully to hide in metaphors. Brutus's sacrificers—who would carve Caesar as a dish fit for the gods, "Not hew him as a carcass fit for hounds"—become in Antony's metaphor and pun the hunters who bay and slay the brave hart: "O world, thou wast the forest to this hart, / And this indeed, O world, the heart of thee" (3.1.207–8). The conspirators are "butchers" (3.1.255), and Caesar's wounds become "dumb mouths [that] ope their ruby lips/To beg the voice and utterance of [Antony's] tongue" (3.1.260–61).

The funeral orations of Brutus and of Antony (3.2) best demonstrate what can be done and undone with words. Brutus's speech is no less rhetorical and no more reasonable than Antony's,[20] but Antony has the advantage of speaking last and thus from the "deconstructive" position. Antony also understands that performative language is "circumstantial through and through. The success of a performative depends on certain things being the case when it is uttered; performatives therefore are appropriate or inappropriate in relation to conditions of utterance rather than true or false in relation to a reality that underlies all conditions."[21] Because Brutus stakes the belief in his words upon the plebeians' belief in his honor, all Antony needs to do is call that honor into question by refuting Brutus's unsubstantiated assertion that Caesar was ambitious. Through repetition and recontextualizing the words "honour," "honourable," and "ambitious" Antony divests them of their meaning in Brutus's oration. Only one of the three points of Antony's refutation is relevant to the issue of the conspirators' cause. The first, Caesar "hath brought many captives home to Rome, / Whose ransoms did the general coffers fill" (3.2.89–90), in fact, suggests that Caesar might well have deserved a crown. The "evidence," "When that the poor have cried, Caesar hath wept" (3.2.92), and the will that gives to each man seventy-five drachmas and to the public Caesar's private parks and orchards, attests to Caesar's compassion and generosity but does not, as Antony illogically implies, refute

Brutus's claim that Caesar was ambitious. The only relevant evidence that Antony offers is the reminder that when thrice offered a kingly crown on the Lupercal, "he did thrice refuse" (3.2.98). Even this evidence is suspect, given Casca's account of the offer and refusal as a theatrical performance staged to win the plebeian audience.

As he denies his intention and ability to sever Brutus's words from their meaning, Antony also fashions his own words as the truth, "I speak not to disprove what Brutus spoke, / But here I am to speak what I do know" (3.2.101–2). By implying that Brutus speaks only "words," he claims the knowledge of what Cicero calls "the purpose of the things themselves." He continues to cleverly construct his words as truth by claiming that they merely reflect what the plebeians already know: "I tell you that which you yourselves do know. / Show you sweet Caesar's wounds, poor poor dumb mouths, / And bid them speak for me" (3.2.217–19). The "truth" resides not simply in what he has told them but in what he is about to show them, a kind of ocular proof that fires their imaginations.

Although all of Antony's rhetorical strategies are effective, his triumph—his ability to stir men's blood—resides in his theatricality: his ability to replay the assassination as he would have his audience experience it. The ultimate irony and triumph of Antony's achievement lies in his theatrical power to deconstruct Cassius's and Brutus's perception of the assassination as a "lofty scene" to be "acted over / In states unborn and accents yet unknown" (3.1.112–13). Antony rewrites (all too suddenly and in language too well known) their metaphoric scene of ritual sacrifice and liberation as literally "a savage spectacle." Like the fine player in *Hamlet* who weeps for Hecuba, Antony breaks his oration to shed tears for Caesar: "his eyes are red as fire with weeping" (3.2.116). With Caesar's will as a stage property, he plays to his audience's curiosity and greed. Generating suspense, he first refuses to read the will, claiming that its contents would sanctify Caesar; a napkin soaked in his "sacred blood" (3.2.134) would become a holy relic to be bequeathed as a rich legacy. This image, like the rest of Antony's verbal refashioning, is an ironic appropriation of Brutus's image of Caesar as a dish fit for the gods. The political is the theatrical—only and all a play.

Antony gives the plebeians a part in his play by inviting them to insist upon the reading of the will. He draws them into the action, collapsing the distinction between player and audience: "Then make a ring about the corpse of Caesar, / And let me show you him that made the will" (3.2.158–59). The written will is merely the device to focus the attention of the plebeians upon the body as text. With the rents in Caesar's mantle and the wounds of the corpse as spectacle, Antony replays and reinterprets the meaning of the assassination. The mantle worn first "That day he overcame the Nervii" (3.2.171) serves to remind the plebeians of the courage and conquest associated with the name of Caesar. Just as he previously named the conspirators as he took their bloody hands, Antony now reenacts the murder by giving the names of the major conspirators to various rents in the mantle. Antony's verbs oblige the plebeians to see the violence of the deed:

> Look, in this place ran Cassius' dagger through:
> See what a rent the envious Casca made:
> Through this, the well-beloved Brutus stabbed,
> And as he plucked his cursed steel away,
> Mark how the blood of Caesar followed it,
> As rushing out of doors to be resolved
> If Brutus so unkindly knocked or no[.] (3.2.172–78)

The last three lines above show that whereas Brutus is governed by metaphor, Antony is its master. Caesar dies not from the many wounds but from "the most unkindest cut of all" (3.2.181), the wound of ingratitude. The mantle as stage property comes into Antony's play once more as he describes Caesar's final gesture: "And in his mantle muffling up his face ... great Caesar fell" (3.2.185–87). The image is particularly effective because it suggests Caesar's acknowledgement of the shame inherent in the assassination and particularly in Brutus's participation. Antony finally fashions the fall of Caesar as universal, something akin to the Judeo-Christian concept of the Fall: "O what a fall was there, my countrymen! / Then I, and you, and all of us fell down" (3.2.188–89). The plebeians now weep not only for the fall of Caesar but for their participation in it. It pays to be "a masquer and a reveller" (5.1.61), one who loves plays (1.2.202–3). Antony's work is done; he need say nothing over the corpse itself, for through his words he has perfectly suited the rents in the mantle to the wounds in the body. Caesar's will at this point is superfluous to the act of stirring men's blood, for the crowd cries, "Revenge! About! Seek! Burn! Fire! Kill! Slay!" (3.2.199). That the will is merely one of a number of devices Antony uses to manipulate the plebeians is apparent in act 4, scene 1 as he commands Lepidus, "Fetch the will hither, and we shall determine / How to cut off some charge in legacies" (4.1.8–9). What is written can always be rewritten.

While the inflamed mob seeks out the conspirators, names again come into play as Antony, Octavius, and Lepidus coldly decide the fate of many senators, including the innocent Cicero. Messala's source tells of a hundred senators, Brutus's source tells of seventy (4.3.171–76), who are reduced to "names" that are pricked and blotted. With his uncreating word, Antony then turns on Lepidus, reducing him by metaphor to a beast of burden fit only to bear "diverse slanderous loads" (4.3.20). He finally dismisses Lepidus altogether by telling Octavius, "Do not talk of him/But as a property" (4.1.39–40). Filling the void left by the death of Caesar, Antony in this scene becomes a kind of parodic Logos declaring, in effect, "Let there be death."

The death-dealing power of Antony's word, or merely the prick of his pen, is juxtaposed with the quarrel scene between Brutus and Cassius in which their words initially have no meaning at all. Because Brutus has come to distrust the word of Cassius, he seeks meaning in gestures instead. When Lucilius, Brutus's officer, describes the cool reception Cassius gave him, Brutus accounts for this change with what by now we might expect: a metaphor, one that is exceedingly ironic in light of the one that Antony has just devised to fashion Lepidus:

> But hollow men, like horses hot at hand,
> Make gallant show and promise of their mettle:
> But when they should endure the bloody spur,
> They fall their crests, and like deceitful jades
> Sink in the trial. . . . (4.2.23–27)

When these brothers (Cassius is married to Brutus's sister) come face-to-face, their accusations and denials carry no weight. We finally do not know if Cassius has taken bribes, if he has "an itching palm" (4.3.10), if he has denied Brutus the funds to pay his soldiers. The quarrel, a form of dark comic relief in a play so focused on demonstrating the power of words, becomes most ludicrous when Cassius declares, "I am a soldier, I,/Older in practice, abler than yourself" (4.3.30–31), an assertion that generates the following exchange:

BRUTUS
  Go to, you are not, Cassius.
CASSIUS
  I am.
BRUTUS
  I say you are not.
CASSIUS
  Urge me no more. I shall forget myself.
  Have mind upon your health. Tempt me no farther.
BRUTUS
  Away, slight man! (4.3.33–37)

When Brutus threatens to laugh at Cassius's waspish words, Cassius is forced to retract his boast: "You wrong me every way: you wrong me, Brutus. / I said an elder soldier, not a better. / Did I say better?" (4.3.55–57). By this time, Brutus no longer cares what he said. To win Brutus back, Cassius must abandon words and take up his weapon ("There is my dagger, / And here my naked breast"; 4.3.99–100) in a highly melodramatic gesture that replays that of Richard, Duke of Gloucester, as he woos Lady Anne in *Richard III*. Where words prevailed not, the threat of violence prevails. Brutus responds to the gesture: "Sheathe your dagger: / Be angry when you will, it shall have scope" (4.3.106–7).

This lovers' quarrel begins with each man addressing the other as "brother" in a context and tone that makes the filial term ironic and empty of its conventional meaning. Proper names signify differently as well; they no longer have the power to conjure, although Cassius claims that the name of Brutus protects Brutus from Cassius, and Brutus claims that "The name of Cassius honours this corruption, / And chastisement doth therefore hide his head" (4.3.15–16). In the first ninety-one lines of this scene, names are used in direct address as each accuses the other. At first, neither presumes to sound his own name by referring to himself in the third person, as both do in the first half of the play. Then finally Cassius refers to himself in the third person as he evokes their former bond by baring his breast to Brutus and inviting the revenge of Antony and Octavius: "Revenge yourselves alone on Cassius, / For Cassius is a-weary of the world" (4.3.93–94). Then, as Brutus reaffirms their bond, Cassius refers to himself and Brutus in the third person, to sound each name: "Hath Cassius lived / To be but mirth and laughter to his Brutus" (4.3.112–13). Once Brutus and Cassius are reconciled, they speak each other's names repeatedly as an affirmation of their bond. In a citational repetition, the filial address returns as well, redressed now in genuine affection: "Hear me, good brother ... O my dear brother ... Good night, good brother" (4.3.210; 231; 235).

This bond between brothers—one of the finest dramatizations of love between men in the canon—is given full expression in their conversation and leave-taking before the battle. Realizing that this may be "The very last time we shall speak together" (5.1.98), Cassius asks the crucial, intimate question: "If we do lose this battle ... /What are you then determined to do?" (5.1.97–99). In response, Brutus voices his condemnation of the suicide of Cato:

> ... I know not how,
> But I do find it cowardly and vile,
> For fear of what might fall, so to prevent
> The time of life ... (5.1.102–5)

That he knows not how he has come by this opinion is both poignant and ironic, for it was precisely "For fear of what might fall" that he chose "to prevent / The time of life" of Caesar. Brutus seems here completely unaware of the verbal process by which he fashioned the justification for Caesar's assassination; he does not recognize how completely his own metaphors have controlled his thoughts and assumptions. Now his words, like weapons, turn upon him to refashion the assassination as cowardly and vile. His response to Cassius's next question, "You are contented to be led in triumph / Thorough the streets of Rome?" (5.1.108–9) surely fashions the time of life for Cassius as well as for himself: "No, Cassius, no: think not, thou noble Roman, / That ever Brutus will go bound to Rome. / He bears too great a mind" (5.1.110–12). He thus equates, as in a metaphor, the name of Cassius with the epithet "noble Roman" and elevates his own name through the use of the third person.

Political realities have been consistently shaped and reshaped by rhetorical figures, particularly by the power of metaphors, and by theatricality. In sharp contrast, the private and personal farewell speeches of Cassius and Brutus—their final utterances to one another—are stunning and deeply moving in their linguistic simplicity:

BRUTUS:
. . .
For ever and for ever farewell, Cassius.
If we do meet again, why, we shall smile;
If not, why then this parting was well made.
CASSIUS
For ever and for ever farewell, Brutus:
If we do meet again, we'll smile indeed;
If not, 'tis true this parting was well made. (5.1.117–22)

They speak as one voice as Cassius repeats the words of Brutus, worthy of citation. The "farewell" is literalized and serves as the performative blessing, "may you fare well."

The process of construing and misconstruing that defines the nature of language and thus the nature of these Romans also defines ultimately the fate of Cassius, Titinius, and Brutus, as they fashion their own retribution. When Pindarus misconstrues success as defeat, thinking Cassius's "best friend" (5.3.35) Titinius has been captured, Cassius accepts this narrative as the thing itself and commits suicide. As he dies, he suits the word to the action: "Caesar, thou art revenged/Even with the sword that killed thee" (5.3.45–46). Cassius's deed is then fashioned by the metaphor of Titinius's encomium:

But Cassius is no more. O setting sun:
As in thy red rays thou dost sink tonight,

So in his red blood Cassius' day is set.
The sun of Rome is set. Our day is gone[.] (5.3.60–63)

Titinius's observation, repeated by Messala, "Mistrust of good success
hath done this deed" (5.3.65–66), recalls the mistrust of Caesar's success,
expressed in Brutus' orchard soliloquy, that leads to the assassination. The
fear that Caesar would be crowned leads to the ironic crowning of Cassius
in death: "But hold thee, take this garland on thy brow; / Thy Brutus bid
me give it thee, and I / Will do his bidding" (5.3.85–87).

Titinius's account of Cassius's fatal error, "Alas, thou hast misconstrued
everything" (5.3.84) applies, like the apothegm of Cicero, to all of the characters and the action of the play. Such misconstruction necessitates further
expiatory sacrifice in the suicides of Titinius and Brutus. The dying words of
Brutus once again constitute a rhyme in a couplet that, with the exception of
Caesar's name, is monosyllabic and deeply moving in its simplicity: "Caesar,
now be still. / I killed not thee with half so good a will" (5.5.50–51). In these
final words, suited to the action, Brutus imagines himself as the exorcist who,
with the sacrifice of his own life, will finally dispel the spirit of Caesar. Exorcism, however, is rewritten by history as conjuration, for the spirit of Caesar is
reified in imperial Rome. Mark Rose observes that "as a representation of the
transformation of the Roman Republic into the Empire, *Julius Caesar* may
be understood as yet another of the many originary myths of the Imperial
Tudor State." He adds that "by transforming the historical fact of the defeat
of Brutus and the republican movement in Rome into a metaphysical confir-
mation of the inevitability of imperial greatness, Shakespeare's play implicitly
confirms the legitimacy of the Tudor state."[22] What Shakespeare does with
words within his own historical, political context thus mirrors the work of
metaphors and theatrical performance in the political world of Rome.

Julius Caesar illustrates the observation of Marion Trousdale that the
Renaissance acquired from Augustine and Erasmus a basic understanding
of the fundamental difference "between divine and human language. God's
word is substance; it is ontologically real. But in man language is accident, not
substance."[23] Language defines us as fallen; it speaks the Fall in the arbitrary
connection and slippage between signifier and signified. In Derrida's words,
the "sign is always a sign of the Fall."[24] *Julius Caesar*, as the dramatization of
the performativity of language, of how we do things with words, illustrates a
fall, nevertheless, most fortunate.

Notes

1. Richard A. Burt, "'A Dangerous Rome': Shakespeare's *Julius Caesar* and the
Discursive Determinism of Cultural Politics," in *Contending Kingdoms: Historical*,

Psychological, and Feminist Approaches to the Literature of Sixteenth-Century England and France, ed. Marie-Rose Logan and Peter L. Rudnytsky (Detroit, MI: Wayne State University Press, 1991), 109–27.

2. Anne Barton, "*Julius Caesar* and *Coriolanus*: Shakespeare's Roman World of Words," in *Shakespeare's Craft*, ed. Philip H. Highfill, Jr. (Carbondale: Southern Illinois University Press, 1982), 24.

3. Ibid., 25.

4. Ibid., 26.

5. Gayle Greene, "'The Power of Speech/To Stir Men's Blood': The Language of Tragedy in Shakespeare's *Julius Caesar*," *Renaissance Drama*, n.s., 11 (1980): 68, 69.

6. Stanley Fish, *Is There a Text in This Class?: The Authority of Interpretive Communities* (Cambridge, MA: Harvard University Press, 1980), 221.

7. Ibid., 231.

8. J.L. Austin, *How to Do Things with Words* (Cambridge, MA: Harvard University Press, 1962), 3–11.

9. Fish, *Is There a Text?*, 198.

10. Madeleine Doran, *Shakespeare's Dramatic Language* (Madison: University of Wisconsin Press, 1976), 224, n.1.

11. R.A. Foakes, "Language and Action in *Julius Caesar*," in *Twentieth Century Interpretations of "Julius Caesar"*, ed. Leonard Dean (Englewood Cliffs, NJ: Prentice Hall, 1968), 58. Foakes observes that the "word Caesar had long been in use to signify an all-conquering, absolute monarch and is used in the play with this implication" (61).

12. I am suggesting here that the difference in ways words work for Caesar and for everyone else in this play fits the following explanation by Austin: "We also perform *illocutionary acts* such as informing, ordering, warning, undertaking, &c., i.e. utterances which have a certain (conventional) force ... we may also perform *perlocutionary acts*: what we bring about or achieve *by* saying something, such as convincing, persuading, deterring, and even, say, surprising or misleading" (*How to Do Things*, 108).

13. John W. Velz, "*Orator* and *Imperator* in *Julius Caesar*: Style and the Process of Roman History," *Shakespeare Studies* 15 (1982): 65.

14. Revels Student Editions, ed. David Bevington (Manchester: Manchester University Press, 1996).

15. Mark Rose, "Conjuring Caesar: Ceremony, History, and Authority in 1599," *English Literary Renaissance* 19 (1989): 297.

16. George Lakoff and Mark Johnson, *Metaphors We Live By* (Chicago: University of Chicago Press, 1980), 3–10.

17. Ibid., 10–13.

18. Greene, "'The Power of Speech,'" 80.

19. Austin, *How to Do Things*, 7.

20. Greene explains that "Brutus's most effective device is to present the issue as though it were a choice between two alternatives which leave no choice but to assassinate Caesar, but which rest on unexamined assumptions concerning Caesar: so that, again, the argument is a self-referential construct that makes sense in its own terms but casts no light outside itself to its supposed subject." His oration is marked by the "illusion of ... logic" and "is far from an appeal to the intellect with 'real reasons' ... It is a brilliant piece of oratory, brilliantly suited to manipulating

a difficult crowd, while resorting to none of the obviously cheap tricks so conspicuous in Antony's performance. Thus it enables Brutus to preserve his conception of
himself in his own eyes and others' as a rational man reasonably motivated" ("'The
Power of Speech,'" 83, 84, 85). Velz contends that "Antony's superiority over Brutus
lies as much in his place in the sequence of speakers as in his oratorical method"
(*"Orator* and *Imperator"* 56).

21. Fish, *Is There a Text?*, 198.

22. Rose, "Conjuring Caesar," 303.

23. Marion Trousdale, *Shakespeare and the Rhetoricians* (Chapel Hill: University of North Carolina Press, 1982), 25.

24. Jacques Derrida, *Of Grammatology*, trans. Gayatri Spivak (Baltimore: The
Johns Hopkins University Press, 1974), 150.

DANIEL JUAN GIL

"Bare Life": Political Order and the Specter of Antisocial Being in Shakespeare's Julius Caesar

Many early modern writers, including Shakespeare, celebrated the state's growing penetration of daily life.[1] On the other hand, because the social imaginary founded on the nation-state was still emergent in the period, early modern writers, again including Shakespeare, could also conceive of alternatives. In that sense, the surviving literary culture of the period is a resource for rethinking some of our most basic modern assumptions about social and political life. My aim in these pages is to disclose an oppositional discourse that declines to assume the nation-state as a basic framework for society. Exploiting the turmoil generated by the state's effort to penetrate and organize social life, this oppositional discourse reimagined the most basic, body-mediated interactions through which people connect to other people outside of political or even social structures. Crucial to this project, however, is to distinguish this early modern approach from our present notions of civil society. In the sense in which the term has become influential in communitarian and antipolitical discourse, "civil society" is imagined to rely on connections between people that operate outside the sphere of state power.[2] Contemporary accounts often draw on Jürgen Habermas's now classic study *The Structural Transformation of the Public Sphere*. Focusing on eighteenth-century England, Habermas describes a public sphere founded on an extra-state society that nurtures a "purely human" use of

From *Common Knowledge* 13, no. 1 (Winter 2007): 67–79. © 2007 by Duke University Press.

communicative rationality.³ So conceived, civil society is potentially universal and, transcending the framework of the nation-state, can subject it to reasoned critique from outside.⁴

Several theorists of state power, notably Giorgio Agamben, have offered a structural critique of these conclusions. In *Homo Sacer: Sovereign Power and Bare Life*, Agamben argues that all political power is "biopolitical" in that it seeks to organize the most basic, biological infrastructure of human life. Thus, Agamben suggests, civil society is not an autonomous social development but a product of state power:⁵

> It is almost as if, starting from a certain point, every decisive political event were double-sided: the spaces, the liberties, and the rights won by individuals in their conflicts with central powers always simultaneously prepared a tacit but increasing inscription of individuals' lives within the state order, thus offering a new and more dreadful foundation for the very sovereign power from which they wanted to liberate themselves.... The fact is that one and the same affirmation of bare life leads, in bourgeois democracy, to a primacy of the private over the public and of individual liberties over collective obligations and yet becomes, in totalitarian states, the decisive political criterion and the exemplary realm of sovereign decisions.⁶

The paradox that Agamben points to is that the private realm liberates itself from the state only by demanding from the state a charter of rights and privileges that involves private life ever more fully in the political order. In effect, Agamben is opposed to any liberal theory that posits a social life that preexists state power and that offers a standpoint from which state power can be criticized from outside. Civil society tacitly affirms state power, he argues, even if it also allows for critical detachment from particular state policies.

The early modern state's effort to organize the details of social life is a central concern of early modern culture. Writers of the period would, typically, have agreed that what we now call "private life" and "civil society" were recent products of the state and its penetration of social life. But Agamben's account of state power as *essentially* biopolitical, as *always* seeking to rationalize and structure the amorphous realm of "bare life," is especially instructive to the student of antipolitics. Bypassing the dyad of nation-state and state-mediated civil society, the early modern discourse of antipolitics seeks to make "bare life" visible as such. To imagine a form of life not mediated by political structures, early modern writers in this line turned their attention to emotions, which they interpreted neither as privileged signs of an inner self nor as merely bodily, humoral imbalances. As distinguished, then, from the ways in which modern psychology and Galenic medical theory regard the emotions, early modern writers tended to deal with emotions as defining bodily states that, in recurring patterns, open and close the body to other, emotionally inflamed bodies. Emotions were treated as a grammar of pre- or nonsocial connections between bodies—connections that become evident only when politically ordered social webs go wrong or collapse.[7] Some early modern thinkers thus opened the door to a phenomenology of "bare life" itself.

Shakespeare is among those thinkers, as evidenced by *Julius Caesar*, one of his most self-consciously political, or rather antipolitical, works.[8] The play registers and theorizes the efforts of the state to reorganize social life, but the play also reveals a deep-seated impulse to break with this emerging political framework. While the conspirators in the play are often interpreted as defining a public sphere that resists Caesar's expansion of state power, the play rather points to a deep complicity between Caesar and the conspirators against him. By forcing social questions into a nationalized political frame of reference, their conflict consolidates and strengthens the national political field, which comes to attain almost a monopoly on the ways in which social life can be conceptualized. Marc Antony's rebellion must be understood against this backdrop. His is a rebellion not for Caesar or against Brutus (conceived as rival political positions) but against politics—against the acquiescence in a politics that orders social life into rival factions demanding personal sacrifice in the name of public goods. Antony teaches Rome a grammar of interpersonal bonding that defines connections between bodies (via emotions conceived as fluids), and these connections are meant to replace any politically mediated public life. Antony's oppositional discourse sounds irrational, unfeasible, or antisocial. But from a standpoint outside the political field (and that standpoint is what I am trying to locate), radical opposition is not antisocial so much as it is antisystemic—a clear break from the emerging, modern assumption of the nation-state as a fundamental condition of social life.[9]

The political field that Shakespeare sketches in *Julius Caesar* is organized around the competing discursive poles of absolutism and elite civic republicanism. Caesar is accused of incipient tyranny, but within the terms of early modern political discourse his reliance on a blend of charismatic popularity and manipulation of aristocratic elites would make him look to Shakespeare's audience very much like an absolute monarch. To secure his grip on the political order, Caesar brings into being an abstract public of more or less formally interchangeable individuals who encounter the state as a spectacle that they either applaud or hoot. Caesar's absolutist program is counterbalanced by the

civic republicanism of Brutus and the conspirators, for whom the state exists
to offer an aristocratic elite opportunities for the exercise of virtue and thus
the pursuit of ethical perfection. From the perspective of the conspirators, the
state is constituted by patricians seeking to maximize their honor. Brutus and
the conspirators deploy this conception of the state to delegitimize the popular public that Caesar has forced onto the political field. But more crucial than
their differences is the similarity of these opponents: each party takes the rival
version of political publicity into account, which attests to their differences
being essentially local variations within a single political field. Caesar and the
conspirators against him share a presupposition that political forms can create publics and structure a nationalized social life. It is this presumption that
Antony will transcend.

A familiar interpretation of *Julius Caesar* is that the conspirators represent a nascent public sphere that checks the dictatorial state power that
Caesar represents.[10] But the conspirators do not see themselves as operating
outside the state or as speaking up for the presumed rights of some extra-state
public; their main difficulty is that they cannot envision themselves and their
exercise of virtue outside the framework of the state. Cassius experiences loss
of political power as a diminution of self because for him the state is a vehicle
to exercise and develop his own virtue. In his initial temptation speech, Cassius reminds Brutus that "I was born free as Caesar, so were you" (1.2.97) and
complains that they have both become Caesar's "underlings":

> Why, man, he doth bestride the narrow world
> Like a colossus, and we petty men
> Walk under his huge legs and peep about
> To find ourselves dishonorable graves.
> Men at some time are masters of their fates.
> The fault, dear Brutus, is not in our stars,
> But in ourselves, that we are underlings.
>   (1.2.134–140)

The fundamental problem is not that Caesar wants too much power but
that he organizes state power on a footing that deprives aristocrats like
Cassius and Brutus of their opportunity to use the state in service of their
own honor. When Brutus invokes the discourse of the "general good" (as in
1.2.85), he refers only to the elite public of patricians that is constituted by,
and constitutive of, the state.[11]

The constitutive role that the conspirators imagine playing in the operations of the state, and their desire to use the state to maximize their own
virtue, are hallmarks of the civic republicanism that J. G. A. Pocock has recov-

ered at the heart of early modern political theory and that he has offered as an alternative to liberal theories of the state.[12] In the civic republican tradition, individual rights are not an issue, though a small public of individual subjects is thought to underpin a state that enables them to pursue individual perfection. Thus, the conspirators in *Julius Caesar* regard plebeians as living an institutionalized, state-regulated life that, as a fundamentally economic formation, is the opposite of their own and improperly involved in public affairs. The play begins with Murellus and Flavius, the tribunes of the people and ideological soulmates of the conspirators, complaining that the workers are swarming into the streets to celebrate Caesar. Part of Murellus and Flavius's complaint is that the political allegiance of the people is fickle since they once loved Pompey as now they love Caesar:

> Many a time and oft
> Have you climbed up to walls and battlements,
> To towers and windows, yea, to chimney tops,
> Your infants in your arms, and there have sat
> The livelong day with patient expectation
> To see great Pompey pass the streets of Rome.
> (1.1.38–43)

But what Murellus and Flavius most object to is the workers' leaving behind their defined roles in the economic realm and asserting for themselves a role in the public life of politics:

> Hence! home, you idle creatures, get you home!
> Is this a holiday? What, know you not,
> (Being mechanical) you ought not to walk
> Upon a labouring day without the sign
> Of your profession? Speak, what trade art thou?
> (1.1.1–5)

The plebeians have left the nonpolitical but state-regulated domain of the economy, where they wore the "sign / Of [their] profession." Now unmarked, they appear to Murellus and Flavius as a shapeless mass that swarms over the architecture of Rome carrying, as an index of vulgarity, their "infants in [their] arms." Flavius promises to "drive away the vulgar from the streets" and advises Murellus, "So do you too, where you perceive them thick" (1.1.69–71).

From Caesar's perspective, of course, the massed people that Murellus and Flavius view as "worse than senseless things" (1.1.36) and try to drive from the streets of Rome, are anything but shapeless: they are a politically effective public that he himself has conjured up to check the power of the aristocrats. The plebeians constitute a rival form of public life whose structural relation to the state is fundamentally different from that of the tribunes and conspirators. Caesar may be a tyrant but he strives to level all other markers of social difference between persons in the population of Rome. One of his methods is to turn holidays (in the case of the play, the festival of the Lupercal) into state pageants. (This was a strategy of Queen Elizabeth's as well.) Festivity converts the finely graded social and economic order on which Flavius and Murellus comment—"Roman civil society," to risk an anachronism—into a disarray of people who, by assembling, can form a public. More or less interchangeable individuals endowed, collectively, with a public life might be termed "citizens," except that they have no recognized political status apart from formal equality; it might be better to call them "protocitizens."

In Caesar's political imaginary, the smallest unit of political discourse is not the face-to-face conversation between aristocrats, nor even a senate-sized debate governed by rules of procedure, but the mass rally, in which anonymous protocitizens gain power by adding themselves, one by one, to the crowd. Caesar is an expert manipulator of crowds, but these assemblies amass a force that can check even Caesar's will—as when a cheering mass appears to compel him to decline the crown that Antony offers. Casca recounts this rally in a highly tendentious form, but it is easy to extract from his words the real political logic of the event. Casca reports that Antony raised the crown to Julius Caesar three times and that Caesar refused it three times:

> And still as he refused it the rabblement hooted, and clapped their chopped hands, and threw up their sweaty nightcaps, and uttered such a deal of stinking breath because Caesar refused the crown that it had almost choked Caesar; for he swooned and fell down at it. And for mine own part, I durst not laugh, for fear of opening my lips and receiving the bad air.
>
> (1.2.242–49)

Casca's contempt for the "stinking breath" this "rabblement" emits is directly proportional to the crowd's political weight, for he believes that Caesar "would fain have had" the crown (1.2.239–40). Caesar was thwarted only by the opposition of the populace. Casca despises the notion of Caesar as king, but he seems provoked even more that Caesar has endowed the people—stripped of their economic markers and converted en masse into protocitizens—with political force. Casca recognizes their power, even as he tries to devalue it by comparing it to the power of approval and disapproval exercised by an audience being entertained: "If the tagrag people did not clap him and hiss him according as he pleased and displeased them, as they use to do the players in the theatre, I am no true man" (1.2.258–61). Casca may mean to say that Caesar's humility was only for show, but his analogy of the new politics to theater nevertheless acknowledges a political mechanism for determining the popular will. Political scenarios are proposed to an assembly of protocitizens and their applause or hoots are measured. Casca's attack on the validity of the crown-offering play is, therefore, somewhat paradoxically, a register of its political force and of Caesar's success in transforming "the rabblement" into a protocitizenry with some effective political power. What makes the analogy to the theater possible for Casca is the presumed vulgarity and rowdiness of the "tagrag" crowd. Where Caesar envisions a large public with a structurally different relationship to the state than the elite public of the conspirators, Casca insists he can see only a swarming, formless "bare life" reducible to its grossest physical manifestation, its "stinking breath."[13]

It is the clash between these opposing, but equally political, imaginaries that causes "bare life" itself to precipitate, as it were, and begin to accumulate on the streets of Rome where it acquires a potentially transformative power. The amorphous crowd that appears in Rome at the margins of competing political visions exceeds all available political forms and yet it finds ways to assert itself more and more radically after Caesar is killed. Immediately following the assassination, Trebonius reports that "Men, wives, and children stare, cry out, and run, / As it were doomsday" (3.1.98–99), and Brutus recognizes the danger: he asks Antony to "be patient till we have appeased / The multitude, beside themselves with fear" (3.1.180–81). Brutus tells Cassius, "go you into the other street, / And part the numbers," while proposing to the plebeians that "Those that will hear me speak, let 'em stay here. / Those that will follow Cassius, go with him / And public reasons shall be rendered / Of Caesar's death" (3.2.3–8). This image of an orderly exercise of public reasoning must warm the heart of Habermasians committed to a universally human exercise of communicative rationality. But while one plebeian does suggest to the others that they listen to both speeches and then "compare their reasons / When severally we hear them rendered" (3.2.9–10), Brutus's clumsy effort to address the mass as though it were a debating club only highlights his inability to come to terms with what the massed populace represents. A clash of rival versions of politically mediated social life has resulted in the displacement of society itself by a feral but now constitutive "bare life."[14]

The brilliance of Marc Antony's funeral oration, in contrast to that of Brutus, derives largely from Antony's exploiting the experience of "bare life" as a source of antipolitical rage. But Antony's oration draws on his own

experience of "bare life," undergone on the death of his friend: immediately
after the assassination, Brutus tells Antony that he too loved Caesar but that
this personal tie was necessarily secondary to public considerations. Antony,
on the other hand, is drawn beyond political logic into rebellion against any
notion of state-mediated social life. He refuses to regard the assassination as
a political act or a political problem, and his irrational commitment to loving
Caesar produces a crisis (or perhaps it is a breakthrough) in his experience of
himself and others. Addressing Caesar's corpse, Antony promises that "a curse
shall light upon the limbs of men," and he calls forth anarchic violence:

> O pardon me, thou bleeding piece of earth,
> That I am meek and gentle with these butchers.
> Thou art the ruins of the noblest man
> That ever lived in the tide of times.
> Woe to the hand that shed this costly blood.
> Over thy wounds now I do prophesy
> (Which like dumb mouths do ope their ruby lips
> To beg the voice and utterance of my tongue)
> A curse shall light upon the limbs of men:
> Domestic fury and fierce civil strife
> Shall cumber all the parts of Italy:
> Blood and destruction shall be so in use,
> And dreadful objects so familiar,
> That mothers shall but smile when they behold
> Their infants quartered with the hands of war:
> All pity choked with custom of fell deeds,
> And Caesar's spirit, ranging for revenge,
> With Ate by his side come hot from hell,
> Shall in these confines with a monarch's voice
> Cry havoc and let slip the dogs of war ...
>   (3.1.254–73)

Antony could have used the opportunity to define a political program or
to demand violence against evildoers—against all who had opposed Caesar.
Instead, his prophecy of violence seems designed only to validate his own
love for Caesar. It is as if Antony feels that politics has split a nuclear bond
between Caesar and himself, a bond whose violation must now release an
enormous burst of energy that will negate traditional social ties. Antony's
cruel soliloquy has the merit of not concealing beneath patriotic rhetoric the
naked reality of fratricide and war. But in precisely its cruelest aspects, his
speech also expresses a wish for transformation of the most basic patterns

of society, including the structure of family allegiances. When Antony looks forward to a time in which mothers are so hardened to violence that they will "but smile when they behold / Their infants quartered," he is imagining a radical (if radically dystopian) change in social life that flows from his own disorienting experience of the body of Caesar. Antony seems drawn and captured by the unsettling gravity of a corpse whose "dumb mouths do ope their ruby lips / To beg the voice and utterance of my tongue." Here the opened body of Caesar summons Antony to enter and occupy it, to speak for it, to mingle with its fluids and especially its blood—a fantasy that had earlier led Antony to wish that he had "as many eyes as thou hast wounds, / Weeping as fast as they stream forth thy blood" (3.1.200–1).

In this fantasy, bodies communicate by means of humoral fluids that produce pre- or extra-social links. Almost the first wish that Antony expresses after seeing the body of Caesar is a desire to be stabbed with the swords still covered in Caesar's blood:

> If I myself [am going to be killed], there is no hour so fit
> As Caesar's death's hour, nor no instrument
> Of half that worth as those your swords, made rich
> With the most noble blood of all this world.
>   (3.1.153–56)

Brutus thinks that Antony is asking for death and tries to dissuade him—"O Antony, beg not your death of us" (3.1.164)—but what Antony is asking for is nothing so simple as death. His phantasmic experience of Caesar's corpse, of bodily fluids that provoke answering fluids from his own body, reshapes a social connection (his friendship with Caesar) into an unsociable intersubjectivity. By means of the funeral oration, Antony's transformative experience of Caesar's body transforms the social world of the play. Antony displays the alluring corpse and calls for fluid to answer fluid, tears to answer blood. The masses are thus infected by whatever has infected Antony and are brought to the same uncanny psychic terrain.

The funeral oration triggers rioting, and Antony celebrates the "it" he has unleashed: "Now let it work. Mischief, thou art afoot: / Take thou what course thou wilt" (3.2.251–2). But however irrational, the rioting has a logic that picks up and extends the body-centered bonding that Antony experiences in relation to Caesar. Here is the beginning of the riot:

First Plebeian
  Never, never. Come, away, away.
  We'll burn his body in the holy place,

> And with the brands fire the traitors' houses.
> Take up the body.
> SECOND PLEBEIAN
>   Go fetch fire.
> THIRD PLEBEIAN
>   Pluck down benches.
> FOURTH PLEBEIAN
>   Pluck down forms, windows, anything.
>   (3.2.244–50)

What begins as a recognizably political impulse—to cremate Caesar's body in the "holy place" and then set fire to the conspirators' houses—turns quickly into an eschatological desire to transcend politics as such. In attacking the benches and the windows (the benches on which they sat listening to competing accounts of the assassination; the windows through which people, not least Portia, glimpse public doings), these plebeians pull down the material infrastructure of the public life into which Caesar and the conspirators have equally drawn them.[15] So seen, the masses' rage is an antipublic rage, a rage against publicity and politics.

Once liberated from any political framework, the riot, it is commonly argued, demonstrates to Shakespeare's audience the dangers of a people unconstrained by law and social order. But even the cruelest and most irrational elements of the rebellion—even the attack on Cinna the poet, mistaken initially for Cinna the conspirator—can be interpreted differently:

> CINNA
>   I am Cinna the poet, I am Cinna the poet.
> FOURTH PLEBEIAN
>   Tear him for his bad verses, tear him for his bad verses.
> CINNA
>   I am not Cinna the conspirator.
> FOURTH PLEBEIAN
>   It is no matter, his name's Cinna. Pluck but his name out of his
>   heart, and turn him going.
> THIRD PLEBEIAN
>   Tear him, tear him!
>   (3.3.29–36)

Though here, once again, the plebeians begin with a nominally political aim—to kill conspirators—by the time they have established that the Cinna at their mercy is not Cinna the conspirator, an undifferentiated frenzy for blood has taken over. On the one hand, there is a social logic to the frenzy, for in rebelling against Cinna's very name the plebeians are expressing resentment against those who have names as opposed to those who have none—the plebeians, after all, are assigned only numbers. On the other hand, the plebeians are not engaged in an act of compensatory status-building: they reduce themselves to the status of bodies (as agents of physical violence) while reducing Cinna to the same level (as an object of physical violence). "Pluck but his name out of his heart" is not an exclamation from a scene of ordinary mob violence. Names represent a basic principle of social differentiation, and this mob wants to reduce names to bodies. It is unclear whether Cinna survives this assault (the stage directions give us only "Exeunt all the Plebeians"). But if he survives and walks (or is even dragged) off stage, it could look, from the vantage point of the theater audience, as though Cinna has been absorbed into the mob.

It is of course only as theater—the theater Antony loves—that violence can stand for a mode of sociability that operates at the level of bodies. When approached as a theatrical spectacle, the civil war that occupies the last two acts of the play seems an irrational outbreak of resistance to the politics of the nation-state—a political order to which Caesar and his assassins, as well as Queen Elizabeth and her antagonists, appear fully committed. Among the disturbing features of Shakespeare's civil war is the way that common-sensical, self-preserving forms of relationship are infected by the marginal experiences of self and other that Antony injects into Rome. The turn away from self-preservation is clear in the rash of suicides that overtakes the play, beginning with Portia's death after she has "swallowed fire" (4.2.208)—said to be burning coals, in Plutarch—and continuing with the suicides of Cassius, Titinius, and finally Brutus. Given the Roman cult of suicide, these deaths could be read as triumphs of personal autonomy over fate. In Shakespeare's telling, however, the suicides are more problematic, for the public prestige of the Roman aristocrats who die is supplanted by perverse forms of bonding. When Cassius cannot find the courage to kill himself, he must beg his slave Pindarus for death:

> Come hither, sirrah.
> In Parthia did I take thee prisoner,
> And then I swore thee, saving of thy life,
> That whatsoever I did bid thee do,
> Thou shouldst attempt it. Come now, keep thine oath.
> Now be a freeman, and with this good sword
> That ran through Caesar's bowels, search this bosom.
>   (5.3.36–42)

Cassius consciously frames the circumstances of his own death as poetic justice: his dying words are, "Caesar, thou art revenged, / Even with the sword that killed thee" (5.3.45–46). But the fantasy of being penetrated by the sword that "ran through Caesar's bowels"—the same fantasy that possessed Antony after the assassination—is a way of reestablishing a relationship with Caesar at a level well below that of political allegiance and class solidarity (or even homosociality: the object of the fantasy is a corpse that Cassius helped to mutilate).

This perverse form of bonding, moreover, depends on the inversion of a functionally hierarchical tie between master and slave. "Go show your slaves how choleric you are," Brutus taunts Cassius for losing his temper, "And make your bondmen tremble" (4.3.43–4). It is to his bondman that Cassius, a Roman lord begging ardently for death, finally turns himself over—and the spectacle is repeated with Brutus begging for death at the hands of his servant Strato (5.5). In both instances, the relationship between master and slave turns out to be the only reliable one. But Shakespeare takes this bond out of its social context, where it has large consequences for both master and slave, and relocates it in a purely emotional space. The mediated aggression of massive class disparity then fuels a lurid exchange between men that combines aggressive passion with passionate aggression. For Cassius, this suicidal inversion is triggered by what turns out to be an incorrect report of the death of Cassius's "best friend" Titinius: "O, coward that I am, to live so long, / To see my best friend ta'en before my face" (5.3.34–35). Having failed to defend his friend in the moment when he is "ta'en," Cassius apparently regards suicide as a way of restoring their friendship. That renewal takes the form of a connection in which the fate of Titinius is registered in Cassius's own body. When Titinius, alive, returns to find that Cassius has "misconstrued everything" (5.3.84), he promptly stabs himself with the sword that killed Cassius: "By your leave, gods. This is a Roman's part: / Come, Cassius' sword, and find Titinius' heart" (5.3.89–90). While Titinius comes closest in this string of suicides to the aristocratic ideal of dying with honor ("this is a Roman's part"), he nevertheless joins Cassius and Antony in affirming a corporeal solidarity that transcends social status: he uses the sword still gory with Cassius's blood (and Caesar's).

The male-male friendship of aristocrats and the asymmetrical bond between master and slave—but also the stoical mastery over self that Cassius and Brutus so spectacularly lack—are social ties and functions upon which real-world status depends. Shakespeare has character after character in *Julius Caesar* reject social expectations and open an alternative way of being, in which bleeding bodies are penetrated by already bloody swords. It is important to read such moments, and indeed the civil war as a whole, for what they open the door to philosophically; or rather, theatrically. Ignited and then pervaded by antisocial and fundamentally perverse desires, the play's civil war is not a continuation of politics by other means but a frantic escape from and replacement for politics. Bringing this war to the early modern stage, Shakespeare offered an alternative to the iron clasp of the state and of state-mediated social order. The seeming inhumanity of the alternative is a measure of how deeply felt the revulsion from that social order could be. Read against the grain of the modern political imaginary, which assumes the nation-state as the basic framework for social life, and social life as a necessity of human beings, this play discloses a passionate dissent of bodies from the political and social penetration of "bare life."

Notes

1. New Historicist critics have made this case well; notably, Jonathan Goldberg in *James I and the Politics of Literature: Jonson, Shakespeare, Donne, and Their Contemporaries* (Baltimore, MD: Johns Hopkins University Press, 1983).

2. For antipolitical discourse in relation to the idea of civil society, see especially György Konrád, *Antipolitics: An Essay*, trans. Richard E. Allen (1983; New York: Quartet, 1984).

3. Jürgen Habermas, *The Structural Transformation of the Public Sphere: An Inquiry into a Category of Bourgeois Society*, trans. Thomas Burger (1962; Cambridge, MA: MIT Press, 1989). This revolutionary formation of the eighteenth century, Habermas says, rapidly decayed into a relatively inert "public opinion" that is molded and managed though techniques of advertising and state propaganda.

4. It is worth pointing out that Habermas himself, schooled as he is in Hegelian dialectic, consistently foregrounds the ways in which civil society and the state are mutually constitutive, though this important nuance is often lost in applications of his basic model.

5. Giorgio Agamben, *Homo Sacer: Sovereign Power and Bare Life*, trans. Daniel Heller-Roazen (1995; Stanford, CA: Stanford University Press, 1998). Agamben's critique of the notion of an extrapolitical civil society is part of a broader effort to revise and expand Michel Foucault's account of the emergence of "biopolitics" (for example, in the introductory volume of Foucault's *History of Sexuality*). Agamben argues that the Western tradition of political theory has been marked by the failure to understand that political power always asserts a claim over an ambiguous and unshaped realm of "bare life" that seems to be independent of or excluded from public concerns. Agamben argues that the unacknowledged grasp of political power upon "bare life" runs through seemingly very different political forms, and indeed one of his goals is to demonstrate continuity between the classical, liberal nation-state and apparently antithetical totalitarian regimes. Agamben regards them as equally biopolitical, a claim that he uses to explain the quick transformation of the Weimar republic into the Nazi state. Nevertheless, he does suggest that the classical era of the nation-state is marked by a structurally specific veiling of the state's grip on "bare life." The end of the classical era of the nation-state is marked, he argues, not

by the invention of biopolitics (as Foucault argues) but by the relative unveiling—in the death camps and in the politicization of biology by debates over issues like euthanasia—of the state's biopolitical orientation. Veiling biopower, Agamben concludes, had the effect of creating "the spaces, the liberties, and the rights" that inscribe individuals in the political order at the most intimate level of their bare existence.

6. Agamben, *Homo Sacer*, 121–22.

7. In making this claim I am drawing on important work on early modern thought about the humors, notably Gail Kern Paster, *The Body Embarrassed: Drama and the Disciplines of Shame in Early Modern England* (Ithaca, NY: Cornell University Press, 1993); Michael Schoenfeldt, *Bodies and Selves in Early Modern England: Physiology and Inwardness in Spenser, Shakespeare, Herbert, and Milton* (New York: Cambridge University Press, 1999); Susan James, *Passion and Action: The Emotions in Seventeenth-Century Philosophy* (New York: Oxford University Press, 1997). I am also building on my own account of the role of emotions in early modern representations of sexuality as unsocial or asocial: see Daniel Juan Gil, *Before Intimacy: Asocial Sexuality in Early Modern England* (Minneapolis: University of Minnesota Press, 2006).

8. My argument that *Julius Caesar* is interesting because it is misaligned with the modern political imaginary is indebted to Richard Halpern's discussion of the play in *Shakespeare Among the Moderns* (Ithaca, NY: Cornell University Press, 1997).

9. I draw the term "antisystemic" from the title of the important study by Giovanni Arrighi, Terence K. Hopkins, and Immanuel Wallerstein, which argues that, when anticapitalist movements have sought to ameliorate the local effects of international capitalism by aiming to gain a measure of state power (through trade union movements, for example), their success paradoxically strengthens the nation-state, which is the key mechanism by which the capitalist world-system operates. Arrighi and company term "antisystemic" those modes of resistance and social organization that do not strengthen the nation-state while challenging the power of international capital. My effort here is to observe an antisystemic moment just when the nation-state arrived on the scene. See Giovanni Arrighi, Terence K. Hopkins, and Immanuel Wallerstein, *Antisystemic Movements* (London: Verso, 1989).

10. All references to *Julius Caesar* are taken from the Arden 3 edition of David Daniell (New York: Thompson, 1998). Citations are given parenthetically in the text.

11. In the scene cited, Brutus tells Cassius that, if what he has to say deals with "the general good, / [then] Set honour in one eye, and death i'th' other, / And I will look on both indifferently" (1.2.85–6).

12. See the classical statement in J. G. A. Pocock, *The Machiavellian Moment: Florentine Political Thought and the Atlantic Republican Tradition* (Princeton, NJ: Princeton University Press, 1975).

13. This friction between ideologies is resolved historically by the modern settlement in which the state is seen to guarantee various rights within a nationalized political field that preexists individual decisions about political allegiances, and these rights, in turn, make various kinds of political opposition possible. It is essentially this settlement (achieved in England through the Glorious Revolution) that is reflected and codified in Habermas's account of an oppositional public sphere.

14. It is as if the aristocratic self-conception as an elite that constitutes the state is transposed onto the abstract, universal field conjured up by Caesar's leveling of

local differences. In making the claim that "bare life" is constitutive in this way, I am drawing on Negri's discussion of the difference between "constituted" and "constitutive" power. See Antonio Negri, *Insurgencies: Constituent Power and the Modern State*, trans. Maurizia Boscagli (Minneapolis: University of Minnesota Press, 1999).

15. Obviously, gender complicates Portia's relationship to the conspirators' ideology of public life in important ways. Being inducted into the conspiracy seems to be a form of liberation from her gendered role in the home, a liberation that she paradoxically completes with her spectacular suicide. In this context, see Cynthia Marshall's discussion of Portia's self-mutilating turn against her gender identity in "Portia's Wound, Calphurnia's Dream: Reading Character in *Julius Caesar*," *English Literary Renaissance* 24.2 (Spring 1994): 471–88. It is worth noting that Shakespeare consistently calls attention to the important role that women play in the life of the massed crowd.

Chronology

1564	William Shakespeare christened at Stratford-on-Avon April 26.
1582	Marries Anne Hathaway in November.
1583	Daughter Susanna born, baptized on May 26.
1585	Twins Hamnet and Judith born, baptized on February 2.
1587	Shakespeare goes to London, without family.
1589–90	*Henry VI, Part 1* written.
1590–91	*Henry VI, Part 2* and *Henry VI, Part 3* written.
1592–93	*Richard III* and *The Two Gentlemen of Verona* written.
1593	Publication of *Venus and Adonis*, dedicated to the Earl of Southampton; the sonnets probably begun.
1593	*The Comedy of Errors* written.
1593–94	Publication of *The Rape of Lucrece*, also dedicated to the Earl of Southampton. *Titus Andronicus* and *The Taming of the Shrew* written.
1594–95	*Love's Labour's Lost*, *King John*, and *Richard II* written.
1595–96	*Romeo and Juliet* and *A Midsummer Night's Dream* written.
1596	Son Hamnet dies.

1596–97	*The Merchant of Venice* and *Henry IV, Part 1* written; purchases New Place in Stratford.
1597–98	*The Merry Wives of Windsor* and *Henry IV, Part 2* written.
1598–99	*Much Ado about Nothing* written.
1599	*Henry V, Julius Caesar,* and *As You Like It* written.
1600–01	*Hamlet* written.
1601	*The Phoenix and the Turtle* written; father dies.
1601–02	*Twelfth Night* and *Troilus and Cressida* written.
1602–03	*All's Well That Ends Well* written.
1603	Shakespeare's company becomes the King's Men.
1604	*Measure for Measure* and *Othello* written.
1605	*King Lear* written.
1606	*Macbeth* and *Antony and Cleopatra* written.
1607	Marriage of daughter Susanna on June 5.
1607–08	*Coriolanus, Timon of Athens,* and *Pericles* written.
1608	Mother dies.
1609	Publication, probably unauthorized, of the quarto edition of the sonnets.
1609–10	*Cymbeline* written.
1610–11	*The Winter's Tale* written.
1611	*The Tempest* written. Shakespeare returns to Stratford, where he will live until his death.
1612	*A Funeral Elegy* written.
1612–13	*Henry VIII* written; The Globe Theatre destroyed by fire.
1613	*The Two Noble Kinsmen* written (with John Fletcher).
1616	Daughter Judith marries on February 10; Shakespeare dies April 23.
1623	Publication of the First Folio edition of Shakespeare's plays.

Contributors

HAROLD BLOOM is Sterling Professor of the Humanities at Yale University. He is the author of 30 books, including *Shelley's Mythmaking*, *The Visionary Company*, *Blake's Apocalypse*, *Yeats*, *A Map of Misreading*, *Kabbalah and Criticism*, *Agon: Toward a Theory of Revisionism*, *The American Religion*, *The Western Canon*, and *Omens of Millennium: The Gnosis of Angels, Dreams, and Resurrection*. *The Anxiety of Influence* sets forth Professor Bloom's provocative theory of the literary relationships between the great writers and their predecessors. His most recent books include *Shakespeare: The Invention of the Human*, a 1998 National Book Award finalist, *How to Read and Why*, *Genius: A Mosaic of One Hundred Exemplary Creative Minds*, *Hamlet: Poem Unlimited*, *Where Shall Wisdom Be Found?*, and *Jesus and Yahweh: The Names Divine*. In 1999, Professor Bloom received the prestigious American Academy of Arts and Letters Gold Medal for Criticism. He has also received the International Prize of Catalonia, the Alfonso Reyes Prize of Mexico, and the Hans Christian Andersen Bicentennial Prize of Denmark.

TERRENCE N. TICE has been a professor at the University of Michigan. He is editor and translator for the Mellen series Schleiermacher Studies and Translations.

ROBERT F. WILLSON JR. is professor emeritus at the University of Missouri–Kansas City. He is the author of *Shakespeare's Reflexive Endings* and *Shakespeare's Opening Scenes*.

165

JAN H. BLITS is a professor in the School of Education at the University of Delaware. He authored *The Soul of Athens: Shakespeare's* A Midsummer Night's Dream and *The Insufficiency of Virtue*, among other works.

NICHOLAS VISSER has taught in the English department at the University of Cape Town. He is a contributor to *Post-Colonial Shakespeares*; his work has also appeared in journals, including *Twentieth Century Literature* and *Studies in American Fiction*.

R.F. FLEISSNER has taught at Central State University in Ohio. He has published *Shakespeare and the Matter of the Crux*.

JOHN ROE is a reader at the University of York. He has edited *Shakespeare: The Poems* and co-edited *Inspiration and Technique: Ancient to Modern Views on Beauty and Art*.

LLOYD DAVIS has been a reader in English at the University of Queensland. He has published essays and books, including *Guise and Disguise: Rhetoric and Characterization in the English Renaissance* and *Introducing Cultural and Media Studies* (which he co-authored).

BARBARA J. BAINES is professor emerita at North Carolina State University. She has published *Representing Rape in the English Early Modern Period* and *Thomas Heywood*.

DANIEL JUAN GIL is an assistant professor at Texas Christian University. He has written *Before Intimacy: Asocial Sexuality in Early Modern England* and also has written on *Troilus and Cressida*.

Bibliography

Alexander, Catherine M.S., ed. *Shakespeare and Politics*. Cambridge, UK; New York: Cambridge University Press, 2004.

Baines, Barbara J. "Political and Poetic Revisionism in *Julius Caesar*." *The Upstart Crow* 10 (1990): 42–54.

Batson, Beatrice, ed. *Shakespeare's Christianity: The Protestant and Catholic Poetics of* Julius Caesar, Macbeth, *and* Hamlet. Waco, Texas: Baylor University, 2006.

Bono, Barbara J. "The Birth of Tragedy: Tragic Action in *Julius Caesar*." *English Literary Renaissance* 24, no. 2 (Spring 1994): 449–70.

Boulukos, Athanasios. "The Cobbler and the Tribunes in *Julius Caesar*." *MLN* 119, no. 5 (December 2004): 1083–89.

Bradley, Marshall C. "Caska: Stoic, Cynic, 'Christian.'" *Literature & Theology: An International Journal of Theory, Criticism and Culture* 8, no. 2 (June 1994): 140–56.

Bromwich, David. "Hazlitt on Shakespeare and the Motives of Power." *Hazlitt Review* 1 (2008): 5–15.

Brown, John Russell. *Shakespeare: The Tragedies*. New York: Palgrave, 2001.

Buhler, Stephen M. "No Spectre, No Sceptre: The Agon of Materialist Thought in Shakespeare's *Julius Caesar*." *English Literary Renaissance* 26, no. 2 (Spring 1996): 313–32.

Carducci, Jane. "Brutus, Cassius, and Caesar in Shakespeare's *Julius Caesar*: Language and the Roman Male." *Language and Literature* 13 (1988): 1–19.

Carpi, Daniela. "Law and Sedition in *Julius Caesar*." In *Shakespeare and the Law*, edited by Daniela Carpi, pp. 103–15. Ravenna, Italy: Longo, 2003.

Champion, Larry S. *The Essential Shakespeare: An Annotated Bibliography of Major Modern Studies.* 2nd ed. New York: G.K. Hall; Toronto: Maxwell Macmillan Canada; New York: Maxwell Macmillan International, 1993.

Chapman, Raymond. "'I Have Seen More Years than You': Youth and Age in *Julius Caesar.*" *The Aligarh Journal of English Studies* 17, nos. 1–2 (1995): 1–11.

Cook, Albert. "The Transmutation of Heroic Complexity: Plutarch and Shakespeare." *Classical and Modern Literature: A Quarterly* 17, no. 1 (Fall 1996): 31–43.

Cora Alonso, Jesús. "'This dream is all amiss interpreted': *Julius Caesar*, Shakespeare's Alchemical Tragedy." *SEDERI* 14 (2004): 17–51.

Corti, Claudia. "Shakespeare's Uncultured Caesar on the Elizabethan Stage." In *Italian Studies in Shakespeare and His Contemporaries*, edited by Michele Marrapodi, pp. 109–27. Newark: Delaware University Press; London: Associated University Presses, 1999.

Diede, Martha Kalnin. *Shakespeare's Knowledgeable Body.* New York; Frankfurt: Lang, 2008.

DiPietro, Cary. *Shakespeare and Modernism.* Cambridge, UK; New York: Cambridge University Press, 2006.

Dillon, Janette. *The Cambridge Introduction to Shakespeare's Tragedies.* Cambridge, England: Cambridge University Press, 2007.

Dobson, Michael. "Accents Yet Unknown: Canonisation and the Claiming of *Julius Caesar.*" In *The Appropriation of Shakespeare: Post-Renaissance Reconstructions of the Works and the Myth*, edited by Jean I. Marsden, pp. 11–28. New York: St. Martin's, 1991.

Drakakis, John. "'Fashion It Thus': *Julius Caesar* and the Politics of Theatrical Representation." *Shakespeare Survey* 44 (1992): 65–73.

Faas, Ekbert. *Tragedy and After: Euripides, Shakespeare, Goethe.* Kingston: McGill-Queen's University Press, 1984.

Garber, Marjorie B. *Coming of Age in Shakespeare.* London; New York: Methuen, 1981.

Greene, Gayle. "'The Power of Speech to Stir Men's Blood': The Language of Tragedy in Shakespeare's *Julius Caesar.*" *Renaissance Drama* 11 (1980): 67–93.

Hager, Alan. "'The Teeth of Emulation': Failed Sacrifice in Shakespeare's *Julius Caesar.*" *The Upstart Crow* 8 (1988): 5468.

Hamer, Mary. *William Shakespeare, Julius Caesar.* Plymouth, U.K.: Northcote House in association with the British Council, 1998.

Hawkes, Terence. *Shakespeare in the Present.* London; New York: Routledge, 2002.

Hopkins, D. J. "Performance and Urban Space in Shakespeare's Rome, or 'S.P.Q.L.'" In *Rematerializing Shakespeare: Authority and Representation on the Early Modern English Stage*, edited by Bryan Reynolds and William N. West, pp. 35–52. New York: Palgrave Macmillan, 2005.

Howard-Hill, T. H. *Shakespearian Bibliography and Textual Criticism: A Bibliography.* 2nd ed. Signal Mountain, Tenn.: Summertown, 2000.

Hutchins, Christine E. "'Who Is Here So Rude That Would Not Be a Roman?' England as Anti-Type of Rome in Elizabethan Print and *Julius Caesar.*" *Ben Jonson Journal* 8 (2001): 207–27.

Kezar, Dennis. "*Julius Caesar* and the Properties of Shakespeare's Globe." *English Literary Renaissance* 28, no. 1 (Winter 1998): 18–46.

Knowles, Ronald. *Shakespeare's Arguments with History.* Houndmills, Basingstoke, Hampshire; New York: Palgrave, 2002.

Leggatt, Alexander. "Roman Plays." In *An Oxford Guide to Shakespeare*, edited by Stanley Wells and Lena Orlin, pp. 231–48. Oxford, England: Oxford University Press, 2003.

Lewin, James A. "Imperious Caesar's Ghost." *Shakespeare and Renaissance Association of West Virginia* 23 (2000): 1–14.

Marshall, Cynthia. "Portia's Wound, Calphurnia's Dream: Reading Character in *Julius Caesar.*" *English Literary Renaissance* 24, no. 2 (Spring 1994): 471–88.

———. "Totem, Taboo, and *Julius Caesar.*" *Literature and Psychology* 37, nos. 1–2 (1991): 11–33.

———. "Shakespeare Crossing the Rubicon." *Shakespeare Survey* 53 (2000): 73–88.

Martindale, Charles, and A.B. Taylor, eds. *Shakespeare and the Classics.* Cambridge, U.K.; New York: Cambridge University Press, 2004.

McDonald, Russ, ed. *Shakespeare: An Anthology of Criticism and Theory, 1945–2000.* Malden, Mass.: Blackwell, 2004.

McMurtry, Jo. Julius Caesar: *A Guide to the Play.* Westport, Conn.: Greenwood Press, 1998.

Mehl, Dieter. *Shakespeare's Tragedies: An Introduction.* Cambridge, New York: Cambridge University Press, 1986.

Miles, Gary B. "How Roman Are Shakespeare's 'Romans'?" *Shakespeare Quarterly* 40, no. 3 (Fall 1989): 257–83.

Miller, Anthony. "'Words Before Blows': Civil and Military in *Julius Caesar.*" *Sydney Studies in English* 28 (2002): 124–35.

Miola, Robert S. *Shakespeare's Rome.* Cambridge, New York: Cambridge University Press, 1983.

Moisan, Thomas. "'Knock Me Here Soundly': Comic Misprision and Class Consciousness in Shakespeare." *Shakespeare Quarterly* 42, no. 3 (Fall 1991): 276–90.

Munro, Ian. *The Figure of the Crowd in Early Modern London: The City and Its Double.* New York: Palgrave Macmillan, 2005.

Orkin, Martin. "Proverbial Allusion in *Julius Caesar.*" *Pretexts: Studies in Writing and Culture* 7, no. 2 (November 1998): 213–34.

Paris, Bernard. "Julius Caesar." *Aligarh Critical Miscellany* 7, no. 2 (1994): 117–49.

Ripley, John. Julius Caesar *on Stage in England and America, 1599–1973*. Cambridge; New York: Cambridge University Press, 1980.

Roe, John. "'Character' in Plutarch and Shakespeare: Brutus, Julius Caesar, and Mark Antony." In *Shakespeare and the Classics*, edited by Charles Martindale and A. B. Taylor, pp. 173–87. Cambridge, England: Cambridge University Press, 2004.

Royle, Nicholas. "The Poet: *Julius Caesar* and the Democracy to Come." *Oxford Literary Review* 25 (2003): 39–61.

Snodgrass, Mary Ellen. Julius Caesar / *William Shakespeare*. Chichester: John Wiley, 2006.

Sohmer, Steve. *Shakespeare's Mystery Play: The Opening of the Globe Theatre 1599*. Manchester, U.K.; New York: Manchester University Press; New York; distributed in the USA by St. Martin's Press, 1999.

Thomas, Vivian. *Julius Caesar*. New York: Twayne Publishers, 1992.

———. *Shakespeare's Roman Worlds*. London; New York: Routledge, 1989.

Wells, Robin Headlam. "*Julius Caesar*, Machiavelli, and the Uses of History." *Shakespeare Survey* 55 (2002): 209–18.

Wilson, Richard. "A Brute Part: *Julius Caesar* and the Rites of Violence." *Cahiers Elisabéthains: Late Medieval and Renaissance Studies* 50 (October 1996): 19–32.

Acknowledgments

Terrence N. Tice, "Calphurnia's Dream and Communication with the Audience in Shakespeare's *Julius Caesar*." From *Shakespeare Yearbook* 1 (Spring 1990): 37–49. © 1990 by the Edwin Mellen Press.

Robert F. Willson Jr., *"Julius Caesar*: The Forum Scene as Historic Play-within." From *Shakespeare Yearbook* 1 (Spring 1990): 14–28. © 1990 by the Edwin Mellen Press.

Jan H. Blits, "Manliness and Friendship in *Julius Caesar*." From *The End of the Ancient Republic: Shakespeare's* Julius Caesar, Rowan and Littlefield Publishers Inc. © 1993 by the Center for the Philosophy of Science.

Nicholas Visser, "Plebeian Politics in *Julius Caesar*." From *Shakespeare in Southern Africa* 7 (1994): 22–31. © 1994 by the Shakespeare Society of Southern Africa.

R.F. Fleissner, "The Problem of Brutus's Paternity in *Julius Caesar* (in Partial Relation to *Hamlet*)." From *Hamlet Studies* 19, nos. 1 and 2 (Summer and Winter 1997): 109–113. © 1997 by *Hamlet Studies*.

John Roe, *"Julius Caesar*: Conscience and Conspiracy" by John Roe. From *Shakesperare and Machiavelli*, D.S. Brewer. © 2002 by John Roe.

Lloyd Davis, "Embodied Masculinity in Shakespeare's *Julius Caesar*." From *EnterText* 3, no. 1 (Spring 2003): 161–82. © 2003 by Brunel University.

Index

Characters in literary works are indexed by first name (if any), followed by the name of the work in parentheses